Playboy's

Single Person's Guide to

Real Estate Investing

BY THE SAME AUTHOR

NONFICTION

The Complete Guide to Real Estate Financing

The Complete Handbook of How to Farm Real Estate Listings and Sales

Building Your Wealth Through Creative Real Estate Investing

FICTION

The Ultimate Game

The Venture

Lauderdale Run

Playboy's

Single Person's Guide to Real Estate Investing

JACK CUMMINGS

PBP
A PLAYBOY PRESS BOOK

 Published simultaneously in the United States and Canada by Playboy Press, Chicago, Illinois. Printed in the United States of America.

First Edition

Library of Congress Cataloging in Publication Data
Cummings, Jack, 1940–
Playboy's single person's guide to real estate investing.
1. Real estate investment. 2. Single people.
I. Title.
HD1379.C78 332.63'24'0880652 80–7790
ISBN 0–87223–621–8

To Miss Brontë

Forever in My Heart

ACKNOWLEDGMENTS

I WISH TO ACKNOWLEDGE the moral support given to me by Nancy Parsegian of Playboy; also, the never faltering support of my staff and associates at Cummings Realty, who are my reflecting pond, in which all ideas and programs are tested and perfected (or discarded). Thanks go to Ray Brown of Radio Shack for his expertise in calculating amortization tables and other real estate analysis.

In particular acknowledgment, I wish to single out the best and most constant motivation to me in this book: my love for real estate.

Contents

Playboy's
Single Person's Guide to
Real Estate Investing

Introduction

Do you know who said, "You have to have money to make money?" It was a rich guy who feared competition.

You don't have to be rich to become rich. This book will show you how. If you are single and hope to become independently wealthy, this book will be more important to you than any investment book you could ever read. It will do more than show you how you can make money without having money to start with. This book will help you to reach your goal, step by step.

There has never been a book quite like this one. It is written primarily for the single person, male or female, young or old. It explains the secrets of real estate investing in clear and easy-to-follow terms that permit you to see how you can attain financial success.

Let's face it: As a single, you have some very special problems that have been ignored until now. You pay more income tax than you should—much more than your married counterpart—and you have more expenses in many areas. On top of that, you do not get the help from Uncle Sam that you would get if you owned and invested in real estate.

As a single you live a life-style that does, in fact, enable you to make it big in real estate—but only if you recognize your special problems and how you can get the edge in investing in real estate.

As a working realtor-author, I know well the need to have something easy to read, with clear and concise steps to follow.

This book is designed and written with that in mind. It will take you from developing self-confidence to giving you basics, then the fine points on the techniques that smart investors use to build and keep their wealth.

1

Why Single People Need to Buy and Own Real Estate

THE SINGLES ERA IS HERE. It sneaked in quietly and has become firmly entrenched in the world as a solid, here-to-stay, economic power. Just look around you. Everywhere you see singles running businesses, spending, enjoying to a degree that astounds business analysts. Merchandising markets have changed, selling strategies have been altered, and new industries have rushed in to fill the demand for new products for the singles market.

THE THIRD NECESSITY OF LIFE: SHELTER

CONTRARY to a great deal of discussion among the Masters and Johnsons of this world, the third necessity is not sex—sex isn't in the top three. The third necessity, behind food and clothing, is shelter—the most tangible and most durable.

Shelter, and the land on which it is built, has long been the toy of the rich and the dream of the poor. Wars are fought over ownership of land and shelter. Revolutions take it away from one group of people and give it to another. Land and shelter are the foundations of all wealth.

While it is true that if you have money you can buy more real estate (or nearly anything, for that matter), it isn't true that the accumulation of wealth must commence with sizable sums of good cold cash. The fact is, real estate is probably the easiest of all forms of investment to get into. In many situations you don't even need *any cash at all* to become an owner.

Real estate is one of the basic necessities. Never forget that. This simple statement is part of the key to your success as an investor. Because real estate is basic and necessary, everyone must utilize it. Some will rent, others will own; a few will live off the owners or renters.

Singles—The New Investors

In the late 1970s the real estate industry saw the sudden growth of the singles market among real estate investors. What had happened almost overnight during the middle '70s was a movement of single people into real estate investing. They were moving out of the ranks of renters and into those of buyers—so much so that by the end of the '70s the singles' buying power accounted for nearly 25% of all recognized real estate purchases. This percentage may not seem impressive, but it was more than double the percentage of the previous twenty years. Also, it does not include the hidden percentage of purchases made in corporate and partnership names, which most certainly had a hefty component of singles ownership.

The good news here was that not only did singles have the money to spend, but that they recognized that they could not afford *not* to buy. They realized that ownership of real estate is not a luxury or a status symbol, but absolutely necessary to their financial existence in this modern world of double-digit inflation.

Yet millions of single people hadn't discovered the secrets to real estate investing. Many of those who did buy found that they couldn't just pick out what they liked and expect to make a profit. Real estate investing is a science, and it requires some specialized techniques to get the edge. Not every home or apartment or lot is bound to produce a profit. It has always been possible to lose your shirt in real estate.

Dozens of books on the market promise success through following the methods used by their authors. But adopting someone else's patterns just doesn't work when it comes to real estate (or, for that matter, any other form of investment). Times change, places are different, supply and demand vary. Success comes quicker to those who know what they are doing than to those who stumble around listening to wrong or misdirected advice.

Personally, I love books that tell how people made millions of dollars by investing in real estate. However, I see not only how the profits were made, but what mistakes were made, which I try to avoid later on myself. There are traps out there, and you want to avoid them whenever possible.

Singles Especially Need Real Estate

"Pardon me. You're single, aren't you?" I asked.

"Yes, I am," he said.

"Do you rent your apartment?"

"Yes. I'd like to own, but I don't have the cash to put down."

"I know the feeling," I said. "You pay tax?"

"Doesn't everyone?" he said.

"No, not everyone. Some people don't because they don't make enough money. Others because they planned it that way—most often through ownership of real estate."

"Yeah. So?" he said.

"So why don't you play the game? I mean, you're single, right?" I asked.

"Yeah."

"Then you can plan too. Only you have more to plan with."

The point of this conversation is this: As a single person you pay more tax; you carry a heavier burden than the guy who doesn't pay any tax. You need to wise up and learn the rich guys' game—to wit: Never use your own money when you can have the other guy(s) pay your bills for you.

The other guy might be you right now if you are paying rent, or it might be you because you pay more tax than you should and the rich guy doesn't pay his share because he owns real estate.

It's worth repeating: The secret to investing in real estate is to get someone else to pay your tab.

10 Reasons Singles Need to Own Real Estate

1. Singles and real estate, as natural a pair as ever devised. As a single you have many things going for you that right at this moment you may not recognize or appreciate as advantages in real estate investing. Yet it's true. As a single you have special abilities, tax consequences, goals, and current problems that differ from those of your married counterpart, of whatever age.

Many people have not accepted the fact that ownership of real estate is within their grasp. Ownership of real property isn't that different from ownership of personal property. If you think cars, then you will own cars. The same thing goes for boats or airplanes. Price isn't a factor. So think real estate.

2. As a single you can't afford not to own real estate. When it comes to your economics, there is only one criterion that is important: How many real spendable dollars did you have during the year? Not how much did you earn, but what was left after you paid your basic nut and the luxuries you indulged yourself in and then paid your year-end tax?

Real spendable dollars are what some accountants and stockbroker types call after-expenses money. They are measurable only in retrospect, because by the time you get to the point of measuring them, you may have already spent them. But you can anticipate them and measure them nonetheless—so much so that if you are now renting, you will be able to calculate just how much you can spend in owning. A simple checklist in Chapter 9 will show you exactly how much more you can spend in cash by owning and still have more left over at the end of the year. Sound like a paradox? Not so. Owning might cost more in the amount of the check you write, but part of that check is being paid by some other guy (Uncle Sam).

3. Real estate is absolute. Not only is it a necessity, but it is absolute. It is the most tangible thing you can put your hands on.

It is right where you find it; it doesn't move around (although some of it might blow away, wash away, burn down, or blow up). Your ownership lasts for as long as you have planned it to, bending only to progress, urban renewal, and eminent domain.

The fact that it is absolute gives it a lasting quality that also establishes its value. Its location *is* its value. The saying that "all land is governed by only three things: location, location, location" is not without merit.

Just because it is absolute doesn't mean it is inflexible. On the contrary. Warehouses can become restaurants, or lofts, or be torn down for high-rise office buildings. Flat land can become airports and mountains vineyards or cottage sites; hotels become schools or schools hospitals; and homes become doctors' offices or whatever the mind can dream up and city zoning ordinances permit.

Because land is both absolute and flexible, it can be made to fit your needs and goals. Best of all, there is some to fit your budget.

4. Real estate is not a burden. Many single people I deal with begin by telling me they want to rent, because they don't want to be tied down by owning real estate.

Joy was an airline stewardess and loved her job. She was senior in the area and had her pick of the best flights to the best places to which her airline flew. She had always rented, and while she made a good salary and had no extraordinary expenses to hold her back, she was convinced she would suffer from the burden of owning. She had ruled out owning a condo (which some of her friends had urged her to get), despite the fact that all she had to do was pay the mortgage payment and taxes, just as she was then paying rent. She ruled out a home for the seemingly obvious reason that it was too much work to keep up a house.

The real fact was Joy was frightened about owning a piece of real estate. But she got to thinking real estate (the first step) and got some solid counseling. What seemed to best fit her needs and abilities was a small apartment building of four units. She was able to afford the property's initial down payment, and with the rent from the three other apartments (the other guys paying her tab) was able to carry the mortgage and throw off some spending money to boot.

Often the concept of real estate being a burden is a rationalization to ease the fear that you can't afford it, or that once you have it you won't be able to hold on to it. It is important for you to recognize that while real estate is not in itself a burden, it is entirely possible for you to get into a situation that is not sustainable, a predicament that causes you financial loss rather than gain.

Investing in real estate has its risks. Once you know all the options available to you, you can reduce those risks. In some cases you can eliminate the risks altogether.

The fear of risk can cause many investors to avoid something rather than take the chance. When it comes to money, doing nothing is sometimes more risky than making a move in a direction that may not be perfect but is positive. Nonetheless, investing in anything involves some risk. However, rich people learned a long time ago that the biggest risk in doing anything lies in not knowing your alternatives. Don't buy anything until you have a good, clear understanding of the ups and downs. The more options you have open to you, the more directions you can take to get from your present point A to your desired point B. In real estate your options, or alternatives, come from knowing as much as you can about yourself, your goals, and the kinds of real estate that might get you what you want. The fastest and most dramatic reduction in risk you can make is to understand as much as you can about what can go wrong. Anticipating the down side, knowing what to do if it comes, in itself removes a great deal of that feared element: risk.

5. Buying, owning, selling—profiting all the while—fits a single's life-style. The pioneering frontiersman led the life-style of the single. In fact, the man who didn't hack a homestead out of the wilderness didn't get married. This left the perpetual bachelor with a novel excuse for not being ready for marriage ("Darling, just give me a few more years to clear the north two hundred and chop up an ample supply of firewood").

Why Single People Need to Buy and Own Real Estate

In many societies the ownership of real estate was essential before a single could become a married member of the community. (Rest assured, however, that owning real estate does not automatically lead to marriage!)

The reasons for ownership of land or shelter prior to marrying are just as valid today as in the past. All other things being equal, a well-motivated single person thinking real estate is better able to prosper in his investments than a married person. I am not arguing against marriage, nor the success that can come from that side of the fence—only pointing out the practical aspects of economics.

Charlie was single, fresh out of Vietnam, young, full of stored-up energy, and ready to go. He thought of many things: girls, booze, having fun, spending all the money he could get his hands on, as fast as he could. He spent it on girls, booze, having a good time, cars, clothes, and more girls and booze. Then he ran out of money and had to go to work.

We met about the time he was growing tired with his job. I recognized Charlie as a natural salesman. He had the ability to sell because you felt comfortable with him instantly. He was bursting with confidence in himself, and that would spread to his clients and whatever product he wanted to sell.

I convinced him he would be good at selling real estate, but only if he could first think real estate, then own real estate.

It wasn't an easy task for Charlie. But he did it, and very quickly began to be the successful salesman I thought he would be. His real success, however, wasn't in selling real estate. It was in buying, fixing up, selling at a profit, and buying some more.

Charlie is still a single; he still thinks of girls and booze and having a good time, which he still does by spending his money on girls, booze, and having a good time. Only this time he isn't going to run out of money.

I know many senior singles who have a much different lifestyle from Charlie's. But owning real estate fits them, too, because real estate is so flexible and there are so many categories and prices that nearly everyone has property out there waiting for him.

Take Ann, for example. Retired, legally blind, and living on a small nest egg and pension, she became frightened of what was happening with the rental market. She could see the handwriting on the wall—soon she would be unable to afford the continuing rent increases.

Today Ann has her own place. She is able to plan her own destiny more freely now, because she has been able to remove a fear from her life.

Both senior singles and young singles have one thing in common: They are able to make economic sacrifices without making others share the burden. This gives the single one hell of an edge in investing in real estate. If the name of the game is profit, real estate is about the surest investment when it comes to buying something run-down and fixing it up.

If you can sacrifice a few hours a week without harming your other employment, or if you are retired and are healthy enough to spend several hours a week working at painting, gardening, general fix-it things, then you qualify as a candidate for profits.

6. Singles can accept the responsibility of real estate. It is possible, as you will see, that under the right circumstances you can buy real estate with nothing down. The fact of the matter is this: The world is full of run-down properties that are in need of TLC. The lack of tender loving care in many cases is all that keeps the property from being valuable instead of next to worthless. Owners of this kind of property can be convinced that selling the property, even for nothing down, is good, sound business because of one thing: the buyer. If the buyer can demonstrate a willingness to turn that "unwanted" property into something of value, then a sale can result.

Of course, this factor depends on your ability as a single to convince the owner of your desire to accept the responsibility. This gets back to the "think real estate" theme that runs through this book. If you can't see yourself buying and spending the time and effort to fix up the property, and then obtaining the profits from that effort, it is doubtful you will be about to convince someone else that you are the guy for that deal.

Being single has nothing to do with the ability to be responsible. All that is needed for that trait is being human. This factor will work for you if you are of the nature to be responsible, or willing to set a goal and then work 100% for it. Here's why. Because there are many people who are less motivated than you, the rewards of the world are never spread on a pro rata basis. The pot isn't open for everyone to dip into. It is there for those who work hard to get it, and the hard worker with a plan and a direction takes double helpings.

Profits in real estate come to those who take the chance, who go that extra mile, who just plain get off their ass and act within their own abilities.

I've never seen anyone lose his place in the line of success because he took a flyer on his own ability. Instead, losses generally come when you bet on the ability of others and not yourself.

As a single you have the advantage of being able to carry the responsibility of ownership of real estate. You can accept it because the rest of the load you carry may be lighter than your non-single compatriot's.

Susan is another example. "Look at me," she said. I saw a single woman who took care of her aged and ill mother. Susan worked at a job in the daytime and at home in the evening. "Where's my ability to take responsibility?" she asked.

That was five years ago. Since then, thinking real estate, Susan and her mother have moved seven or eight times. They pick up unfurnished condos. Using her mother's uncanny ability to plan a color-coordinated redecorating of the apartments, they have made a nice profit on each one. It was all in the life-style. The mother doesn't seem so aged or ill now, by the way.

7. Owning real estate can provide needed cash. Some kinds of real estate are "alligators." This means the property eats more cash than it produces. While that isn't always bad, it is a problem if you need to pay back borrowed money, or invest in rebuilding, before the property can produce income.

Other properties are cash machines. The property just seems to manufacture money all by itself. These income-producing properties are not always what they first seem to be.

For example, owning a duplex (a house with two living

units) and having one side available for rent might be an added way to help the duplex pay for itself. One unique way of increasing the value of that simple duplex is seen in what Brad did.

Brad had a nice duplex in Lauderdale By The Sea. He lived in one side and rented out the other. He even had a roommate who shared his side, to generate even more cash.

Brad found that he could get more rent from the other side by furnishing it and renting it not year-round but only during the winter season. He could make more during four months this way than he could the whole year on an annual rental.

He was able to pick up some off-season rent, too—and to cap it off, he reserved one off-season month for himself, joined a timeshare organization, and each year exchanged the use of that unit for another somewhere he wished to vacation.

Brad simply took more options and applied them to his benefit. He generated far more cash than he had been able to do by following the easy route.

Cash comes in very different packages when you own real estate. Transferring your tab to another guy effectively generates cash. After all, if you don't spend your own money on the bill, then you can use that cash somewhere else.

Receiving income is part of the real estate cycle.

Having some extra spending money can be the biggest advantage of all. There are many ways to turn land and property into cash, and with a little ingenuity, such as Brad used, you can benefit too.

8. **Real estate is a wealth builder.** All the truly great fortunes in this world have come from land. Nations fight for it, individuals die for it. Oil is found under it, gold in it, wheat springs from it. You can see it, smell it, walk on it. Its value is governed by where it is and the demand for it.

The economics of real estate is the most simple of all forms of investment. Two basic factors govern the ultimate price to which land will rise: supply and demand. Because land is absolute, the supply is limited by many factors.

A shortage of rental apartments in a period of heavy demand will really drive up the price or value of these units. Developers will notice this, of course, and if possible will develop more units.

However, the developers must be able to find a site for these new units. Suitable vacant sites might not exist, and demolition of existing structures might be a prerequisite for the new development. This form of development is expensive and often not warranted.

Thus, the supply of real estate is limited. This is not true of stocks, bonds, and other investments.

The best time to begin getting wealthy is now. Take stock of what you have going for you. How much cash can you pull together? How much can you afford to spend on fixing up a run-down property? Are you ready to think about real estate?

Saul bought a six-unit apartment house for $3,000 down. The total price was $54,000. (I think the owner, a woman of substantial means who was tired of looking after the apartments, took a liking to him.)

The apartments had always been rented unfurnished on an annual basis, and were a bit run-down. Saul threw a couple of beer parties and had the building painted inside and out. He then furnished the apartments, one by one, not with cheap motel-type furniture, but by following the household classified ads. He bought solid furniture, much of which he finished himself.

The furnished apartments rented for much more money, and for three years Saul poured every dime from the rent into the mortgage and upgrading the property.

By the fourth year he had reduced the original mortgage to $46,000. He then sold the units for $95,000. This cleared him $49,000, out of which he paid about $7,000 in commission and expenses of the sale. The $42,000 left was his return on the original investment of $3,000 and another $2,500 out-of-pocket. All other cash poured into the property came from other people. Remember, Saul let other people pay his tab as rent for his apartments.

The reason someone would pay Saul $95,000 for those units was the multiplier effect that occurs in real estate. The return on the cash invested, from the buyer's point of view, has to meet his demand requirement. If the investor demanded a 10% return on his cash invested (and if he were paying all cash), then for each $1,000 invested the cash flow would have to be $100.

Because of leverage, which increases the return by allowing the investor to buy without putting all cash down, the advantages to the cash flow are only part of the investor's total return. The multiplier effect is seen by Saul taking a property and increasing the gross rent.

Saul's method was simple and required only a bit of cosmetics and changing the apartments to furnished instead of unfurnished. As he increased the gross rents he also increased the bottom line. Yet because a buyer would ultimately buy based on the return (10%), for every $100 of increased annual rent at the bottom line, the value of the property had increased $1,000.

If you can buy any property that can have its bottom line increased, you are on your way to profits. A 5,000-square-foot building renting for $4 per square foot per year net (the tenant paying all expenses) will have a gross rent of $20,000. If you were looking for a 10% return on your money and you didn't have any mortgages, the value of this building would be $200,000. If you paid $200,000 and got $20,000 in income at the end of each year, you would be getting a 10% return.

If you can increase the rent to $5 per square foot per year, your income is now $25,000 and the value of the property is $250,000. With a simple $1-per-square-foot increase, you've made a fast $50,000.

Remember that it is the bottom line that is important, and when the rent is net, net, that usually means the tenant is covering all the other expenses. (A word of caution at this point. Terminology in real estate is not uniform across the country. To a possible tenant from California and a property owner in New York, *net, net* might not mean the same thing.)

9. Singles can protect their new wealth with real estate. You've heard the term *tax shelter* before. There used to be a number of different ways to invest to shelter your earned income from taxes. Many have been closed down by the IRS. The best of them remains, and that is real estate.

Because singles pay more tax than married people, singles

have an extra reason to look to ownership of real estate for their personal shelter as well as a place to protect their savings.

After all, it is one thing to make money, and another to keep it. Real estate has the ability to convert earned income into capital gains income, to generate paper losses that wipe out tax liability, to throw off cashless benefits.

Martin had made a killing in entertainment, rising from a little-known recording artist to the hit of the year. The cash rolling in was great, but what about taxes? His accountants advised real estate. He bought a 200-unit apartment complex with only 20% down, and took all the advantages of the depreciation. Martin used all the alternatives he could, and saved enough on his taxes that year to cover the down payment on the apartments. For Martin, the apartments didn't really cost anything because it was wealth he would have lost.

It's not always the big bucks that you will be protecting. It isn't a question of how much you protect, really. The question is: Is it worth my while? Am I protecting anything?

Not all real estate provides the immediate cash protection that Martin found. Some property required additional capital expenditure each year, without improving the year-end after-tax dollar. That doesn't mean that kind of real estate is bad, only that it may not suit your needs. If you need shelter, if you need to protect your wealth, then try to solve *that* problem.

By the time you finish this book you will have dozens of alternatives which will help you decide which way you need to go.

10. You need to buy real estate now, before you can't afford it. It is safe to say that not everyone in the United States will own real estate. Not all singles will be able to get their act in gear to be able to buy real estate. Married people will find they can't save enough to buy. Whatever the reason, there will be those people who don't own, and they help others to own.

The question isn't whether you will be able to afford to buy real estate. That you, as an enterprising single, will always be able to do.

Working your way up the economic ladder is something you do with the set of circumstances you have before you. Each of you reading this book is different, unique, personally you. There is no fifth-quarter game plan, no nineteenth-hole chance to pull it out of the bag. You are here right now, and what your future has in store for you will depend on the direction you take.

If you are beginning to think real estate, then owning it will more than likely be a result. But that result will occur because of what you do now and in the future.

As an investor in real estate, I've heard people tell me they could have bought this or that parcel ten years ago. They say it like this: "Hell, Jack, see that corner over there, the one with the bank on it? I could have bought that corner, let me see, ten years ago for only $50,000. What do you think it's worth now?"

I don't bother to ask them why they didn't buy it ten years ago because I already know the answer. They were busy telling someone else about another corner they could have bought ten years before that.

Everyone reading this book who is going to be more wealthy ten years from now will be able to tell that kind of story. Let's face it, some purchases must be lost because you can't afford them now. The trick is to know what you can afford and not let those investments slip past. If they slip past now, then you may never be able to afford them in the future.

Most investors starting out don't know what they can afford. That might sound strange but it is the truth. In Chapter 9 you will see how to determine how much more you can actually pay in monthly payments by owning in comparison to renting—without reducing your yearly after-tax spendable cash.

The main idea is to have a goal and to work for it. If you are confused about this, then take this test to ascertain whether you are the kind of single who should buy real estate.

Are You Ready to Buy Real Estate?

Rules: Answer each question yes or no. Do not look at the scoring method prior to answering the questions.

1. Do you currently rent your shelter?
2. Do you carry the responsibility of the rent alone?
3. Do you want to be more financially fit?
4. Have you ever owned a car free and clear?
5. Do you consider yourself the kind of person others can rely on?
6. Do you have eight months' rent or more saved up?
7. Do you have ten hours a week available for a better cause?
8. Can you close your eyes and see yourself five years from now?
9. Do you like what you see?
10. Do you consider yourself a hard worker?
11. Do others consider you a hard worker?
12. Are your living expenses average?
13. Are you working less than 42 hours per week in a steady, well-paying job?
14. Are you willing to sacrifice to improve your present living standard?
15. Is your health average or better?

How to Score:

For each yes, give yourself 10 points. For each no, deduct 5 points. You get a bonus of 50 points if you have answered yes to 13, 14, and 15.

If you score less than 90, you are not ready to buy real estate. It might mean that you will never be ready, that you are destined to be one of those who help the owners of real estate because you pick up their tab. Or it might mean you just need to think real estate some more.

2

Who Should Buy and How Much Cash Does It Take?

If you begin with the premise that not everyone is destined to own real estate, which is a fact, then it is possible that some readers of this book will simply *not* be ultimate owners of this wonderful commodity. You, perhaps.

Let me see. I believe I can think of some occupations that people follow that would rule out the need for ownership of real estate. A priest, for example, or a dedicated evangelist, or a resident of a monastery, or a member of a commune, or a career soldier, or a lifer at one of the nation's penal institutes. Or the free spirit who isn't any of the above, but just couldn't quite get a minimum score of 90 points in the readiness test in the first chapter.

Differentiate Between *Can* Invest and *Should* Invest

A person on his last leg of life, looking the hereafter straight in the face, is a person who should not invest in real estate (for his own benefit), unless it is an eternal resting place. On the other hand, the college student attending classes all day and working at night is more than likely a person who cannot invest.

Economics plays a part in all of this, of course. Yet the

economics of the buyer is more of a qualifier than a prerequisite. The money part of investing enables the buyer to pick and choose with more to select from. It's like the buyer of a car with only $500 in his pocket. He doesn't have the choice of models that the person with $15,000 has.

Yet there still remains a difference between who can invest and who should invest. Let's narrow it down. Any prospective investor who didn't score 90 on the readiness test is in my opinion an absolute 100% nonbuyer. In this case, both the can't and shouldn't would apply unless (a big *unless* coming up) the person is a politician or was born with a silver spoon in his mouth (or both). Politics and inherited wealth negate any test of responsibility or good setting.

Of those who scored 125 or more, it now narrows down to can you or can't you? You should, but are you able to?

Once you've determined that you should buy real estate, then the crucial decision to be made is can you get into the market now, or are circumstances not right? These circumstances might center around you. You have started a new job and need to devote all your energy to that for a while. Or you are holding down a job or two while finishing up your education. It might be something more personal. You aren't sure if you are going to get married—or divorced—or there's an impending illness, or some other imminent change in your life-style because of an outside force.

Jose bought about everything which could be bought, except outright ownership of real estate. He did break down and buy a co-ownership in a condo, but only because a buddy owed him some money and taking the share in the condo was the easiest way to collect.

Jose's reason for not buying real estate was the fact that there was an imminent change in store for him. He was in line for a whopping inheritance and he wanted to be free to enjoy it. The only problem to this was it was his father's estate that he was to inherit, and his father wasn't planning on kicking the bucket.

You've played Monopoly, right? It's a real estate game that

is real in many aspects. You can go for broke by holding out for the cream of the crop. Buy Park Place and Boardwalk because you collect most from your opponents when they land there. Or you can nickel-and-dime your way to wealth by holding on to the low-rent areas.

Your game plan in investing and the tremendous flexibility of the real estate market allow you to start small and grow. Holding on to all your cash and starting big in one fell swoop is okay too if that suits your style and ability.

So we know you should buy. Now, can you or can't you?

How Much Money Is Needed to Begin Building a Real Estate Empire?

HOLD ON here a moment. Who said you had to build an empire? Who said you had to make a mint of money in the first place? Not everyone has that in his game plan. Having a home, a family, a comfortable and happy life might be part or all of your plan, and that's great. The home part of that is the real estate, of course, and that may require money, but not necessarily.

If you are a veteran, however (and there are millions of veterans out there, both men and women), you can take advantage of your VA loan entitlement to buy a home, a duplex, or a small apartment building with little or no cash down. Not all vets know this.

Another thing many vets don't know is that the entitlement, which is continually going up, doesn't expire. The entitlement is a monetary amount which the U.S. Government will insure to a lender against a loss. In the late 1970s the entitlement went to \$25,000. Based on this insurance, which is on the top of the loan, most lenders would lend up to \$100,000 (four times the entitlement), and some even more for income-producing properties, such as duplexes or four-unit apartments. All this with nothing down.

Many vets don't know this, and they don't know that if they had taken advantage of an entitlement at a lower amount (say, back when it was only \$10,000, which would support a \$40,000 loan), they now would have an additional amount of entitlement they could use.

If you are a vet, call your nearest VA office to get the latest scoop on the VA loans. Don't have the guy at the VA office send you a brochure. Their brochures were written by the same cat that wrote the 1040 income tax form, and whatever they send you is apt to be out of date because they change their entitlement and programs rather frequently (which accounts for my being vague here).

How Any Single Can Buy Real Estate With Nothing Down

This one section might be worth a thousand times what you paid for this book. It might start you on the road to becoming an owner of real estate.

I've already mentioned the VA loan, which will enable a qualifying GI to buy with little or no cash down. But what about the non-vet, or the vet who has used up his entitlement? What about you?

6 Sources of Real Estate That Can Be Bought with Nothing Down

1. Properties going into foreclosure. There are a million reasons why some people fail to meet their financial obligations and let properties go into foreclosure. Sometimes it actually benefits the owner to let the property slip into default, because the loss is more attractive than a potential sale. Whatever the reason, one person's problem might be your gold mine.

Where do you find foreclosure properties? Lenders are one place to look. Banks, savings and loans, and other institutional lenders will do almost anything to avoid having to foreclose on a loan. It looks bad on their lending record, and as they may have sold the loan to an insurance company (or be trying to), their service of a foreclosure is expensive and distasteful.

So here you come. You're bright (you scored 90 or more,

didn't you?), full of promise, and you are ready to take on something that needs tender loving care to be pulled out of the well.

Let the lenders in your area know who you are. Pay them a visit and ask them to pass on to you potential foreclosures in the kind of property you are interested in.

If they do (and they will if you establish some rapport there), you can sometimes make a deal with the owner of the property. A property owner looking foreclosure in the face may have no choice but to take your offer. After all, you are willing (perhaps) to give the seller some ultimate return on his hard-earned capital, even though you aren't giving him a down payment.

2. Watch the courthouse. You can find potential foreclosures by watching the lien recordings in the courthouse. Or become a subscriber to one of several court recording publications that will show you all the legal events going on in your county, from births to deaths to foreclosures.

A lien or series of liens being filed against a property owner is a sign this person may not be prompt with his payments. The mortgage company doesn't act as quickly as an unpaid worker, and this preliminary indication can give you a chance to contact this owner to see if he has any real estate he is interested in selling. Keep in mind, however, the foreclosure may not have been filed, nor are you assured there will ever be a foreclosure. You will call a lot of people this way and hit only a few prime candidates. After a while, however, you get the knack of being able to tell who is more likely to be going under.

3. Company-bought homes. If you live in an area with one or more sizable companies, it is likely the company has been forced to buy one or more homes (or apartments) from time to time. This occurs because key employees are transferred and the company agrees to take over the house the employee owned. This is often your chance to make a very good deal. These companies will usually have one person in charge of real estate. This is the guy or gal you need to meet. Again, establishing rapport is your key. It's like going to apply for a job, but more important. Remember, you will be asking the seller to take a flyer on *you* and not your down payment. If you were ever an altar boy, now's the time to whip out the photo of you in your white robe.

4. The newspaper—watch for ads or run your own.

> ARE YOU PROPERTY POOR?
> I'll take over your mortgage, give you paper, and we'll both be happy. Call Jack at . . .

or sometimes you see this:

> HELP!!! I've been transferred. I'll hold 100% mortgage to the right buyer. Call "Moved."

The local newspaper can be your mine, so give it a look. The trick here is to be flexible with your needs but at the same time selective. You don't want to be sidetracked just because the property can be purchased with nothing down. You might be paying far too much for it as a penalty. I know hundreds of sellers who would sell you or anyone their property with nothing down—and that's no big deal.

However, ads in the newspaper will pull in responses. You should try to negotiate the best deal you can, of course. It isn't a question of being fair. The alternative which the owner of the property faces might be a virtual total loss in the very near future. No seller will take a deal you offer unless there isn't a better deal in the wind (or in his hand). The seller who tells you, "Charlie, I like you and I'd rather you get this property than anyone else I know . . . so just pay me $150,000, okay?" may be sincere, but try to set your emotions aside.

5. The general marketplace. Some sellers don't even tell their brokers everything. In fact, pending foreclosure is often the last thing the broker finds out about. Because of this, don't hesitate to look around with a broker. Don't worry about his commission. He'll figure a way to get it.

Bruce was a good client of mine and wanted to buy a beautiful homesite on the ocean in Fort Lauderdale. His lovely wife, Nancy, had always wanted a place on the beach, and when I showed her an old home that could be remodeled, she and Bruce were ready. The price was $200,000, and by the time I was finished, Bruce had bought it with nothing out of his pocket. In fact, he walked out of the closing with the property and $50,000 cash in his own pocket.

Here's what happened: Bruce bought the property by giving the seller the following: 1) a $100,000 second mortgage on his current house. The idea was, the second mortgage would be paid off when Bruce's house was sold. 2) At the closing the seller would get another $100,000 in cash.

This cash was going to come from a new first mortgage Bruce was going to put on the property he was buying. I was able to get him a first mortgage of $150,000. Of that, $100,000 went to the seller at the closing—and Bruce had bought the property with nothing down and was, in essence, paid $50,000 to do it.

Another client, David, was able to buy a warehouse for $120,000 by obtaining a new first mortgage in the amount of $127,000. He, too, walked away from the closing with cash in his hands.

Both of these examples are current, and the techniques will produce amazing results for you. They are simply deals made within the options available to you. Financing a property sometimes entails guts more than anything else.

6. Exchange clubs. Exchange clubs are scattered around the country. These are organizations which consist of professional real estate exchangers, who deal in both buying and selling real estate as well as exchanging it. Later on you will see the advantages of exchange and why it should become one of your options. But for the moment consider that within these clubs there are many property owners, sometimes brokers themselves, as well as their clients, who would rather sell—even for nothing down—than hold on to their property.

You find these clubs by calling one or more real estate brokers until you find one who knows where the nearest such club is. There may not be any in your town, and if that is the case call or visit several brokers, asking for a salesman who deals in exchanges. By the time you have read the section on exchanges in this book, you will quickly discover if the salesman you are talking to knows as much as you do about exchanging. If you know more than he does, then look harder.

Exchanges, like other marketplaces in real estate, are almost solely controlled by brokers. If you can't get access to professional exchangers, you may have to forget about this option.

The Down Payment

For you to be selective in buying property, cash becomes necessary. You can't always make a no-cash-down deal. The question, then, is how much cash do you need to put down?

One Theory: Borrow as Much as You Can Because Its Cheap Money

Borrowing money from a lender, or entering into deals where the seller holds paper, is a customary way to buy real estate. The ability of buyers to finance a high portion of the purchase price is much more common than in most other kinds of investment.

One investment theory tells investors to use as little of their own money as possible in buying their real estate. The concept is based on the past history of the money market and the rising value of real estate. The theory goes like this: If you have a quantity of money to invest and you invest it all in one item without financing any portion of the purchase, then you have one free-and-clear item. (Sounds simple so far, doesn't it?)

Gwen had $30,000 from a trust fund. She needed a place to live, so she decided to buy an apartment instead of renting. She found one for $30,000 and bought it. (This was the simple part.) A few years later she sold it for $38,000. By now she had some smarts about these things. She took the $38,000 and put that down on a ten-unit apartment building. The apartment building was priced at $190,000, so she paid 20% down and financed the balance.

Tax shelter investors take this concept of borrowing to the hilt to an extreme, buying with a down payment of 5% or 10%. The other guy contributes 90% or 95% of the money; then other other guys pay off the mortgage.

A Second Theory: Maximum Leverage Doesn't Mean Maximum Mortgage

This is a more conservative and, in my opinion, sounder approach to arriving at the proper balance between cash down and amount to be financed. It is based on the following premises:

1. You have the luxury of being able to put a varying amount of cash down on the property of your choice. You could, if need be, put at least 29% cash down. Some properties could take more.

2. The availability of financing or terms provides you with the potential option of having a spread of terms. There is no sense going into a discussion on a situation that is closed with the seller standing firm on at least 25% down. (That doesn't mean you can't offer less, however.)

3. The exercise you are undertaking is for the benefit of making the deal better for you, or to clinch the deal in the first place. The idea of leverage is that you want to get the maximum benefit from the financing.

The financing you place on a property can affect its present value and its future value. You should attempt to look at what effect every mortgage will have, now while you hold on to the property and later when you plan to sell it, hopefully at a profit.

Tabitha bought a six-unit apartment complex, paying all cash. Her $90,000 investment gave her a place to live and an $8,000 return at the end of the year.

Jill bought a similar complex, paying $95,000. However, Jill's complex had an old first mortgage on it, and the seller took back some additional paper (a second mortgage); Jill put down only $20,000. Jill, too, had a place to live, and after paying the mortgages (from the rent that she collected from the other guys), she had $2,500 left over.

Tabitha invested $90,000 and got back $8,000. Jill invested $20,000 and got back $2,500. Who had the better deal?

Jill, of course. Her annual return on $20,000 was 12.5% cash-on-cash, plus the equity buildup of her mortagages as the $75,000 balance was paid down by the other guys. Poor Tabitha got less than 10% on her invested capital, and no mortgage pay-down because there was no mortgage. Even though Jill paid more, her place was worth more and her benefit was much greater. If Tabitha had done the same thing, she would have had $70,000 additional cash to put somewhere else.

Financing is what did the trick. In Jill's case, it was an advantage. But it isn't always such a beneficial thing.

Page and his pal Philip bought a small building with the idea of converting it to a flower-and-houseplant shop. It was a good idea for the area, and it should have been a success. They put only 20% down on the building because they convinced the seller they had to spend a lot of money on the building to get it ready for business. The seller agreed, but to make the deal, Page and Philip signed a second mortgage for $35,000 payable over five years at 14% interest. What happened, of course, was that Page and Philip overburdened themselves with debt service. The amount of mortgage wasn't the problem, it was the way they had to pay it off, which was more than their business could handle. The financing they created buried them.

The Best Theory: Finance the Deal to Suit Your Needs

You may have to be flexible; the seller may have to be flexible. It's a give-and-take game to some degree. "I'll let you have two free stops at Boardwalk if you agree not to collect the $3,000 I owe you for stopping on your hotel-covered Marvin Gardens . . ." Each deal, each buyer will have a new set of circumstances. But in each case, one should look to the future.

Gaspar was so anxious to buy his own home he ignored my suggestion that he wait a few months. "Look, Jack, I've got the down payment in the bank now. If I wait the prices will go up."

Prices may go up some of the time, but there are times they go down, too. You always have to look at what is going on. I advised Gaspar to hold off. "Interest is at 14% now," I told him. "If you put a mortgage on the property now, you will saddle the home with a mortgage that will hurt the future value of the property."

Gaspar went ahead and bought the home of his dreams.

Take a look for a moment what happens when the interest

rate goes up 1% over the term of a mortgage. The chart below shows six mortgages. They range from 9% to 14%. Each is for thirty years and the principal amount is $80,000. You will note that the total paid over thirty years for $80,000 at 9% is $231,840. Of that, $151,840 is interest. At 14%, the same mortgage costs a total of $341,280—almost *$100,000 more* in interest.

TABLE 1.

MORTGAGE COMPARISON CHART

(*Principal* = *$80,000*)

ANNUAL INTEREST CHARGED	MONTHLY PAYMENT[a]	ANNUAL PAYMENT[a]	TOTAL PAID[b]	TOTAL INTEREST[b]
9%	$644.00	$ 7,728	$231,840	$151,840
10	702.00	8,424	252,720	172,720[c]
11	762.00	9,144	274,320	194,320[d]
12	822.66	9,872	296,160	216,160[e]
13	884.66	10,616	318,479	238,480[f]
14	948.00	11,376	341,280	261,128[g]

[a] Principal and interest.
[b] Over 30 years.
[c] Increase of $20,880 over 9% mortgage.
[d] Increase of $21,600 over 10% mortgage.
[e] Increase of $21,840 over 11% mortgage.
[f] Increase of $22,320 over 12% mortgage.
[g] Increase of $22,648 over 13% mortgage.

In reviewing the chart, it should be clear that if you bought the property with a 9% mortgage you would do much better in the long run than if you had bought it with a 14% mortgage. The advantage you need to see here is that current financing on a property might make it far more valuable to you. If there is a toss-up between two or more properties and one of them already has some older financing at lower rates, you can save a lot of money by taking advantage of that existing financing. Better yet, when you go to sell you will still have profit available to you because you won't have burdened the property with a mortgage that took a lot of your own cash to carry. Note that the 10% mortgage takes $8,424 per year to carry. The 13% mortgage takes over $2,000 more. In ten years, if you had saved that two grand, you would have earned well over $20,000 at modest interest rates.

Know Your Options

This book will give you some of the best techniques for financing your purchases. It will show you not only how to make your deals work for you, but how to set them up so you can make the best profit later on.

Think real estate . . . and think ahead.

Financing is more than taking out a mortgage. It is something that rides with the property until it is paid off. It is a continuing cost of the property and must be reckoned with. If the mortgage is being paid off by the other guys, then you have less to worry about. The ability to make the best deal with the financing will generate money in your pocket.

You would buy the office building that gave you a fair return on your cash down, even though the mortgage rate was 14%. However, if you could get a 12% mortgage rate you do two things—increase your return because your mortgage payment is less, and increase the potential profit by ten or more times the increased return to you. If you now get another $1,504 income each year because of the lower interest, the value of this property has now increased at least $15,040.

All the best plans can be underestimated when it comes to the cost. Because of this, you will want to hold on to some capital and not commit it all to mortgage payments. Don't do what Philip and his pal Page did, and string yourself out until you are eaten alive by debt.

On the other hand, some singles have cash flowing in like water over the dam. It's true. I know many singles who have good jobs or professions and few responsibilities. One friend and client is a deep-sea diver who is on job sites for about four months a year, spending almost nothing. Another swinging single is a first mate in the merchant marine; he spends six months going around the world, at no expense, and saves a bundle. The same can be said for airline personnel and doctors and the like--lots of money coming in. The ability to carry heavy payments gives these investors more choice. They have added incentive to invest in real estate—the tax the top single earners pay is so high that shelter is a must.

I've asked many singles how they got into real estate and what happened to them. Some tell horrible stories of making mistakes, getting overburdened by heavy mortgage and upkeep payments, unable to carry the property. Others have much more pleasant stories. Many even made it to the top of the heap. For instance, Harry came to the United States at eighteen. He had $50 in his pocket. He got a job doing manual labor for a construction company and saved his money.

He started fixing up old warehouses into lofts, and after ten years he bought forty-three acres on Long Island. He began building homes and bought some more land. When he married, at the age of thirty, he was worth over $8 million. Not bad, not bad.

Owning your own shelter or your own income property is a solidifying experience. You begin to see and feel things you never did as a renter or user of someone else's property. You now pay real estate tax, and feel direct effects of the county and state governments that use your money. You get benefits and see benefits eroded. You watch while local governments pass laws that limit your property value by changing zoning, or density use, or some of a hundred other variables.

If you approach each purchase viewing as many of your options as you can, then you will have reduced your risk. You may, in fact, make a killing on the deal.

Not every purchase will make you a profit all the time. It is true that some people never have a loser. But perhaps it's because they never really take a chance.

Real estate is unlike any other investment commodity. Stocks are never so visible, so real. Real estate simply *is*, and it is where all the smart money is.

Big profits go hand in hand with big risks. If you limit your risks by knowing more about the alternatives than the next guy, then you have the edge. So bet on yourself.

3

Building Your Fortune Through Real Estate

Look around you. What you see is real estate—real property that is owned and used by people like yourself. It's time you got a piece of the action. Stop being one of the other guys.

To begin, you need to examine some of the foundations that are the keys to investing in real estate so you can profit and profit big. You will build your fortune, not by haphazard investing, but by selecting from the alternatives available to you and understanding the simple secrets of buying and making money through real estate investing. The place to bein is with our own basic need: your shelter.

Back up and take a look at your own present status with regard to real estate. If you own some, it is possible you don't own enough, or perhaps you own the wrong kind and need to upgrade your portfolio. But, if you are an average single, you don't own any. You are a renter of your own very basic need—your shelter.

Renters seem to fall into four categories:

1. The "I'd like to own my own place but I can't afford it" person.

2. The "I prefer to rent because I don't want the responsibility of owning my own place" person.

3. The "I should be renting because that is the best thing for me to do" person.

4. The "I've got to buy, renting is bad for my health" person.

People in the first category usually lack the knowledge to tell how much they could afford.

The second type of renter is often rationalizing a perceived financial inability.

Many people in the third category indeed should not buy. Somebody has to be the other guy.

You might just be one of those people who really should rent. But, unfortunately, there are many people who honestly feel they should rent when they would be far better off if they bought. The last category is, of course, where I feel many renters belong —those of you who realize buying is the thing to do.

GETTING STARTED

YOUR FUTURE as an investor in real estate will depend on many factors. The crucial part is getting started. Buying real estate frequently requires sizable front money as a down payment, and money is the usual problem faced by investors of any age or category.

This book has already covered how you can buy real estate with nothing down. Soon to come are many proven methods on how to buy with very little down. So don't worry about money for the moment. There are other things you need first.

This country got its start as real estate. It was built by people who came from far-off places in search of land they could own for themselves. In fact, in the very early days the promise of land was about the only way you could get people to come here.

"What! Leave the comforts of London to live with those savages?"

"We'll give you one hundred and sixty fine acres of timber and pasture."

"Well, then, sign me up."

It worked time and time again. But although the land was free, it was hard work keeping it. It is still hard work keeping your land, so you need to have everything going for you when you go out and buy.

Believe it or not, a lot of real estate investors used to pick their properties virtually by throwing darts at a map. Many still do. This is the "you can't fail no matter what you do" approach, based on the premise that real estate as a whole just keeps going up in value so you don't have to be a genius to make money at it.

It is true that intelligence is not a prerequisite to making money. Many people who aren't quite as "smart" as others do very well in real estate investing because they develop a sense of what is important and don't analyze the deal to death. Time and time again I've seen prime properties snapped up by savvy buyers who knew they liked the property, believed they could afford it, and had a gut feeling it was going up in value. While these people are buying the property, some smart, sophisticated investor is still checking with his lawyer or accountant about a dozen different things that might go wrong.

You don't need to be a graduate of business school, a bookkeeper, a CPA, or a lawyer to make it big in real estate. Look around and see who has been successful. More often than not, it is the hardworking guy who takes a chance on his own intuition and ability to put things together. It takes courage, but you can make it.

The 6 Magic Factors of Real Estate

Any real estate investment should be analyzed by what I call the six magic factors of real estate. They are what gives real estate the edge over other forms of investment. They are the very foundation on which even the simplest investment is judged.

Two of the elements are absolute and predictable to the penny. The other four can only be estimated in projecting what any investment will do.

1. Equity buildup. When part of the purchase price is covered by a mortgage, you will have a predictable annual equity buildup as you pay down the mortgage balance.

If you bought a $50,000 home and put $10,000 down, you would have a mortgage of $40,000 to pay off. As you reduced the amount you owed, the value to you of the property would grow.

This occurs even if the value of the property itself doesn't increase at all. When, ten years down the road, you have reduced the mortgage to $30,000, your equity is now at least $20,000—double the original equity.

TABLE 2.

EQUITY BUILDUP THROUGH MORTGAGE REDUCTION

In this example, a $50,000 home is purchased with a first mortgage of $40,000 at 10% for 30 years; monthly payment (principal and interest) is $351.

END OF YEAR	BALANCE OWED ON MORTGAGE	EQUITY BUILDUP
0	$40,000	$ 0
1	39,773	227
5	38,642	1,358
10	36,373	3,627
15	32,651	7,349
20	26,557	13,443
25	16,517	23,483
30	0	40,000

As you can see, the amount of principal reduction in the mortgage increases as the mortgage matures. While the payment itself doesn't change over the thirty years, the amount applied to interest is greater in the first years. The end of the first five years shows a principal reduction of only $1,358, while the last five years pays off $16,517. Ah, if we could only turn this around the other way!

Equity is your monetary benefit in the property after you have subtracted the balance you owe on the mortgage from the present market value.

2. Appreciation.

"What did you pay for that apartment, Jack?"

"It came to $70,000."

"Any mortgage?"

"Sure," I said. "I put 20% down—that came to $14,000. The balance was a mortgage for $56,000."

"Your equity, then, was your down payment of $14,000."

"Right," I said.

"And you just sold it for $90,000?"

"I sure did."

"How much did you owe when you sold?"

"$50,000."

"So while you owned the property you added $6,000 to your equity by the reduction of your mortgage?"

"Right," I said.

"But you sold for $90,000?"

"Yep," I said with a smile.

"Let me see. You paid $70,000. You owed $56,000. You had equity of $14,000. You then added $6,000 to your equity by paying down your mortgage by $6,000. That totals only $20,000 in equity."

"Right," I said again.

"But you sold for $90,000 and owed only $50,000, so you had to clear $40,000."

"That's right," I said. "Got back my $20,000 invested plus $20,000."

"If your original equity was $14,000 and you built it up by $6,000, to a total of $20,000 . . . where did the other $20,000 come from?"

"Appreciation," I said. "Good old appreciation."

In this transaction, appreciation didn't come from the reduction of the mortgage, but it was equity nonetheless. It was simply the value of the property increasing relative to everything else.

Had the property been bought originally for $70,000 all cash and then sold for $90,000 all cash, the change would have been the effect of appreciation alone. But I had not bought for cash.

Appreciation is, then, a highly sought after factor of investing in anything. You don't buy diamonds or gold or real estate hoping it will go down in value. You want it to appreciate.

This element is one of the magic factors that cannot be predicted with any exactness. Some land goes up very rapidly and creates very large gains. But the secret here that some investors never seem to grasp is that the value of the property doesn't have to double for you to double your investment. In fact, small gains in the appreciation can double or even quadruple your equity.

TABLE 3.

EQUITY BUILDUP THROUGH APPRECIATION

Again, the price of the home is $50,000, with a 30-year mortgage of $40,000 at 10%. The second column is based on a simple 5% per year increase in value.

End of Year	Assumed Value	Balance Owed on Mortgage	Equity
0	$ 50,000	$40,000	$ 10,000[a]
1	52,500	39,773	12,727
5	62,500	38,642	23,858
10	75,000	36,373	38,627
15	87,500	32,651	54,849
20	100,000	26,557	73,443
25	112,500	16,517	95,983
30	125,000	0	125,000

[a] Down payment.

If this property were a house rented to one of the other guys and the rent just covered expenses and mortgage payments, so that you just broke even, you could retire $115,000 richer than when you started. This is a benefit you don't get by paying rent—and the mortgage payments came out of someone else's pocket.

It is possible, of course, for the market value of the property to decline, and then reduction of the mortgage may not increase equity. However, reduction in value rarely occurs if you have followed the simplest investment techniques. In a depression, of course, real estate holds on better than most investments, because it is a necessity.

One tract of land that I put a group of friends into, taking a part of it myself, was a twenty-seven-acre parcel out on the edge of growth in the Fort Lauderdale area. The land was on a major road and adjoined a condo project that hadn't quite gotten off the ground yet.

I had seen the land literally a thousand times without giving it any thought. Then, everything just seemed to point to this area as a future hot spot, I analyzed the tract and decided that it would double in price within five years at the most.

This analysis wasn't as scientific as you might think. I knew the county was going to build several new roads in the area, and that three large real estate projects had been assembled several miles farther out from the center of things, making this site no longer on the edge but inside the edge of progress.

We bought the land with 20% down. The total purchase price was just about $450,000, so the down payment of $90,000 was spread among eighteen friends, seven of whom were singles on the way to building their fortunes. The initial investment per investor was $5,000. In addition, I anticipated our paying down the mortgage for at least five years before the property could be sold. In essence, I projected an average growth of 20% in the property over each of the next five years so we could cash out at the end of that time.

What actually happened was that we sold all but three acres at the end of the first year for about $835,000. We still owed $360,000 on the first mortgage, so our equity picture at purchase and later at the sale looked like this:

At Purchase		At Sale
$450,000	Price	$835,000
360,000	–Mortgage	360,000
$ 90,000	Equity	$475,000
	–Original Investment	90,000
	Gain	$385,000

The return on our original investment of $90,000 was $385,000. In terms of yield, the investor who had put up $5,000 got back over 400% of that amount in one year. Also, we still had three acres of land, which were sold several years later for over $150,000 additional return. This was appreciation at its best. Notice that the property itself had not doubled in price, yet the return was over five times the original investment.

Not all of your real estate transactions (or mine) will be so spectacular. However, you will frequently have deals where the value can go up only 15% or 20% in one year and still reap wild returns—for example, if you were able to take an option on a property and tie it up for a year. Say there's a residential lot you feel is a good investment, and you know you could buy it a year from now, on terms, but you can't quite scrape up the down payment now. In this situation, you can try the option-to-buy method of locking up the future value at today's price. I've done this by offering a fair option amount to the owner of the land, telling him that I wasn't sure I was going to buy the lot but I was willing to risk the option money to reserve my right to buy at the end of a year, with the option money to be applied to the purchase.

One such deal I made involved a lot on the water in Fort Lauderdale. The lot's value was $30,000 and I put up $5,000 on an option. To buy the lot, I'd have to come up with $25,000 at the end of the first year. In essence, what I did was buy an interest-free term while I hoped the value of the lot would go up.

If the lot had gone up in value only 10%, from $30,000 to $33,000, I would have had a potential gain of $3,000 on my $5,000 option money. That's a 60% return.

If the lot went up 20% in that one year (not at all uncommon if you are following the rules and tips in this book), I would have had a lot worth $36,000, and my equity would look like this:

Price	$36,000
I owed	−25,000
Equity	$11,000

In this instance, with a 20% increase in the value of the lot I would have had over a 100% return on my $5,000 option money.

The end of this story is, I closed on the lot at the end of the twelve months, coming up with the $25,000. Within two months

I was offered $60,000 for the lot. (I didn't sell, however, but built a home on the lot and moved in.)

Play around with this growth factor that makes millions of dollars for the investors who recognize that only if you pay all cash do you lose out on this leveraging effect of letting someone else's money (the seller's or mortgage holder's) build your wealth.

Watch out for the opposite of appreciation, which is *not* depreciation (which is a benefit, not a handicap) but devaluation. Depreciation involves another magic factor of real estate.

3. Tax shelter. You have heard of people, often doctors and other professionals, buying into tax shelters. You might have bought into one yourself. There used to be lots of different kinds —movies, books, cattle, oil, art expeditions, charities, and, of course, real estate, just to name a few. One by one the IRS has been knocking them off, until the only one left that makes any sense is real estate.

This is how a tax-shelter deal works:

John Ford, a general contractor, has nearly finished building a two-hundred-unit garden-apartment complex, and he is interested in forming a limited partnership to sell a major portion of the project in order to generate some quick and ready cash for his other operations.

Ford has estimated that the project will be worth $6,000,000 when completed; these numbers are justified by the rental picture of the area. Based on this figure, Ford has obtained a construction loan, with a permanent loan from a major insurance company to replace the repaid construction loan. The amount of the permanent loan is $4,500,000.

The actual cost to buy the land, build the building, and carry the construction interest will total $4,650,000. This is nearly $200,000 more than Ford had anticipated when he started the project a year earlier. He was planning on mortgaging 100% of the cost, but overruns dictated that he put some of his own money into the project.

Ford structures a limited partnership so that he will attract thirty investors each with $50,000 to invest (half now, the other half next year). This will generate $1,500,000 for Ford.

The terms of the deal are these:

1. As limited partners they will have 75% of the interest in the complex.

2. They will have 100% of the tax shelter.

3. He will give them preferred income at the rate of 9%.

4. He will operate the property for a 5% management fee.

Here's what has happened: Ford, in selling his complex this way, will get $1,500,000 above the mortgage. This is all the property is worth anyway. He still has 25% of the complex, and is paid 5% to look after it.

The investors will have 100% of the tax shelter. The shelter comes from those items of real property which are depreciable. It is from the annual depreciation which IRS allows owners of real property to deduct from their income that the term *tax shelter* is derived. Depreciation is taken just like any other normal operating expense. The only difference is, it is a paper expense. Depreciation does not have an actual expenditure of money tied to it. Interest, for example, is also deductible, but you have to actually pay interest.

Virtually everything except land is depreciable under guidelines which we will discuss later and which you can note on the depreciation chart at the end of this chapter. Ford determined that his investors were most interested in a fast tax shelter, so he decided to take the greatest amount of depreciation early. From the investors' point of view, they see Ford's tax shelter deal as giving them $4,800,000 of actual depreciable property (out of the $6,000,000 value). The accountants have set this up, counting the first-year extra allowance for the personal property (furniture and fixtures) in some units and a double-declining-balance form of depreciation (one of the fastest—to be explained shortly), so the first year will have a depreciation of $400,000, or over $13,000 per investor. This $13,000 is a paper loss to offset income. That is to say, it will show up on each investor's income tax return as a loss and will shelter $13,000 of actual income.

If the investor is a young, single doctor paying 75% of his nonearned income to Uncle Sam, he can "hide" $13,000 of that income behind this tax shelter and avoid paying an additional

$9,750 in tax. The second year he may have a similar depreciation, and his total actual expenditure (without any consideration for income coming in from rent) is $30,500, as he has saved $19,500 in taxes. Uncle Sam paid nearly 40% of the investor's purchase price.

Ford has given the investors a preferred income at 9%, which means he will see they get that return on their invested capital out of rents before he takes anything on his remaining 25% interest in the project.

This kind of tax shelter transaction is not difficult to follow, and the benefits are easy to see.

A tax shelter is a trade-off and conversion of ordinary income to income taxed at lower, long-term capital gains rates. Over the years as you depreciate a property you reduce your book value in it. This book value is called your *basis*. This is important to know when you refer to tax shelter deals because if there is no ultimate conversion of ordinary income into capital gains, the tax shelter may not be a very good one.

When you sell a property, the gain is the amount of money you get above your basis. Remember, basis is not the price you paid for a property. Take a good look at how basis is determined:

1. Start with the price you paid.
2. Add any closing costs which are part of the acquisition of the property.
3. Add any capital improvements while you own the property (buildings, repairs of a capital nature which you do not take as expenses for the year).
4. Add expenses such as taxes and interest which you have not taken as a deduction from earned income.
5. Subtotal the amount to this point.
6. Subtract from the subtotal all depreciation you have taken while you have owned the property.
7. What's left is your basis.

You can see that the only deduction in arriving at basis is, in fact, depreciation. Because depreciation is your tax shelter, and what you are sheltering is ordinary income, when you sell, the amount of the capital gain (assuming that the income qualifies as a long-term capital gain) which is above your basis will include this depreciation.

Also, because you can pick your own time to sell, you can convert and move the income from one year to another. Sometimes you postpone the conversion well down the road to when your ordinary income tax rates will be much lower (in retirement, for example).

Keep in mind that the best tax shelter is one that shelters most of its own income. Several years ago syndicates were putting together deals that gave investors a lot of instant shelter but no long-range conversion. Properties were being front-loaded with heavy mortgages that not only were nonamortizing but actually led to the principal balance being built up. The pro forma (a projected analysis) of the income properties was often overstated, and deal after deal got into trouble. Many tax shelter deals failed because the property was so heavily mortgaged the income could not support the expenses, and there was no other benefit to balance the loss of income.

When it comes to income-producing property, take advantage of the kind of tax shelter that most benefits you. The fast write-down through depreciation may not be the answer to your problem. You might do better to remember that for most people the best tax shelter is a new source of income with which to pay the tax. In selecting a property you have to look at *all* of the magic factors of real estate.

Remember also: Whenever you can get Uncle Sam to kick in and pay part of your investment, take advantage of this.

4. Cash flow. If someone pays you for the use of some of your real estate, you may have cash flow.

Cash flow is the money you have in your hand at the end of each month (or year) as a direct result of your real estate investment. Ready cash is something everyone can use.

In essence, cash flow is the bottom line. It's what's left when you begin with gross income and deduct actual expenses and make mortgage payments.

For example, assume you own a duplex and you rent out one side for $400 per month. You live in the other side with a friend, who pays you $175 per month for that privilege. Your gross income would be $575 per month, or $6,900 per year. Your upkeep and expenses for the duplex might run you $1,500 or more; let's say you can pay your real estate tax, keep up the yard, and maintain the property in good repair for $1,850 per year. Assume your total mortgage payment of principal, interest, and insurance ran you $375 per month, or $4,500 per year. With this information we look at the cash flow analysis:

Gross income		$6,900
Less:		
Expenses	$1,850	
Mortgage	4,500	
		6,350
Cash flow		$ 550

While $550 may not seem like an enormous amount of money, in addition to the cash flow you are: 1) living free, 2) building equity, 3) seeing your investment appreciate, and 4) sheltering not only income from the investment but perhaps other income as well.

When you progress in your investment capability you will see that there are many properties that will score highly on the four magic factors of real estate discussed thus far.

5. Inflation fighter. Take a look again at the three basic necessities of man—food, clothing, and shelter. These three items share many similarities. Each is subject to the supply and demand rules that regulate their values. Each involves the input of raw materials and the manipulation of people to create the finished product. Each item can be bought, held, used, traded, and to some degree used up.

The first two, food and clothing, are needed in a steady flow. Who would say "I've bought all the food I'll ever need" or "Well, I don't have to buy any more clothes" (unless he said this on the fast way down from the Empire State Building)?

Because it's impractical to stockpile a lifetime supply of food and clothing, you will constantly be at the mercy of inflation when you *do* go out to buy these two necessities. The food or clothes you buy today will certainly cost more five years from now to replace. Yet the five-year-old loaf of bread, the five-year-old suit of clothes, will be next to worthless. If you don't consume these two necessities, you may not have any value at all.

(There are exceptions to this, of course. I understand that some furs, if kept in like-new condition, are more valuable because of inflation. Also, it is possible to store some food stocks that will reach maturity at an increased price over a period of years, such as wine and fine brandy.)

Real estate is an absolute item. It simply *exists*, and it *exists* in a certain location. If this sounds like double talk, don't be misled. Real estate is valuable not because of the space it occupies on this earth, but because of its location in relation to other locations.

A given duplex will vary in value depending entirely on which of a thousand different places it happens to occupy in the United States. It is possible to set this duplex on land that costs the same in different locations and still end up with different values, simply because location is what you pay for.

Because all real estate does begin with land, and because land, and its location, will largely determine ultimate value, real estate is not only unique but is also the only true inflation fighter.

The fifth magic factor of real estate is the combination of all, or most, of the first four. It is important for you to recognize that all of the first four factors will not always occur in all real estate transactions. Investment in vacant land, for example, will not necessarily produce cash flow. By itself this is no reason to avoid purchasing vacant land. What is needed is some counterbalance. There must be the promise, at least, of a greater benefit from one or more of the other factors.

6. Emotion—the mystery factor. There's a modern approach to investing in real estate, or at least in some kinds of real estate: "If you like it and you can afford it, then buy it." The concept here is there will be times when you just want to own whatever it is. There may be no logical economic reason. The cash flow may be nonexistent, there may be no hope of appreciation, and the only tax shelter might be the loss you take when you have to give it away.

People react emotionally when buying other commodities, don't they? How about those fancy cars, or expensive designer clothes, or dinner at the most expensive spots in town? Emotion is a real factor when you buy something you can use.

Don't let your analytic mind get you so bogged down with the economics of an investment that you overlook this most important aspect of all. Do you like what you are proposing to buy? If not, then you should ask yourself the next question: "Am I forced to buy something I don't like because there is nothing around I can afford that I do like?" If the answer to this last question is yes, then you simply need to work hard at building your portfolio so you will eventually be able to afford what you like.

Three Basic Methods of Depreciation, the Source of Tax Shelter

1. Straight line.
2. Declining-balance methods.
3. Sum-of-the-years digits.

Any real estate improvement can be depreciated over its useful life. The IRS Code provides a guide to useful life. This guide doesn't have to be followed to the letter, but any difference should be explainable to IRS or court satisfaction or the depreciation will be disallowed.

The IRS allows depreciation on this basis of useful life: apartments (40 years), banks (50), factories (45), garages (45), hotels (40), office buildings (45), stores (50), warehouses (60).

The IRS also permits a component depreciation. Specific items within the building are broken out of the total package and depreciated separately: structure (40 years), electrical (15), plumbing (15), roofing (15), heating (10), air conditioning (10), carpeting (5), painting and decorating (5).

What Can Be Depreciated with What Method?

1. Straight line. All improvements can use this straight-line method. The useful life of the entire property is determined (either in total or by component), and once the land and salvage values have been deducted, the useful life is divided into the remaining value to determine the depreciation.

$$\frac{\text{Basis} - (\text{Land value} + \text{salvage value})}{\text{Remaining life}} = \begin{matrix}\text{Annual} \\ \text{depreciation deduction}\end{matrix}$$

For example, if you buy a property for \$100,000, your beginning basis is \$100,000. If the useful life remaining is forty years, the land value is \$20,000, and the salvage value of the improvements at the end of forty years is \$5,000, here's what the depreciation would look like:

$$\frac{\$100{,}000 - (\$20{,}000 + \$5{,}000)}{40 \text{ years}} = \$1{,}875 \text{ per year}$$

Note that \$1,875 is 2.5% or one-fortieth, of the improvement value of \$75,000.

2. Declining-balance methods. These methods permit write-offs as great as double the straight-line rate. The three forms most commonly used are 125%, 150%, and 200% rates. These are in essence a multiple of the straight-line rate. However, you do not take into account salvage value in the declining-balance methods. Table 4 offers comparisons of these various rates of depreciation.

When You Can Use the Different Declining Methods

125%: Can be applied to used real property acquired before July 25, 1969, and used residential rental property acquired after July 24, 1969, with a useful life of twenty years or more.

150%: This is the fastest depreciation method available for used property acquired before July 25, 1969, and new nonresidential rental property built after July 24, 1969.

200%: This is available for new real estate constructed before July 25, 1969 (you have to be the first user), and new residential rental properties.

3. The sum-of-the-years digits. How it's figured: The total of all the years is found and then used as the denominator of a declining fraction.

$$\frac{\text{Years} + 1 \times \text{years}}{2} = \text{the denominator}$$

For example, if the mortgage was for twenty years, then years 1, 2, 3, 4, and so on to a total of 20 are added up. The above formula is a shortcut:

$$\frac{20 + 1 \times 20}{2} = 210$$

Therefore, as the years pass, the depreciation would slowly decline. Here is the rate for the first five years:

Year 1 = 20/210
Year 2 = 19/210
Year 3 = 18/210
Year 4 = 17/210
Year 5 = 16/210

As you can see, the depreciation for the first year, 20/210, will be much greater than that for the last year in the term, 1/210.

The sum-of-the-years digits can be used only for new real estate built before July 25, 1969, and new residential rental properties. This is the fastest write-down of any of the methods, and throws off high amounts of tax shelter in the early years.

However, there is a danger in fast write-off of property with the accelerated methods. IRS gives and takes away. It permits the fast write-off in the cases indicated, but if the property is sold the IRS will want you to calculate to see if you took excessive depreciation (a larger amount than you would take in the straight-line method). If you did, such excess is subject to tax at earned-income rates and not at a capital-gains rate.

You should be aware that on commercial-type property 100% depreciation taken in excess of the straight-line method would be counted as earned income in the year of the sale. This factor must be considered when you are buying with an eye to selling in the near future.

Residential rental property is less restrictive. In residential rental property 100% of excessive depreciation is taxed at earned-income rates for the first 100 months, declining 1% each month thereafter. After 200 months there is no tax on the excessive depreciation.

Qualified low-cost rental properties: The recapture is 100% for the first 20 months, then a decline of 1% for each month thereafter.

Watch for new and special deals coming out of IRS. The country is going into a changing cycle of rental development and urban renewal, and there are likely to be many new programs to give incentives to the builders of such projects. Ask your accountant to explain the latest data on historical sites, rehabilitation of ghetto areas, low-cost rental projects, etc.

Review Table 4. You can use this to get your act rolling.

TABLE 4.

Percent of Depreciation

Method→	Straight-Line		125% S.L.		150% S.L.		200% S.L.		Sum-Years Digits	
Year	Annual %	Cumulative %	Annual %	Cumulative %	Annual %	Cumulative %	Annual %	Cumulative %	Annual %	Cumulative %
15-Year Useful Life										
1	6.67	6.67	8.33	8.33	10.00	10.00	13.33	13.33	12.50	12.50
2	6.67	13.33	7.64	15.97	9.00	19.00	11.56	24.89	11.67	24.17
3	6.67	20.00	7.00	22.97	8.10	27.10	10.01	34.90	10.83	35.00
4	6.67	26.67	6.42	29.39	7.29	34.39	8.68	43.58	10.00	45.00
5	6.67	33.33	5.88	35.28	6.56	40.95	7.52	51.11	9.17	54.17
6	6.67	40.00	5.39	40.67	5.90	46.86	6.52	57.62	8.33	62.50
7	6.67	46.67	4.94	45.61	5.31	52.17	5.65	63.27	7.50	70.00
8	6.67	53.33	4.53	50.15	4.78	56.95	4.90	68.17	6.67	76.67
9	6.67	60.00	4.15	54.30	4.30	61.26	4.24	72.42	5.83	82.50
10	6.67	66.67	3.81	58.11	3.87	65.13	3.68	76.09	5.00	87.50
20-Year Useful Life										
1	5.00	5.00	6.25	6.25	7.50	7.50	10.00	10.00	9.52	9.52
2	5.00	10.00	5.86	12.11	6.94	14.44	9.00	19.00	9.05	18.57
3	5.00	15.00	5.49	17.60	6.42	20.85	8.10	27.10	8.57	27.14
4	5.00	20.00	5.15	22.75	5.94	26.79	7.29	34.39	8.10	35.24
5	5.00	25.00	4.83	27.58	5.49	32.28	6.56	40.95	7.62	42.86
6	5.00	30.00	4.53	32.11	5.08	37.36	5.90	46.86	7.14	50.00
7	5.00	35.00	4.24	36.35	4.70	42.06	5.31	52.17	6.67	56.67
8	5.00	40.00	3.98	40.33	4.35	46.40	4.78	56.95	6.19	62.86
9	5.00	45.00	3.73	44.06	4.02	50.42	4.30	61.26	5.71	68.57
10	5.00	50.00	3.50	47.55	3.72	54.14	3.87	65.13	5.24	73.81

Method→	Straight-Line		125% S.L.		150% S.L.		200% S.L.		Sum-Years Digits	
Year	Annual %	Cumulative %	Annual %	Cumulative %	Annual %	Cumulative %	Annual %	Cumulative %	Annual %	Cumulative %
					25-Year Useful Life					
1	4.00	4.00	5.00	5.00	6.00	6.00	8.00	8.00	7.69	7.69
2	4.00	8.00	4.75	9.75	5.64	11.64	7.36	15.36	7.38	15.08
3	4.00	12.00	4.51	14.26	5.30	16.94	6.77	22.13	7.08	22.15
4	4.00	16.00	4.29	18.55	4.98	21.93	6.23	28.36	6.77	28.92
5	4.00	20.00	4.07	22.62	4.68	26.61	5.73	34.09	6.46	35.38
6	4.00	24.00	3.87	26.49	4.40	31.01	5.27	39.36	6.15	41.54
7	4.00	28.00	3.68	30.17	4.14	35.15	4.85	44.22	5.85	47.38
8	4.00	32.00	3.49	33.66	3.89	39.04	4.46	48.68	5.54	52.92
9	4.00	36.00	3.32	36.58	3.66	42.70	4.11	52.78	5.23	58.15
10	4.00	40.00	3.15	40.13	3.44	46.14	3.78	56.56	4.92	63.08
					30-Year Useful Life					
1	3.33	3.33	4.17	4.17	5.00	5.00	6.67	6.67	6.45	6.45
2	3.33	6.67	3.99	8.16	4.75	9.75	6.22	12.89	6.24	12.69
3	3.33	10.00	3.83	11.99	4.51	14.26	5.81	18.70	6.02	18.71
4	3.33	13.33	3.67	15.65	4.29	18.55	5.42	24.12	5.81	24.52
5	3.33	16.67	3.51	19.17	4.07	22.62	5.06	29.18	5.59	30.11
6	3.33	20.00	3.37	22.54	3.87	26.49	4.72	33.90	5.38	35.48
7	3.33	23.33	3.23	25.76	3.68	30.17	4.41	38.30	5.16	40.65
8	3.33	26.67	3.09	28.86	3.49	33.66	4.11	42.42	4.95	45.59
9	3.33	30,00	2.96	31.82	3.32	36.98	3.84	46.26	4.73	50.32
10	3.33	33.33	2.84	34.66	3.15	40.13	3.58	49.84	4.52	54.84

Method→	Straight-Line		125% S.L.		150% S.L.		200% S.L.		Sum-Years Digits	
Year	Annual %	Cumulative %	Annual %	Cumulative %	Annual %	Cumulative %	Annual %	Cumulative %	Annual %	Cumulative %
				33⅓-Year Useful Life						
1	3.00	3.00	3.75	3.75	4.50	4.50	6.01	6.01	5.93	5.93
2	3.00	6.01	3.61	7.37	4.30	8.81	5.65	11.65	5.75	11.69
3	3.00	9.01	3.48	10.84	4.11	12.91	5.31	16.96	5.58	17.26
4	3.00	12.01	3.35	14.19	3.92	16.84	4.99	21.95	5.40	22.66
5	3.00	15.02	3.22	17.41	3.75	20.58	4.69	26.63	5.22	27.88
6	3.00	18.02	3.10	20.51	3.58	24.16	4.41	31.04	5.04	32.92
7	3.00	21.02	2.98	23.50	3.42	27.58	4.14	35.18	4.86	37.79
8	3.00	24.02	2.87	26.37	3.26	30.84	3.89	39.07	4.69	42.47
9	3.00	27.03	2.76	29.13	3.12	33.95	3.66	42.73	4.51	46.98
10	3.00	30.03	2.66	31.79	2.98	36.93	3.44	46.17	4.33	51.31
				35-Year Useful Life						
1	2.86	2.86	3.57	3.57	4.29	4.29	5.71	5.71	5.56	5.56
2	2.86	5.71	3.44	7.02	4.10	8.39	5.39	11.10	5.40	10.95
3	2.86	8.57	3.32	10.34	3.93	12.31	5.08	16.18	5.24	16.19
4	2.86	11.43	3.20	13.54	3.76	16.07	4.79	20.97	5.08	21.27
5	2.86	14.29	3.09	16.63	3.60	19.67	4.52	25.49	4.92	26.19
6	2.86	17.14	2.98	19.60	3.44	23.11	4.26	29.75	4.76	30.95
7	2.86	20.00	2.87	22.48	3.30	26.41	4.01	33.76	4.60	35.56
8	2.86	22.86	2.77	25.24	3.15	29.56	3.79	37.55	4.44	40.00
9	2.86	25.71	2.67	27.91	3.02	32.58	3.57	41.11	4.29	44.29
10	2.86	28.57	2.57	30.49	2.89	35.47	3.36	44.48	4.13	48.41

Method→	Straight-Line		125% S.L.		150% S.L.		200% S.L.		Sum-Years Digits	
Year	Annual %	Cumulative %	Annual %	Cumulative %	Annual %	Cumulative %	Annual %	Cumulative %	Annual %	Cumulative %
					40-Year Useful Life					
1	2.50	2.50	3.12	3.12	3.75	3.75	5.00	5.00	4.88	4.88
2	2.50	5.00	3.03	6.15	3.61	7.36	4.75	9.75	4.76	9.63
3	2.50	7.50	2.93	9.09	3.47	10.83	4.51	14.26	4.63	14.27
4	2.50	10.00	2.84	11.93	3.34	14.18	4.29	18.55	4.51	18.78
5	2.50	12.50	2.75	14.68	3.22	17.40	4.07	22.62	4.39	23.17
6	2.50	15.00	2.67	17.34	3.10	20.49	3.87	26.49	4.27	27.44
7	2.50	17.50	2.58	19.93	2.98	23.47	3.68	30.17	4.15	31.59
8	2.50	20.00	2.50	22.43	2.87	26.34	3.49	33.66	4.02	35.61
9	2.50	22.50	2.42	24.85	2.76	29.11	3.32	36.98	3.90	39.51
10	2.50	25.00	2.35	27.20	2.66	31.76	3.15	40.13	3.78	43.29
					50-Year Useful Life					
1	2.00	2.00	2.50	2.50	3.00	3.00	4.00	4.00	3.92	3.92
2	2.00	4.00	2.44	4.94	2.91	5.91	3.84	7.84	3.84	7.76
3	2.00	6.00	2.38	7.31	2.82	8.73	3.69	11.53	3.76	11.53
4	2.00	8.00	2.32	9.63	2.74	11.47	3.54	15.07	3.69	15.22
5	2.00	10.00	2.26	11.89	2.66	14.13	3.40	18.46	3.61	18.82
6	2.00	12.00	2.20	14.09	2.58	16.70	3.26	21.72	3.53	22.35
7	2.00	14.00	2.15	16.24	2.50	19.20	3.13	24.86	3.45	25.80
8	2.00	16.00	2.09	18.33	2.42	21.63	3.01	27.86	3.37	29.18
9	2.00	18.00	2.04	20.38	2.35	23.98	2.89	30.75	3.29	32.47
10	2.00	20.00	1.99	22.37	2.28	26.26	2.77	33.52	3.22	35.69

4

Singles' Special Problems

SINGLES face special problems that the rest of the population only occasionally come up against. It's time we attacked these problems with specific battle plans. But first we have to identify the problems and see if they fit your situation.

CREDIT

WE LIVE in a credit society. The plastic cards that enable us to buy by charging have made merchandising and banking what they are today. There is hardly a shop or business establishment that won't accept payment in credit cards.

Many cards are valid only in one shop. Others are meant to be used all over the world. They are convenient, they are useful, they are in demand.

But that is only one kind of credit. To get a credit card isn't as easy as many people think. We see them advertised on TV, in newspapers, in magazines. Whatever is advertised must be easy to get . . . as long as you have the price. Right?

Not so. No doubt many of you reading this book have applied for a credit card and been rejected. An oil company, MasterCard, or American Express are all alike. Burned by the "bad credit risk," they are being much more selective in handing out their cards. It isn't the annual card holder's fee that the card companies are really interested in, but the fee merchants pay for the convenience of having ready buyers for their merchandise. No waiting for the end of the month to go shopping now, not with that card in your pocket.

Credit card companies and other members of the banking industry are growing more and more concerned with the condition of their accounts receivable and their ultimate collection. Uncollectible debt increases each year. The bad debt, or uncollectible charge, is a billion-dollar problem, and the costs are spread among the users. One effect is to make it harder for the marginal credit risk to get credit.

And who bears the brunt of this? The singles! And most of all, the single woman. At the top of the list is the recently divorced, now single woman.

Joanne was a hard worker—so hard, in fact, that she was supplying about 60% of the income of her union with Rick. Their marriage was headed for the rocks, but Joanne was not overly upset about her future. After all, she had a steady job, she had a good position in the community, she was social-minded, and all in all was an asset to her employer and the community. It looked as if Rick was going to be the big loser.

When the marriage ended, Rick decided to hang on to their apartment; his name was on the lease. Joanne was glad to get out of the place anyway. She went to stay with a girl friend until she could find a place. Hell, that shouldn't be hard.

Mind you, things had changed. Rick had the credit. Rick had the credit cards. Joanne had her maiden name back again.

In the eyes of the credit world, Rick hadn't undergone any change for the worse, whereas Joanne was now single. Toughsville, when it came to getting credit.

Without credit, Joanne had to live on cash at hand. She had to put up cash for nearly everything she did.

A single moving up in the world, easing out of family life, also faces the rude awakening that somewhere down the line there is going to be a credit check. That check and the report that comes back can affect the future of this single in far more ways than the ability to get a credit card.

Good Credit Is a Prerequisite in Demonstrating Responsibility

There are plenty of people who pay their bills but are irresponsible in other ways, but when it comes to becoming a financial success in this good old U.S. of A., you play the game with the current house rules. Begin right now to establish yourself as a good credit risk.

Note that I said *establish* yourself as a good credit risk. You might be the greatest, most dependable person, and the lowest credit risk in the world. But that won't do. It's like being a great lover—you need to have others appreciate that fact.

When it comes to real estate, being a good credit risk is essential. Let's take a look at the things you can do to make yourself a *bad* credit risk.

- Be a single woman living alone or with friends in a new town. (Score 30 points, then deduct 5 points for each six months at the same address.)
- Be a single guy just out of the submarine corps. (Score 10 points plus 5 points for each six months you've been without a woman.)
- Run up hefty bar tabs around town and not pay them off. (Score 10 points for each bar.)
- Constantly be a month behind on your car payments. (Score 20 points for each month behind, and a 50-point bonus for each additional car.)
- Owe back rent. (For each month not paid you get 20 points.)
- Get turned down for auto insurance. (Score 10 points each time.)
- Never have borrowed money. (Score 25 points, then deduct 5 points for each $10,000 you have loaned someone else [who paid it back].)
- Have no charge accounts anywhere. (20 points.)
- Have no payment record on the charge accounts you do have. (20 points. Score 15 points for each card that you haven't used in the past six months.)

• Tell everyone you just got out of prison. (Score 15 points for each five years in the slammer.)

• Have just been sent to prison. (Send this book back to the warden and score a bonus of 100 points.)

• Have your checks bounce back NSF (nonsufficient funds). (Score 5 points for each check in past twelve months.)

• Have a mortgage foreclosed on you. (Score 5 points for each $10,000 of mortgage.)

• Be behind on your mortgage payments. (Score 25 points for each month behind for each mortgage.)

• Don't return a rented car. (50 points.)

• Have less than twelve months' job experience at your present place of employment. (25 points.)

• Earn less than welfare gives for being unemployed. (50 points.)

• Spend more than you earn. (Score 5 points for each $10 you spend in excess of your monthly earnings.)

• Sell books door to door—books which you checked out of the local library. (Score 15 points for each book.)

You may be a bad risk if you score 50 points. If you score over 200 points and don't have a big bank account, your credit is low-low-low.

Only one of the Catch-22's of credit is having credit. I've heard credit managers tell a credit applicant that it was necessary for him to have three other credit card references. My God! If you have to have a credit card to get a credit card, how'd anyone ever start?

If you don't have a credit card, you can't have a history of good payment on your charges. A history of paying all cash for everything you have ever bought doesn't count because there is no record of that. Sorry—cash doesn't count.

Things You Can Do to Build Your Credit

1. Get a credit card. Find a commercial bank that is a member of one of the major credit cards—Visa or MasterCard, for example. Open a checking account there. Put all your money in that account. If you have a savings account, draw it out and put it in the checking account. Then write a check back to your savings account. If you don't spend much, run money through each account (savings and checking) several times to build up the level. The charge for the checks you write might run a few dollars for the month, but the idea is to show that you are a spender.

Cashing a lot of checks made out to you in large sums, depositing the cash in the savings account, then drawing out the savings and depositing it in your checking isn't all that time-consuming and can help build your money flow at the commercial bank. After three months of this, apply for a Visa card at the bank. Don't be surprised if you have already received an invitation to do so, but don't take advantage of the invitation until you have demonstrated a money flow ability. Sometimes the bank's computers send out the applications to everyone. Hold off, you aren't ready for the credit check.

2. Pay your bills fast. Build a record of fast payment on your monthly statements from any credit card company. You should pay all your bills promptly, of course, but be overly fast with credit cards. Avoid establishing any bad vibes here.

3. Borrow money. I know a contractor who goes into his commercial bank and borrows $20,000 every few months. He does it on his signature, without having to pledge anything. He is that well thought of, even though his net worth isn't all that hefty. He does this and within a few weeks he pays back the money—all of it, with interest. When it comes time for him to build some houses, and he's at the same bank talking about several hundred thousand dollars of construction money, he is treated royally. By the way, never once has he had a need for the $20,000 he borrowed. That is just his way to keep his credit at the top of the list.

The fact is, it isn't the borrowing of money, it's the paying it back that's important. When you can demonstrate you've done that, then you have a feather in your good-credit cap.

4. Don't run up big bills. The idea of developing credit isn't so you can use it to the hilt. The idea is to develop some record of yourself as a good credit risk.

Therefore, you should avoid using the credit cards to borrow money. Don't charge something and then, instead of paying the bill in full when it comes in, take the option of paying the "easy monthly amount." Millions of dollars each month are piling up in these credit card loans at monumental interest rates. The high interest that credit card companies are allowed to charge simply adds to the cost of what you buy.

The pattern you establish in your payment record also includes the amount of money you continually borrow in this way. Using your credit for convenient purchasing is one thing; borrowing at these excessive rates can be improper management of your funds. If it isn't an absolute necessity and you couldn't afford it now if you had to pay cash, then why pay the extra price by charging it and paying it back at the credit rate? Developing sound management of your funds is part of good credit. Work at being dollar wise.

5. Know your limits. Of all the ways to build up a good credit standing, the most difficult for many people is to know and live within their limits. The abuse of credit is a danger that has affected many people to the point where they have become creditholics. They suffer much as gamblers except that they can walk out of the store a winner . . . until the bills come.

Setting and maintaining a budget is very hard. Singles on their own for the first time have the special handicap that often their income won't support the living standard they were used to while living with their families. Older senior singles, with the loss of income resulting from retirement, face the same problem. But it is something that must be done. You and I don't have the luxury of being able to print our own money as the government does. A deficit budget will quickly take you into irretrievable debt. So don't try to print your own money by using credit cards.

If you see a friend going wild and having a week-long binge with his credit cards, make a strong cup of coffee, take away the cards before someone gets hurt, and call a cab to take him home.

6. Don't be too proud to have a cosigner. Many first homes and apartments are bought with the additional credit push of someone else. Using a relative's or friend's credit as a supplement to yours so you can qualify for a mortgage is not uncommon. It happens all the time and is not the big deal that many people make it out to be. Don't have the attitude "I couldn't ask Mom and Dad to sign on that mortgage." If the real estate is a sound deal and you are able to come up with the down payment, then Mom and Dad aren't risking anything at all. What is actually happening is that the lender is now willing to make the loan because you, Mom, and Dad together have met his requirements. No lender will comfortably make a loan to someone who has no discernible credit, unless the credit is created by an extra-large down payment. If you are putting 40% or 50% down, then that alone might be all you need. "To hell with the credit check, boys, make that loan."

On the other hand, if your deal is more normal and you are going in with no more than 20% down, then you alone might not be enough.

If you are buying property for the first or even the last time, you might need a partner in the deal. It is common now, for example, to have several partners buy duplexes or small apartment buildings together. Each then takes one of the units as his home. In this way the combined credit of the partners supersedes that of the single individual.

Those six tips for building better credit are easy to follow. However, if you are already considered a bad credit risk you have a more serious problem. One of the unfortunate aspects of this modern world is the tenure of records kept in computers. Bad news about you will hang around for a long time. To add to this, records from one part of society—say, the automobile-insurance sector—are easily shared by another computer operation across the country—say, the XYZ Credit Bureau.

You have read of cases where people have had their lives disrupted by an incorrect or damaging bad credit report. Fortunately, these things aren't common, but almost everyone who has used a credit card for several years has experienced the computer error.

Dear Customer:

You have failed to pay the balance due of $37,560. Please forward your payment to us within 5 days from this date or we will be forced to turn this collection over to our not-so-nice roughnecks.

Dear Computer:

I've sent eight letters to you (copies enclosed) telling of your computer error in my billing. The balance due was $37.56, not the amount the statements have shown. Besides, I had paid that amount prior to receipt of your first bill. Please take care of this matter.

Very patiently yours,

Dear Customer:

Your account has been credited with the payment of $37.56. Your past unpaid balance, however, has been charged with $1,589 of late-penalty interest on the previous balance of $37,560. You now owe $39,111.44. Because this amount is past 90 days due, this is your final notice.

One thing to remember—a computer has far more patience than you do, so don't play their game. By the way, it does no good to staple, bend, fold, or mutilate the computer card that comes with your bills. None of that really means anything. It's the computer's private joke. When the cards come back filled with staples, all bent and folded and mutilated, the computer knows it is getting to you.

Emerging from being a bad credit risk is not easy. Some people have even moved away and changed their name. Don't underestimate the power of bad credit. It's like acne. Its scars may stay with you for a long time.

BE YOUR OWN BOSS

WHY NOT? Isn't one of the major problems of a single the job you have (or don't have)? Real estate can solve that.

There was a time, back when this country was getting started, when all anyone needed was real estate. Just give me my homestead and I'll be all right. If I can get hold of a bit of dirt I can grow a living, raise a living, dig a living. Whatever you or I really needed could come from the land or in exchange for produce.

Farmers, cattle barons, miners, wildcatters, developers, all took land and made it produce for them. You can do the same. In fact, look around and you will see that one of the most profitable products to come from land is organically grown food. This "new" way of farming isn't new at all, of course, but it is different, and in many respects impossible for the giant farmer to do because of the nature of big farming.

Organic food products are more costly to produce in big quantities, but when grown in small quantities they yield a high return to the grower. Because of this, many singles are turning back to the basics and farming this "ancient" way and at the same time becoming their own boss.

Getting Down to the Basics

THE LURE of land was all it took to entice people to the New World, to Australia, to South Africa, to places where land was available and people weren't. While it's true that the government no longer gives away free homesteads, it is still possible to have the use of land on a nearly free basis.

Many farmers utilize land at a fraction of its value by leasing it from someone else. While this might seem to make them one of the other guys in this respect, they can turn a profit by growing more than they would have had they bought it at its real value.

Ownership of real estate comes in two basic forms—ownership of the fee and leasehold ownership. Let's take a look at these two forms, because you will have the opportunity in the future to decide which form you want to pursue. There is a tremendous difference in the short- and long-range costs of these forms.

By the way, don't think this is simple despite the fact that it is basic. In years of lecturing before professional real estate groups of salesmen, brokers, lawyers, and accountants, I saw many of these professionals who had not grasped the concepts about to be unfurled before your very eyes.

Ownership of the Fee Simple

In legal talk the fee is the title to the property. Ownership in fee simple is ownership of the property with the fewest restrictions possible on the title. Ownership of real estate in fee simple is therefore the best possible form of ownership.

Outright ownership of the fee, or title, to the property you have purchased is, of course, the way you can benefit in all the rewards the property can bring. You have the use as well as the ownership. Yet ownership of your real estate doesn't give you all the rights you might have thought you had. All real estate has restrictions that limit your free use of the property. Your rights to land aren't absolute. The extent to which your use is limited or regulated may ultimately cause you to decide that *ownership* of the property is no longer desirable. Table 5 shows some (not all) of the restrictions that are found on real estate. You will see the sources of these restrictions and what you can do to reduce their effect.

Many restrictions are set with the idea of protecting the local values by causing a standard of development to be adhered to. In nearly all cases the restrictions imposed on your land will have this effect. It isn't a matter of the effect being beneficial to your intended use, but more a set pattern that you can view in anticipating the long-range use of a parcel of property. If you are buying raw land in the middle of the country, you might have the thought that someday, when the growth from the nearby city gets out that far, you will have a great site for a shopping center or housing subdivision. If you were to see, however, that the land next to this proposed purchase of yours was zoned in such a way as to permit its use as a garbage dump, then you might invest elsewhere. It is absolutely necessary that you become familiar with zoning laws and land-use plans. However, the "trend" is also important, because cities and other local and national governing bodies change their minds from time to time. Such trends, therefore, need to be watched carefully.

There are some restrictions placed by local governing bodies (as well as state and federal agencies) that are so idiotic that you may be able to obtain special exceptions to them. These special exceptions are generally referred to as variances, which are granted by the agency which has control over that particular restriction. While the ability to win relief over a restrictive law is some help, sometimes you win, other times you don't. When you are buying

TABLE 5.

Restrictions on Use

Restriction	Origin	What You Can Do
Road easement	1. Subdivision developer. 2. Local governmental action.	(1 & 2) Hard to get around as the restriction is already there. If it isn't being used, petition the city or county for it to be vacated.
Utility easement Deed restriction (1 & 3 only)	3. Seller you bought from.	(3) Seller may have wanted it to protect access to adjoining property. You must negotiate such matters at the time the property is bought.
Mineral rights Water rights Air rights	1. A previous owner. 2. Local, state, or federal government.	Frequently you can buy the mineral or other rights from the owner. Remember, the person you buy the real estate from may not have owned these rights himself and you may have to deal with another person. *Always ask about this.*
Building and zoning restrictions	Local, state, and federal governing agencies.	These change from time to time in your area. The most restrictive is that which affects the building you can do, as it is the hardest to combat. Local governmental restrictions are tough as well but can sometimes be overturned. The problem is that governmental restrictions tend to become progressively stronger over the years.

real estate, anticipate what restrictions you are going to have to deal with before you buy.

Most of the restrictions you will be able to live with. Sometimes, in fact, it is the restriction that makes your property valuable.

I have a tract of land which is zoned B-3, which in Broward County, Florida, means the highest possible commercial and business zoning. It is in essence the least restrictive form of such zoning. The property will thus support a wider variety of use than other forms of B-zoning (B-1 and B-2 in Broward). If all the land in the area were zoned B-3, there would be no particular edge in my land. However, it turns out there is no more B-3 land for a half mile in either direction on this busy highway. Some similar land right across the street that had been zoned B-3 was recently down-zoned by the city to B-1. Simply because of its zoning, therefore, my land is more valuable.

On the other hand, the land across the street did not become more valuable as the zoning restrictions were increased. Note I didn't say the *value* of this changed land was lessened. That was not the case here. The zoning was still permissive enough to maintain the value it had previously, when there was a great deal of B-3 zoning. What happened was that the elimination of most of the B-3 increased the value of the sole remaining B-3 parcel (mine).

Thus, restrictions imposed by the local governing bodies can increase your values tremendously.

One client came to me several years ago and wanted me to help him rezone some land he had. It was zoned for apartment development, but due to a new main highway that was constructed along one side, it was not as well suited for apartments as it had been previously. After a dozen or so meetings with the proper governing agencies, we had the property rezoned to highly restrictive commercial use. This use, although quite restricted in the commercial categories, was far more practical than the apartment use zoning. The value then went from $45,000 per acre to $165,000 per acre three years later.

But everything that is given can also be taken away. I've been on the losing side occasionally and had property become more restricted because of a new zoning ordinance, or building law, or platting law, or some such thing.

You must constantly be on the alert for the erosion of your property rights. Laws enacted for special reasons, which at the time might not seem to apply to you, later can be interpreted so that it will seem that the law was passed just because of you!

Ownership of the title isn't always the right thing for you. Sometimes control of the real estate is far more desirable than owning it.

Leasehold Ownership

When you rent an apartment, you in effect have a leasehold interest in that apartment for the term of the lease. You are benefiting from the use of the apartment without having ownership of it.

In short leases, this benefit is usually not as great as the ownership of the apartment itself. However, if you have a lease which is long enough and the terms are favorable enough, then the value of the lease might be worth more to you than ownership of the property.

For example, if you were able to obtain a lease (with a sublet clause) on a nice one-bedroom apartment for twenty years at $250 per month, and the rental market went to $450, your ability to profit in the rental market by subletting the apartment would be assured. For twenty years you would pocket the difference between what you collect from the subtenant and what you pay to the landlord—$200 per month, or $2,400 per year, or $48,000 over twenty years—and the landlord still carries the expenses. Your use of the property at the lower rent of $3,000 per year keeps the owner of the property from enjoying the benefits of increased income as the rental market goes up. The moral is, owning property can sometimes be less desirable than leasing it.

In large transactions, where the values are in hundreds of thousands or even millions of dollars, there is another consideration that is important: Land is not depreciable.

To understand the effect of depreciation, let's look first at a normal ownership situation to see the effect depreciation has on the actual spendable cash left at the end of the year. Remember, tax shelter is the sole effect of depreciation. The paper loss created by the expense that isn't really paid that year causes real estate to have its very attractive shelter effect, and the tax shelter from real estate comes from the buildings.

Dina owns a duplex for which she paid $60,000, putting $15,000 down. She used to live in one side and rent the other, but moved out a year ago and is fixing up a home she bought for resale. She rents out both sides of the duplex for a total rent of $800 per month. Each side is furnished.

Dina owes $45,000 on the 9% mortgage, and her payments total $4,500 per year to the savings and loan. Her expenses to keep up the duplex come to an additional $3,000 (taxes, maintenance, etc.). Dina's cash flow picture looks like this:

Rent collected		$9,600
Mortgage payments	$4,500	
Operating expenses	3,000	
Total cash paid out		7,500
Cash flow		$2,100
Tax she'd have to pay		765[a]
After-tax income		$1,335

[a] Tax calculation:

Gross rent		$9,600
Interest on mortgage	$4,050[b]	
Operating expenses	3,000	
Total deductible, not including tax shelter		7,050
		$2,550
Her tax bracket (30%)		× 0.30
Tax		$ 765

[b] 9% of 45,000 is $4,050.

But Dina has some tax shelter. She paid $60,000 for the duplex and her accountant set up $48,000 of the value in depreciable items. (The other $12,000 was the estimated value of the land alone.) Because the $48,000 was partly furniture and other items which have short lives, her depreciation schedule, based on the straight-line method (book value divided by remaining years of useful life), looks like this:

Item	Remaining Years of Life	Book Value[a]	Year's Depreciation
Furniture	6	$ 6,500	$1,083
Carpets	6	2,500	417
Drapes	5	900	180
Kitchen appliances	10	4,000	400
Building	30	34,100	1,137
			$3,217

[a] Less salvage value.

This was paper expense. That is, she didn't actually write a check to anyone for this amount, but the IRS will allow her to deduct it just as though she did. Dina's income calculations now look like this:

Gross income		$ 9,600
Interest on mortgage	$4,050	
Operating expenses	3,000	
Depreciation	3,217	
		$10,267
(Loss for the year)		($ 667)

According to proper IRS calculations, Dina has *no* income. She will pay *no* tax on the income she might have put in her pocket. Yet the cash flow picture shows that Dina did actually put cash in her pocket—$2,100, to be exact. Without tax shelter she would have seen that drop to only $1,335.

Because of tax shelter, Dina has the full $2,100 to spend. On top of that, the loss ($667) will offset other income. At her tax rate it's like giving her another $200 ($667 × 30% = $200.10). After all tax considerations, Dina now has $2,300 spendable for the year ($2,100 + $200). Considering that she put only $15,000 down, she has an exceptional return on her capital investment.

What If She Leased Instead of Buying?

Assume that instead of buying the duplex for $60,000, Dina was able to buy title to the duplex and lease the land portion, which had a value of $12,000, for $1,200 per year. The new transaction looks like this:

Purchase price of duplex (leasehold equity)	$48,000
Cash down (much less now!)	3,000
Mortgage (at 9%)	$45,000

The cash flow analysis looks like this:

Gross rent		$9,600
Mortgage payments	$4,500	
Land lease payments	1,200	
Operating expenses	3,000	
Total cash paid out		8,700
Cash flow		$ 900

Before, Dina had a cash flow of $2,100, which represented 14% of her total invested cash of $15,000. In this case, her cash flow is only $900—but her return has more than doubled, as $900 is 30% of her invested capital of $3,000 in the land lease transaction.

Let's follow through with the income calculation. The depreciation will remain the same as before, because the land does not add to the tax shelter. Thus, when we take the land away it doesn't reduce the shelter. Here is her spendable cash analysis:

Gross rent			$ 9,600
Mortgage interest	$4,050		
Land lease	1,200		
Operating expenses	3,000		
Depreciation	3,217		
			11,467
(Loss for the year)			($ 1,867)
Cash flow		$ 900	
Benefit from leftover tax shelter[a]		560	
Spendable cash		$1,460	

[a] $1,867 × 30%.

This is nearly a 50% after-tax return on the invested cash of $3,000.

The United States has few land leases under single-family homes, duplexes, and small apartment buildings. However, as the value of these properties continues to rise you will see that the land lease can be a very attractive alternative to other financing techniques. It benefits the buyer because it enables him to afford the property. It may well suit the seller because of the high tax penalty which might be realized in a sale.

Land leasing should be viewed as an alternative financing tool, and considered for its impact on the bottom line. The idea here is not to get hung up on ownership for ownership's sake. Look to the use, the benefits, the flexibility. It is very nice to say, "I own this," but it is all right to say, "I own this building, and because it was better for me, I'm leasing the land."

5

How You Can Become Rich

Now is the time for all potential real estate investors to come to their own aid.

There are no real secrets in real estate. It is all basic stuff. Yet some of the most elementary opportunities in life are often overlooked. Opportunity doesn't hang around hoping you will be the one to grasp it. Opportunities must be recognized, taken, then cashed in.

Here I assume that you are interested in investing in real estate for the purpose of becoming rich. Whatever rich means to you, shoot for it. To help you, here are some things about real estate that you might not have known before.

The mortgage-to-price ratio is the single most important factor in making a fast profit in real estate. What I'm talking about is the amount of the other guy's money you are able to use to purchase the property you want. When you use only 10% of your own money and borrow 90% from another guy (the seller, a bank, someone else), you can reap returns that are sudden and tremendous.

If you pay 100% down, then for you to double your investment, the value must double. This sounds reasonable, doesn't it? If you buy a $50,000 lot and want to hold it until it returns 100% on your investment, you need to hold it until you can net a sale of $100,000. Of course, you will have some annual expenses to add to your investment, so in fact you constantly need to get more than double your investment to have the desired effect.

There are many times you will consider buying this way. If the property is what you want and you can afford it, then why not? But enough time later on for that, once you have made your wealth.

Let's carry through on this for a moment, however. Take a lot I once purchased for $30,000. I felt the lot was going to go up in value at the rate of 15% to 20% per year. It did much better than that in reality. But take a look at the chart below to see how the value changed over the five years I held on to the lot.

TABLE 6.

INCREASE IN VALUE FROM $30,000

YEAR END	% OF INCREASE OVER PREVIOUS YEAR	VALUE
1	20	$36,000
2	20	43,200
3	25	54,000
4	30	70,200
5	35	94,770

Now I do admit that this lot turned out to be an exceptional investment. Its fantastic rise in value was attributable to three things:

1. The lot was a deep-water residential lot in Fort Lauderdale, two blocks from the beach, in a solid, close-to-it-all subdivision, a scarce combination of desirable features. In fact, there was only one other such lot in the immediate area, and it was not for sale.

2. I did my homework and realized that in all of Lauderdale there were fewer than thirty such lots still vacant. The lot purchased was larger than more than 50% of those. It was closer to the beach than over 50% of those available and was lower in price than 80% of those available.

3. The year I bought my lot, more than twenty of the other remaining lots also sold (our office sold our share of them). This made a sudden and dramatic shift in the supply of this commodity. The demand picked up and resales started. Soon all the

lots were spoken for, and buyers were forced to buy older homes just to get the location under the home. Once that happened, the value shot up.

All this is good, of course. But what about the mortgage-to-price ratio that is the key to making fast bucks?

I bought this lot on terms. Beyond enabling people to buy property when they can't pay all cash, the importance of terms is that it enables you to use the other guy's money while you make your own.

Mind you, I didn't know how much the lot was going to increase in value, and you won't know what will happen to your investments until later on. But you can learn from the past; you can anticipate. History does repeat itself.

Being cautious, I was able to negotiate the following mortgage:

I tied up the property for twelve months by giving the seller $5,000 cash in the form of an option payment. If I didn't exercise my option at the end of twelve months, I lost the cash. If I did exercise the option, then the $5,000 counted toward the purchase price and I had to pay another $5,000 down. I would owe $20,000 and could pay that at any time over four years at 8% interest. All I had to pay was quarterly interest payments for four years.

I had other costs too, of course, as once I took title I had to pay the taxes and insurance on the land. Here's what my total investment and carrying costs looked like:

TABLE 7.

Year End	Equity	Principal	Interest	Expenses	Total Cumulative Investment
1	$ 5,000	$ 5,000	$ 0	$ 0	$ 5,000
2	10,000	5,000	1,600	600	12,200
3	10,000	0	1,600	600	14,400
4	10,000	0	1,600	650	16,650
5	30,000	20,000	1,600	700	38,950

To see the relationship between investing with 100% equity and the way I actually bought the property, look at Table 8. It brings together the rising value (Table 6) and the cumulative investment actually made in the property, including expenses (Table 7). Also compare gain which could have been realized in 100% ownership and the actual form of ownership and the corresponding yield for each investment format.

TABLE 8.

VALUE AND YIELDS BASED ON ACTUAL INVESTMENT

Year End	Value	Investment (Cumulative)	Owed	Gain	% of Yield on Investment
0	$30,000	$ 0	$ 0	$ 0	0
1	36,000	5,000	25,000	6,000	120
2	43,200	12,200	20,000	11,000	90.2
3	54,000	14,400	20,000	19,600	136.1
4	70,200	16,650	20,000	33,550	201.5
5	94,770	38,950	0	55,820	143.3

At 100% equity at purchase (no mortgage)

Year End	Value	100% Equity + Costs (Cumulative)	Owed	Gain	% of Yield on Investment
0	$30,000	$ 0	$0	$ 0	0
1	36,000	30,600	0	5,400	17.6
2	43,200	31,200	0	12,000	38.4
3	54,000	31,800	0	22,200	69.8
4	70,200	32,450	0	37,750	116.3
5	94,770	33,050	0	61,720	186.7

The first thing to notice is that in all situations the investment is a very good one. This is because of the tremendous rise in value. Most investments won't be that dramatic.

However, look at the first year-end in each form of investment. In the actual method, with only $5,000 put down (as option), were there to be a sale at the end of the first year, I would have had a return of 120% on the investment. Had I instead paid cash for the property that same year and then paid the taxes, I would have had an investment of $30,600 and a yield of only 17.6%

The peak year in this analysis is the end of the fourth year in the actual method. Had a sale resulted, the yield would have been over 200%.

The Magic of Leverage

LEVERAGE will make you a fortune if you understand it and put it to work for you. If you can borrow money at a rate that is lower than what you can earn on the amount borrowed, the difference is the leverage, which means extra profit for you.

This is in essence what a bank does. It borrows from its depositors and then lends the money out at a higher rate. For example, you give me (the bank) $10,000. I promise to pay you interest at, say, 7% per year. This means it costs me $700 for the use of your money. With that money, I buy an apartment house that is throwing off a net of 12%. I am now earning $1,200; after deducting the $700 I have to pay to you, I'm left with $500. This is my benefit, the amount of leverage I got out of the transaction. When you borrow money at a lower rate than you can earn, you are creating positive leverage.

Not all leverage is beneficial, however. In this case the leverage was positive. That is, there was a benefit out of the transaction. The apartment was rented so it would clear 12% of the value, and I was able to borrow at a rate less than that. It is possible, however, for leverage to be negative. For example, if I borrowed the $10,000 at 15% interest, I would have to pay you $1,500 each year for the use of your money. If I made only $1,200, then I would have to kick in another $300 out of my own pocket. In this instance instead of benefiting from the financing, I'm losing $300 in cash flow because of it.

Another example: I might be able to get you down to a 10% interest rate, but you might demand I pay you back $500 of principal each year until I have paid back the entire $10,000. (Starting to look more like a mortgage now, isn't it?) So each year I would pay you both principal and interest. The first year it would be $1,500 ($1,000 in interest and $500 of principal). I would again have to pay $300 out-of-pocket, and again the leverage would be negative.

Leverage is determined on the basis of the entire payment against the debt, not just the interest. If you pay only interest, as in the first case, and the rate of payment is less than the return from the borrowed money, then you are getting the most out of your borrowed money and your leverage is positive. If you borrow money and then still have to go out-of-pocket because the income from the borrowed money doesn't equal the cost, then you have a negative leverage.

Because leverage is so important, you need to examine the situations in which you can accept negative leverage:

• **Single-family home (your own residence).** You won't have any direct income coming in to offset the cost of the money, so if the total benefits of ownership don't equal or exceed the mortgage cost, then you have made a bad deal.

• **Any investment with short-term debt.** If part of the financing includes a mortgage that will retire soon, you may accept a negative leverage that will become positive in a year or so. Sometimes the existing financing is desirable even though it causes negative leverage in the first years of the investment.

• **A hot growth investment.** If you have solid reasons to project a growth in appreciation that is in excess of the debt cost rate, you can accept a constant out-of-pocket cost until you sell. Vacant land is usually bought with this in mind.

• **A property you are planning to develop.** If you are setting aside a site for future development, then your criterion is simply, will the added cost of the financing be overly burdensome to the development, or will you still come out well despite the financing cost?

• **When debt offsets price.** Sometimes you negotiate a deal that has a heavier debt load than you wanted, but as a trade-off in the deal you got a more attractive price. Remember, each deal will have its terms and its price, and often they are flexible. I like to think of it as "I'll pay your price if you accept my terms."

The Basics of Leverage

If the total price of a property is $150,000 and you buy it with 20% down, you have invested $30,000 right off the bat. If the value goes up 10% to $165,000, you have made $15,000 on an investment of $30,000. That is a 50% yield. Now I'll admit that this sounds very simple, and you might think everyone in the world knows this. Not so—everyone doesn't know this.

Making Positive Leverage Work for You

If you have $10,000 to invest and want to double it, you have several choices. Of them, compare these three:

1. For $10,000, all cash, you can buy something that will go up to $20,000.

2. You can buy something for $30,000, putting only $10,000 down, and have it increase to $40,000 in value.

3. You can buy something for $50,000, putting $10,000 down, and have it increase to $60,000 in value.

Which of the three has the greatest risk? The answer is number 1, because that outcome is the least likely to occur. Yet most investors would say the greatest risk is with the third option. Number 3 is risky only if you can't afford to pay off the $40,000 owed on the transaction. You risk too much by demanding that a property double in value in the short run.

Understand that financing can be your friend or your enemy. The measure by which you judge financing is the leverage you can obtain. There may be a point at which you can go from positive leverage to negative leverage by trying to get too much out of financing. Remember, the maximum loan is not always the best loan. If you have the flexibility to vary your down payment, look at the effect on the deal of several different percentages of loans. You can often negotiate a better loan rate and term at a slightly lower mortgage-to-price ratio.

In my book *The Complete Guide to Real Estate Financing,* I use a leverage-calculation chart (Table 9) which will enable you to analyze one deal with several different mortgages. Table 10 shows the chart filled out with eight different forms of finance. You can copy Table 9 and use it to compare your own mortgage benefits.

Let me set the stage for the use of the leverage-calculation chart. You are thinking of buying a small apartment building that you believe can be bought for $100,000. The asking price might be more, but this is the top line you feel it is prudent for you to pay.

The apartments throw off $11,000 after all expenses are taken out. The existing financing of $50,000 takes another $7,000 in annual principal and interest payments from net income, leaving a cash flow of $4,000.

Net operating income[a]	$11,000
−Debt service[b]	7,000
Cash flow	$4,000

[a] N.O.I. = gross rent less operating expenses.
[b] Principal and interest.

The existing financing already on the property consists of a $50,000 first mortgage at 8½% interest per year. The annual payment as shown above is $7,000. The current constant rate on this mortgage is 14%. (Constant rate is the percent which represents both the principal and interest, and is found by dividing the balance of the principal owed at any moment into the total annual payment of principal and interest.)

In the analysis of what options are open to you in the financing of this property, you see there are five mortgages which have potential:

1. You can pay cash to the existing mortgage. You will note in Table 10 that with $50,000 down you would have a yield of 8% on your invested cash. As the net operating income rate is 11% (N.O.I. rate is found by dividing the net operating income by the price you will pay; it represents what return you would have if you paid 100% equity and had no mortgage), from the

TABLE 9.

Leverage-Calculation Chart

Asking Price $______
Present Finance $______
Equity $______

N.O.I. $______
Debt Service $______
Cash Flow $______

N.O.I. Rate ______%
Property ______
Date ______

Cash Flow Yield ______%
N.O.I. Rate ______%
Leverage ______%

Leverage Calculations

Method	Amount of Mortgage	Years	%	Constant Rate	N.O.I.	Debt Service	Cash Flow	Cash Down	Additional Cash for Financing	Total Cash Down	Yield on Cash	N.O.I. Rate	Leverage Rate
1													
2													
3													
4													
5													
6													
7													
8													

Explanation of Finance Form Used Above

1. ______
2. ______
3. ______
4. ______
5. ______
6. ______
7. ______
8. ______

Prepared by: ______ Date: ______

TABLE 10.

Leverage-Calculation Chart

Asking Price	$ 100,000	N.O.I.	$ 11,000	N.O.I. Rate	11 %
Present Finance	$ 50,000	Debt Service	$ 7,000	Property Date	Jan. 4, 19xx
Equity	$ 50,000	Cash Flow	$ 4,000	Cash Flow Yield	8 %
				N.O.I. Rate	11 %
				Leverage	−3 %

Leverage Calculations

Method	Amount of Mortgage	Years	%	Constant Rate	N.O.I	Debt Service	Cash Flow	Cash Down	Additional Cash for Financing	Total Cash Down	% Yield on Cash	N.O.I. Rate	Leverage Rate
1	$50,000	11.2	8½	14	$11,000	$7,000	$4,000	$50,000	0	$50,000	8	11	−3
2	80,000	30	9¾	10.32	11,000	8,248	2,752	20,000	3,200	23,200	11.86	11	+0.86
3	80,000	40	9½	9.72	11,000	7,776	3,224	20,000	500	20,500	15.73	11	+4.73
4	85,000	30	12	12.34	11,000	10,489	511	15,000	3,400	23,400	2.2	11	−8.8
5	85,000	40	10	10.19	11,000	8,661.50	2,338.50	15,000	500	15,500	15.08	11	+4.08

Explanation of Finance Forms Used Above

1. The existing situation.
2. New loan, over 30 years at 9¾%, closing cost 4%.
3. A wraparound mortgage over 40 years, balloon 11.2 years at 9½%, closing cost $500.
4. New loan, over 30 years at 12%, closing cost 4%.
5. A wraparound mortgage over 40 years, balloon 11.2 years at 10%, closing cost $500.

Prepared by: ____________ Date: ____________

return point of view you could do better than buying with this financing. In short, the existing financing has a negative effect on the return desired. Score the existing financing a minus 3.

2. A normal conventional loan of 80% of the purchase price. Your second option, then, is conventional financing, and while markets change and vary, in this case what was available was a thirty-year loan at 9¾% interest per year. This term would have a constant rate of 10.31% (see Table A in the Appendix). The annual payment on this mortgage is quickly found by multiplying the constant rate by the amount of the mortgage ($80,000 × 10.31% = $8,248. To arrive at the cash flow, deduct the debt service just found from the net operating income.

Net operating income	$11,000
−Debt service	8,248
Cash flow	$ 2,752

Continuing with the chart: With an $80,000 mortgage you would be putting down $20,000. Additional cost to get the mortgage in this case would be another $3,200. So now your total down payment would be $23,200. As the cash flow is $2,752 and your total invested capital is $23,200, your new yield is 11.86%. Because this new yield is more than the N.O.I. rate, the financing has benefited this deal. The positive leverage is slight, but it is positive. In fact, 0.86% positive—a definite improvement in many respects over the first option.

3. A wraparound mortgage. This keeps the existing mortgage and its interest intact for the benefit of the seller. To make the deal even more attractive for the seller, you agree to balloon the mortgage (see Chapter 20) in 11.2 years, at the time the existing first is paid off. In turn, the seller would give you an 80% loan over a pay-out schedule of forty years at a contract rate of 9½%. The seller is apt to do this because he is going to get much more than 9½% with the wraparound and can afford to let you have a break too. (See Chapter 20 for details on this magnificent form of financing.)

The wraparound is a wonderful tool to use in many situations and should be one of the first techniques that you master. Because of the ability to leverage up over the existing financing, the seller can actually earn a greater return by offering a lower than current interest rate.

In this case, you are setting up a wrap at 9½% with an amortization over forty years. This is done to hold down the constant rate and therefore keep the payment down. With this mortgage and a $20,000 down payment plus a small setup cost for the mortgage (and the lawyer to write it), you would have a total investment of about $20,500 in the property. The cash flow of $3,224 at this invested capital shows a 15.73% return.

Note very carefully that due to changes in financing this property has gone from an 8% return to a 15.73% return, without changing in price. This mortgage shows a positive 4.73% leverage. Very good.

4. This is a conventional loan of $85,000—not easy to get, and more costly than the others. At a 12% interest rate and a thirty-year term, the mortgage will result in a cash flow of only $511 and a yield on the investment plus cost of 2.2%. A negative leverage of −8.8%.

5. The last mortgage is another wrap, this time increased to 85%, and at 10%. This is a possible fallback in the event the seller won't buy the earlier one (number 3). To trade off on giving the seller higher interest, you ask for a larger loan. This loan has a positive leverage of 4.09%, which is only slightly lower than number 3.

The leverage chart will show you which mortgage is going to give you the most economic benefit. Leverage calculations are not a decisive factor in determining which property to buy—only which mortgage will provide the major effect over its term.

The idea that should stick with you is this: You want to develop financing that is good for you. Your financial condition may be such that you would prefer to carry the heavy load now so you can have no load in the relatively near future. In this case you would accept a negative leverage, as that would indicate the likelihood of a faster pay-out.

Your goals are important and should not be minimized. ("If

you like it and can afford it, then buy it.") All the leverage calculations in the world won't stop you from getting what you want if you have the cash to buy it.

Yet it is clear that the largest mortgage is not necessarily the best. The greatest return, 15.73%, comes with the $80,000 wrap, rather than the $85,000 one. It's true that this is because the interest rate is higher in the larger mortgage, but that's generally the way it will be.

What Happens When You Just Break Even?

Many purchases will just break even—there will be no cash flow. If the debt service took all the available cash, then there would be a rather large negative leverage working. But many times that is just fine and is good not only for the property but for you.

Cash flow is only one of the benefits of real estate. If there is none, it would be folly to automatically assume the deal is a bad one.

For example, Chuck bought a warehouse that was divided into three bays, each 2,000 square feet. They were rented out at a gross income of $18,000 per year. After expenses, on the average Chuck had a net operating income of $12,800. This transaction was made on a shoestring, as Chuck had bought the place with only $1,000 down. But when he bought it it was a real dump. He had to work hard to clean it up, paint it, and get it rented out. The mortgage he made when he bought it had a six-month moratorium on principal and interest payments, but they were added to the balance owed. He got it rented and his rent paid the mortgage—but that was all. Chuck had to sweat out each month, sometimes coming up with a few bucks from his own pocket. This property just broke even. It would now be worth around $128,000, based on its N.O.I. rate of 10%. But for Chuck it was showing a negative leverage of at least 10%.

Still, it was a terrific deal. Chuck owed only $62,000, and at the 8% mortgage rate he would have the property paid for in less than six years. All he had to do was struggle a little and in just six years he'd have at least $12,800 rolling in each year on the free-and-clear property.

Leverage is using the other guy's money, and using it to the best of your ability. Knowing the options, seeing the alternatives, understanding what is going on, not being frightened by the math of finance, holding your own with the big boys—all of this is available to you. Why? Not because you need to be smart . . . but because it is simple. Just don't tell too many people this secret.

6

How to Establish Goals

THERE ARE SEVERAL THINGS you need to know and understand about goals. The first is that if you have a clear, well-defined goal you will have a far easier time than if you wander around not knowing from day to day or year to year where you want to be. The second thing is that not everything that is good will take you directly to your goal. There are times when it is important and necessary to take a few steps backward to eventually move forward.

I believe these two aspects of goals are worth mentioning in this chapter because the most successful investors knew they wanted to go from the present to a defined place in the future. They didn't know exactly what the in-between stops were going to be, but they had a vision of where they want to be.

Let's face facts: Not everybody knows where he wants to be. Many people haven't had enough experience to discover their ultimate goal in life, or for that matter an intermediate goal. Perennial students go on from one degree to another, constantly finding more reasons not to ultimately strike out on their own to *be* what they have been training for. Of course, it isn't necessary to be in college to fit this description. There are people who go from job to job, reaching a level of mediocrity before moving on, never attaining any level of success—or, worse, reaching a level of success only to move away from it because of the inability to recognize and enjoy it.

What do you see yourself doing five years from now? I frequently ask would-be investors this question. It is interesting to hear the replies, and I can tell you that there is a big difference between the responses from married and single people.

The idea isn't to try to tell the future, but to get you to think about the future. Setting goals is that way. If you can't see yourself achieving the goal, then you more than likely will never make it.

The one most overwhelming item that causes people not to set goals (or not to attain goals they are "forced" to set) is the lack of self-confidence. Investing in real estate is a path to a goal, and your success in your investments will be greatly improved if your sight is set solidly on a goal. Selecting the goal in the first place will depend on your own inner confidence.

Here is a profile of a person with little or no self-confidence:

- He will set a goal well below his real capability.
- Fearing failure, he may not set any goal at all.
- He will develop a negative attitude about the attainment of the goal he has set.
- He will constantly look for rationalizations as to why he couldn't attain the goal, even before he has failed to reach it.
- He will procrastinate in making decisions out of fear that he will make the wrong choice.
- He will rely heavily on others to help in his decision-making, but will rarely give his advisers complete and correct information to work with.
- He won't risk taking a chance on his abilities.
- He usually doesn't recognize that he hasn't enough self-confidence.
- He usually can build his own confidence level once he is truly aware of his problem.

Now take a look at the person who is bubbling with self-confidence. You see a decisive person who may have ups and downs, but seems to constantly bounce back. Innate ability isn't the answer either. You know truly successful people full of self-confidence who from a physical and mental point of view are no more adept or talented than others who can't seem to get their act together. Confidence, then, is more than a direct comparison. It is a full mixture of the right attitudes about what success means.

It is the acceptance of failure as a part of success, and the realization that failure is absolutely necessary to succeed. That's right—you and I and everyone who is out to succeed must have a mix of failures.

Look at the top in any profession. How did they get there? How is their performance while they are there? Is everything 100%? Hell, no—not by a long shot.

The best quarterback in the world doesn't have a 100% pass completion in a season; even the world's best running backs fumble, and baseball players commit errors as well as hit home runs. All successful businessmen know that a wrong decision from time to time is better than no decision at all. The most successful writers have received their share of rejections. Perhaps the most dedicated of all is the artist, who usually has to die to become successful.

All this is important because self-confidence, and the right attitude about success and failure, is something that is there in the beginning. It doesn't come after success.

As you embark on the way to building your fortune in real estate or by any other method, you had best accept the inevitability of obstacles that are bound to stand in your way. The secrets to success are easy, but success is damn hard to get.

There is no way for you to become confident in your abilities overnight. That is something that you must work on and develop. But never underestimate the need to *know* that you can succeed.

How to Develop Short- and Long-range Investment Goals

Real estate is a form of investment that does different things for different people. Often the same property can serve two separate and diverse needs and goals when viewed by different investors. For example, an apartment complex might be bought by an investor with a heavy income tax load, and he will set up a depreciation schedule that will provide the maximum tax shelter possible. That same apartment complex might instead be purchased by an investor who had no such tax problem and would look more to the long-range goal of having a retirement income by holding on to the apartment complex for the rest of his life.

As you develop an understanding of the options and alternatives available, you will see how specific techniques and often specific properties have different results. Planning your future by the most efficient use of these options will put you far ahead of the investor who shotguns his way along the investment trail.

The Short-range Goal Is the Most Important

Long-range planning is like the guy that wants to be sure he goes to heaven but doesn't want to die to get there. Your best long-range plan more than likely will be so vague and general that it wouldn't be very motivating on a day-to-day basis. Any long-range planning or analysis stands or falls on clearly defined short-range goals.

I started writing in high school and was sure writing was what I was going to do. In college, however, my professors discouraged me. I changed my major several times, ending up in business. From there to graduate studies in Europe and another attempt at writing as a livelihood. Again failure. Then, returning to the U.S.A., I entered real estate.

I was away from writing for ten years, working and succeeding in the real estate profession. Then one day I was asked to write a book on finance, which became *The Complete Guide to Real Estate Financing,* which was followed by five novels, then *The Complete Handbook of How to Farm Real Estate Listings and Sales,* and now this book, with more books to follow.

The point is that when I made the decision to go into real estate back in the early '60s, I wasn't taking a step backward in terms of my writing goals. Through intermediate goals I have been able to progress to a point I would not have thought possible. The same will happen to you.

Build toward the long-range goal with short-range goals, and the place to start is the most basic of all: your shelter. If you presently own a home or apartment, look at an immediate need you may have. A cash flow problem, excessive tax to pay at the end of the year, a capital gains problem that can be solved with a real estate exchange—whatever your current problems, you may have a solution in real estate.

Once you have begun to solve your current problems and needs, you can concentrate on the longer-range goals. But before you buy, there are some things that you must do.

8 Key Factors Which Precede Investing in Real Estate

1. Plan ahead. That's what we've been talking about these past few pages. Do some thinking about what you want and need before you rush into anything. Occasionally an opportunity will come up that just doesn't fit the game plan. That doesn't mean that you can't change the game plan. Flexibility will aid you in getting and holding on to the edge that will make your investments more productive. However, you need to recognize there will be times when you must stick to your plan and the opportunity should be passed up.

There will be times when the only *plan* that is important is the "If you like it and can afford it, then buy it" point of view. Plans should have a sound basis, however, and your plans will come along best when you are comfortable at what you are doing.

2. Be comfortable. You must be comfortable in what you are about to do. Don't invest in real estate because I tell you to. Invest because you have read this book and understand what you are getting into. When you sign offers and put up money you are risking hard-earned capital, and if you are making a mistake you might lose it. That doesn't mean you want to lose it or can afford to lose it, only that it is possible to lose it. You reduce or eliminate the risk of loss by being comfortable with the investment.

By the way, the level of comfort you reach will depend on the depth to which you invest. Many people buy real estate every day with no knowledge of what they are doing. They are simply satisfying their need for a shelter or a place for their business. Your quest for wealth will depend on your ability to go beyond that level of comfort. You are already on that path by reading this book.

3. Have alternatives at your fingertips. Everything you do is that much closer to success if you have a chance to view more alternative routes than if you can choose from only one or two options. Knowing the rules of the game is very important when it comes to investing in anything. In real estate the rules are many and the adaptations of the rules endless. You will profit simply because you will know of a method to put the deal together that has eluded another investor. The alternatives and options available to you may be in part obtained from this book. Some of them will be the personal adaptation you give to them by combining two or more aspects, creating something that is unique to you and the deal at hand. But options and alternatives go beyond the techniques you will use. What types of property you invest in is itself an option. How you choose the property and how you expand upon your investment choices may give you a decided competitive edge.

Something will happen once you begin to be comfortable with the real estate market and begin to see all the options available to you. That something is confidence.

4. Understand the relationship of time to investing in real estate. Many different kinds of investing are crucially governed by time. The stock market is no exception. However, the real estate market is a product of time. In time, nearly all real estate will go up in value . . . but when? how long will it take? You buy and sell through other people. The time element is crucial to them, too. They need to sell so much that time is against them, and because of that you can buy at a good price. They need to buy now so time is against them and you can sell at a good price. You make a call at the right time and get the inside data on a parcel of land or a building you want to buy. People make up their minds now and change them tomorrow, so time is important.

It is also the one element that will determine how much of a yield you ultimately make. For example, Charles bought a property for $100,000. He put $25,000 down and agreed to pay off the balance on an interest-only mortgage for ten years at 10% per year, with the balance of $75,000 being paid in full at that time. Brad bought a similar property a mile down the road under the same terms. Each sold his property for $175,000. What was their yield?

You don't know, do you? Of course not. That's because I haven't told you the time element. Let's say Charles couldn't find a buyer for ten years, and had to pay off the land in full. Assuming he would have paid $75,000 in interest plus the $100,000 (plus taxes), he wouldn't have made any profit at all.

Brad sold his land in two years. His total investment was his down payment of $25,000 plus two years of interest, or $40,000 plus taxes. His profit before tax was a clear $60,000 over his invested cash. This return is purely a function of time.

Each property has its time, and that time depends on each investor. What you do to market your property is as important as your motivation to sell. Time will be your friend or your enemy depending on how you approach it.

You should never enter a transaction that turns on the ability to sell at a fixed time in the future in order to produce a profit. Time is never so obligingly reliable.

Many times opportunity will come knocking at your door. Many times you will be unable to take advantage of that opportunity because of other commitments. But when opportunity does knock and you can move, take it and cash in.

5. Learn how to recognize an opportunity. Good real estate deals are hard to come by. Some market areas produce more good buys than others, of course, but in general you need to look around before you buy. The act of looking is essential to acquaint you with the run of the market. There is no reason you can't do the same thing the professional realtor does when he is learning a new market: look, compare, check values.

It will pay off for you to know something about the market. Sure, you may have a savvy broker who is guiding you, but you need more than that. The broker might be giving you the best and most current information available, but it won't do for you what a few weeks of hard looking and comparing and checking values will do. It establishes and clarifies in your own mind what is going on.

It might seem strange that I, a realtor, would give this advice. Not so. The kind of looking I'm advocating doesn't mean driving around to see open houses, or shopping around with a dozen brokers to feel out the market. What I'm talking about involves really learning what is going on in the market. Check out some properties in a variety of categories. Many newspapers publish the real estate sales for the day or week. Check them out, get an idea of the trend. It's like watching the stock market for a few months before you jump in. If you can't find the information in the newspaper, call a lawyer in your town and ask him for the name of the local publication that publishes the deed transfers. It will give you all the data you need to know what is going on.

Research the kind of real estate you think you want to buy, but also check into the other kinds. You might see a trend that will cause you to shift to another kind of property if what you thought you wanted is dropping in value and other things are going up. Real estate is funny that way.

6. Don't look for "the best." Investing in the best property in town may not be the best way to profit. Sound like a paradox? Look at it this way—if it is already the best, is there room for an increase? The chances are that there will always be some room for increases over a period of time. But you don't have the kind of time it might take. Buying at the top is not for the guy trying to build his fortune. That's for the guy who has his fortune and now wants to sit around and say, "Hell, son, see that building? I own it." Thank goodness there are plenty of those rich guys around, as they keep up a good market for those top properties.

You increase income the most when there is the most room to increase it. Real estate is in a way a people problem. That is, people cause the problems with real estate and not the other way around. A problem for one person might not be my problem, or your problem.

Buying "edge" property will give you the chance to fix up the problem, plush up the exterior and interior, raise rents, and reap the profits because of what *you* have done.

"I don't like that building, Mr. Cummings. The tenants are

paying well under what they should be, the place needs a painting badly, the landscaping is in terrible shape. Sure the price is attractive, but it needs a lot."

"Absolutely, Mr. Buyer. Have you ever seen such an opportunity?"

Open your eyes and you will see around you the problems other people have that will be your pathway to wealth.

7. **Control your emotions.** There are times for you to fall in love with a property; of that there can be no question. To paraphrase, I never saw a property I didn't like, but love, now that's another matter.

Emotion is the ally of the real estate salesman. For the investor, emotion must be carefully controlled.

There are times when you go bananas over what you just saw —a lot with a fantastic view, an office building that will suit your needs perfectly, a home that you can afford and is just right for your life-style. But you must control your emotions when you talk to the real estate salesman showing you the property, or get into discussions over price and terms. The reason is simple: You should always maintain a certain element of doubt as to your final move in the mind of the salesman.

This step isn't necessary if you are dealing with an experienced salesman who knows that no buyer or seller is so predictable as to know in advance what he might do under every circumstance. However, some salesmen can get carried away and think they've sold the property long before they really have.

Emotional involvement on your part is usually the best reason to have an agent work your deal. When you buy you should refrain from any contact with the seller over the business portion of the sale. In fact, it is a good idea to avoid all contact whatever with the seller unless some good reason compels contact. The reason is very clear—buyers and sellers have conflicting emotions about the transaction. One word, one glance, an insignificant comment can set those emotions against each other.

"Mr. Seller, I've offered $10,000 less than you've been asking because I must replace the entire houseful of these old carpets."

("What! My wife just picked out those carpets last month!")

When it comes to the negotiation of your deal, in either buying or selling, the agent can earn his fee by doing not much more than keeping things moving without the buyer and seller coming into direct contact. ("You take that back about my wife's taste in carpets, buddy, or I'll give you the front of my fist . . .")

8. **Learn the rules of the game and play by them.** Investing in real estate is more of a people-to-people game than any other kind of investing. The impersonality of the stock market makes it rather dull and uneventful. You call your broker and ask him to buy or sell what you or he suggests. You never see the seller or the buyer. In many instances you never know anything about the deal except the name of the company, the amount you paid, and the profit or loss which resulted.

Real estate is you against them. A person owns that home you are buying. A person is the president of the corporation that is buying your apartment complex. People.

And people like to play a game called "negotiation." Because it is a real game, you should be ready for it. How well you negotiate will depend on many factors, the most important being your patience and knowledge of the way to play the game.

I have seen many sellers unable to make a deal because they were unable to close the gap. They would become insulted at what they thought were ridiculously low offers and not counter-offer.

This shows an inability to grasp the fact that this is one way the game is played. On the other hand, I've made deals that involved months of going back and forth from buyer to seller and back again to offer after counter-offer until the gap was closed.

But alas, there is a time when the game ends. The fact is, simply, there is no overtime and the game can be called due to previous sale or one party growing weary of the game and moving on to another property.

The way to avoid this is to keep the playing time down to a minimum. If you really want to buy and the market is really hot, then you might have to wait for another time and place in which to show how well you play.

Often the back-and-forth of offers is the result of the buyer and seller trying to work out a deal that will simply solve each other's problems. Sometime the problem is one of saving face.

Learning the rules of the game will allow you to play correctly, of course, but knowing all the alternative plays you can call will cause you to ultimately win the game.

Working with these eight key factors will help you develop a strong foundation for becoming rich through real estate. As you continue through this book you should constantly remind yourself that real estate is controlled by people. Its value is determined by its location, and your profit from that property will be the product of time and money. These elements—people, location, time, and money—are all related to whether you did or did not profit.

Of the above four elements, there will always be one which is the most crucial to you for a specific deal. It might be the person, or perhaps the location. Other times it will be the time or the money. But always different, always varied.

These are the things that make investment in real estate exciting and challenging.

7

Investment Strategies for the Single Woman

STATISTICS INDICATE that most of the real estate in the United States is owned or controlled by women, and while much of this wealth can be explained by the death of a husband (or two) or the tax and legal advantages to the male of putting real estate in the wife's name, the real truth is women and real estate are naturals. If you are a woman who is into this book because you want to get the edge every place you can, then take heart. Women have some very solid natural advantages that work for them in the real estate game.

Women who don't do well in real estate, or don't invest in real estate at all, can blame one or more of these following hurdles as the culprit.

1. The "man's world" syndrome. This takes its toll in many a deal and is often manifested in the "I'm a woman and everyone takes advantage of me" attitude. To many women this "man's world" syndrome is the most convenient excuse.

It is a natural, human trait (for men, too) to seek a reason for failure other than one's own failings. This rationalization is one way people try to cover up their mistakes. And it isn't limited to past mistakes. Indeed, it is most often a preventative form of cover-up. "I'm not a college graduate, so I'm not going to make it . . . I come from a poor family, so I'm not going to make it . . . I'm black so . . . I'm Jewish . . . I'm a woman . . ." The idea is to build such a good case for your uphill struggle that when you fail you've got a good out.

"Look, as a woman I can't be expected to make it big, right? I mean after all I've got to buck it all uphill to boot and so if I don't make it it won't be because I didn't try hard . . . everyone was against me right from the start, so if I fail it's not my fault." When the woman with this attitude happens to make it big (by some fluke in the uphill struggle), she is apt to say: "I made it despite the fact that they were against me all the way."

Now don't jump to conclusions. All women will have hurdles placed in their path from time to time. The successful woman simply passes over the hurdle or she ignores it and doesn't acknowledge its existence.

The "man's world" syndrome is the rationalization that many women use to explain the problem *they* are having in any given circumstance, falling back on the defense that it is because they are women that they might not succeed.

It is possible that there are many things in this world that are indeed part of a "man's world," but investing in real estate is not one of them. It does not depend on the sex of the investor, nor does it require a man's or a woman's touch, although each does have special attributes he or she can use. Yet countless times I've heard women say they couldn't even begin to contemplate investment in real estate because it was a man's business.

The hurdle of the "man's world" syndrome is believing that as a woman you can't succeed in investing in real estate because you aren't a man. Your attitude toward your ability to succeed in investing is essential to attaining that success; if you don't have confidence in your abilities, your success will be severely limited. There are many other brick walls for you to overcome, and you should not begin by creating an out for yourself in the event you don't succeed.

How to Overcome the "Man's World" Syndrome

If you have been postponing a move into real estate because you feel it's a man's game, or have been investing reluctantly, using the rationalization that it's all uphill for you, then you are suffering from the "man's world" syndrome. It's a wrong and false illness that has no place in the world of investing (or anyplace else). Face the fact that you *will* make mistakes, and unless you are cured of the "man's world" syndrome, you will convince yourself that it wasn't your mistake at all but was due to "them." In this way you won't recognize your failings and will continue to make the same mistake again and again.

What can you do about this? Simple—learn exactly what kind of game real estate is. You need to see who the players are, what makes them good, how they succeed and why. Take a look at their profile.

Profile of a Successful Real Estate Investor

• **Keeps her investments within her grasp.** This is the investor who won't go beyond the comfort boundary in a geographic sense. To some investors this might mean thousands of miles, to others it's only a few blocks. The reason for this is equally simple: You must know what is going on in the marketplace, and the more you know about the marketplace, the greater the edge you have. If you can find an area in your town that has good investment property (which you will be able to identify by the time you finish this book), then the place for you to begin your investment portfolio will be here after you learn everything you can about the area. That means knowing the streets, the governmental restrictions, the zoning laws, the water and sewage problems, the building setbacks, the . . . well, everything you can learn about the physical aspects of the area. Then learn about the market aspects of the area, such as what has sold, how much, when, what's available on the market now, where, how much, why.

While this might sound like a lot (and it is, it is essential for any successful investor to know or to know someone who does. Probably the best situation would be a combination of the two. Know as much as you can about the areas in which you hope to invest, and know a broker who is *the* expert in the area.

• **Has a goal and works toward it.** We've covered this but it bears mentioning again. Having a direction is the only way to quickly get to a destination. Your goal must be personal, attainable, and measurable. Of these three, attainable is the most elusive. What is attainable? When is a goal high enough? What happens if I can't attain my goal? These and other questions come out of improper goal-setting. Setting goals by yourself can be difficult; while you may have no problem establishing a goal, you may not have a clear understanding of what is needed to attain that goal. The goal of owning a million dollars' worth of real estate might first require a sub-goal: learning what you need to know to buy real estate.

That your goal be measurable is absolutely necessary. If your goal is not measurable, then you have no way to tell where you are in the program. The ability to tell how far along you are will aid in realizing that goal.

All goals should be written down (at least, all important goals). I don't care if you look at the goal every morning, as many people advocate; however, I'm not against that either. The written goal is good because it will cause you to make a decision, and have proof of that decision. And all goals should have a timetable written into them. This timetable will help you set values on your time as you progress toward your goal.

• **Is flexible.** I've never met a successful investor who didn't have the immediate future clearly in sight and a definite path to follow. This definite path, which comes from forethought of where you want to be and how you want to get there, will keep you from being sidetracked. Real estate is a varied form of investing, and you can easily be sidetracked unless you firmly keep in mind some designated goal. Having a goal won't stop you from being flexible, however, as flexibility is the next attribute you will find in successful investors. Goal setters are able to be flexible in the path they might take to the ultimate goal, or in reevaluating their goal.

In real estate, as in other forms of investment, the opportunities that cross your path will be opportunities only if you can recognize them as such *and* take advantage of them. Flexible people are able to because they see more than one way to fit the pieces into the pattern. It is only the inflexible who are often unable to take advantage of an opportunity when it arrives. Many times the immediacy needed to act on an opportunity causes it to pass into another's hands. Yet there will be many times you see the opportunity, and you know you are able to make the investment—but you don't because you are unable to see how this opportunity will get you closer to your goal. Or, worse, you have no goal and can see no ultimate benefit in obtaining the property you have just seen.

Flexibility is an attribute that you will achieve only by trying to establish goals, then exploring all the ways to attain them.

• **Is a positive thinker.** The world is full of negative thinkers. Thank goodness for that. If the world weren't that way, everyone would be successful, and because there is only so much success to go around, the positive thinkers would have to take a drop in pay.

If you are positive about yourself, your goals, and the way in which you attain them, then you will have the edge. Having the edge is what this book is all about. You beat out the other guys by having something on your side they don't.

Positive thinking comes easier to men than women, I've found. I'm not sure of the reason for this, but I believe it might have something to do with the competitive spirit in which many men are brought up. Whatever the reason, developing a positive attitude will help you not only in investing but in everything.

Successful people aren't dissuaded by the fact that life isn't a constant "up." There are downs for all of us, even the most positive thinkers. These downs are natural and essential in a way. Your ability to live through a down will give you the advantage on the next up. This is a fact, and that thought in itself will help you through the next down you experience.

2. The lack of knowledge. The next hurdle that single women often face is that of inadequate background in the field of investment. This is in essence the lack of knowledge of the foundations which make for successful business decisions. This is the biggest hurdle, for two reasons. First, it is a terrifying experience to be thrust into something you know nothing about. It doesn't matter that the knowledge is easily available or that the concepts themselves are very simple; these aspects only make it all the more frustrating. The second reason this hurdle is the biggest is that it can stop you dead in your tracks.

Of all the aspects of real estate investing, the math is the most difficult. It is also the least important, as you need only to understand what it tells you, not how to figure it out. You can hire experts for that. Take, for example, a friend of mine who was buying land for $500 per acre and selling it for $5,000 per acre a few months later. "Hell, Jack," he told me, "I'm doing pretty good making only 10% a year, aren't I?"

All the knowledge needed to put you on your way to being a success in real estate investing is contained here in this book. As you begin to make your positive moves you will begin to experience for yourself the ups and downs of the market and the people you will be dealing with. You will learn real estate is not just a "thing" business, that there are people attached to real estate. They will work for you, rent from you, buy your property at a profit for you, and if you're not careful they will foreclose on you, not lend you money, and run out in the middle of the night with your carpet rolled up in the back of their car and sell your furniture to the apartments down the block. People and this book will be your first guides. You will learn and profit from each.

The biggest part of the knowledge hurdle isn't obtaining the knowledge. Nearly anyone can do that. The biggest part is realizing that you can become as knowledgeable an investor as anyone in a short period of time. You will never know it all, of course. You are fortunate to have this book, because it gives you something that wasn't available to the current big shots in real estate investing. Take advantage of this book. But don't get cocky. Knowledge must be tempered by experience; you can benefit from the mistakes of others, but you will make some of your own. You are bound to, but be sure to benefit from them and not make them too frequently. Learning should be continuous. You will want and need to be current on the factors that control *your* market area. Knowledge is at your doorstep. Make your move to take advantage of it.

3. A lack of borrowing power. Women, and most particularly single women, are not generally viewed as good credit risks. Some of this has already emerged in the chapter on credit. Of all the obstacles you will encounter, the worst may be the loss of borrowing power that all single women face simply because they are single women. Why? Because most single women are thought (by male lenders) to be: potentially unreliable borrowers, likely to have a poor pay-back record; likely to be more interested in "other things" than real estate loans; lower wage earners than their male counterparts; not as stable in employment over a long time period.

I won't defend these attitudes, but they do exist in varying degrees. Most lenders won't admit to being biased toward men in the loan process, but lending money is a business, and for the moment most lenders see their funds better placed in the hands of male borrowers.

The recent advances women have made are outstanding. For the first time in history women are a major economic force due to their own will and abilities. No longer are women with money women who have (had) rich husbands. Because of this, lenders will change their policy, but that's later and not now.

So what do you do when you can't get the loan to buy? The first thing you should do is find out exactly why you didn't get the loan. If it is a matter of your being a genuinely poor risk, then you may not have many alternatives left. On the other hand, if your "risk" is contrived you will have to enter into a "war" with the lender. Alas, when you lose this battle your options dwindle, so you should give this one all you have. Your weapons of war will include:

- A talk with the senior loan officer to discuss your case and go over the reasons why your loan was turned down. Often the reason given will be "it wasn't you but the property." It is true that low appraisals can kill some loans from some lenders, so it is possible that you have a contract to buy that is in excess of what the lender feels is a good price for the property. On the other hand, when lenders are running out of money they will give nearly any reason *except* the fact that they are out of money.

When you feel you have the "right" reason and are still not satisfied that you are being treated fairly, speak up and let your feelings be known. Request another appraisal, ask him to send the loan request back to the loan committee, give him more information on your stability of employment and the like.

Sometimes it's a case where the loan officer didn't try hard enough. If you deal with a real estate broker, make sure you have one who knows the ins and outs of dealing with the lenders in the area.

• Going to another lender. In fact, it is a good idea to shop around for lenders. They are in business like anyone else you know, and they are competitive in many ways. Always apply to three or more lenders.

• Getting a cosigner. It might be a friend, a relative, or a partner in the real estate venture. Often single women band together this way to buy jointly. It is okay to ask Mom or Dad to cosign the mortgage. They really aren't risking that much. Ask your lawyer about your state's laws on this aspect—most states have eliminated deficiency judgments in the event you default on the loan, so the cosigner is really more of a symbol than an actual additional security.

• If you feel you really have been taken, go to court. Many single women in this country have better jobs and make more money than their male counterparts who are getting loans. When you've been at the poked end of the stick, poke back.

4. A flaw in the competitive spirit. Competitive spirit is not athletic ability. The natural competition that arises in the heat of a sports event is not lacking in single women. In fact, women may be more competitive in many sports than men.

On the other hand, when it comes to investing many women, and in particular single women, find decision-making difficult. Laying it on the line, risking hard-earned cash, is difficult for many people, and more so for single women.

There are a number of reasons for this. I believe that the pressure placed on single women to make it in what is in some respects a man's world is an added (and unwarranted) burden that makes such women unnecessarily cautious. This caution, while not in itself bad, can many times lead to lost opportunities. The inability to come to a decision until the moment is lost is common with many people.

A lack of final drive in the competitive spirit, coupled with prudent caution, is the fear of making a mistake. This is the flaw that many singles need to face up to to be successful in real estate investing. While that drive might be evident in the tennis match, it can disappear when it comes time to decide if you should put down nearly all of the hard cash you've saved up over the past three years to buy a duplex or some other property.

Indecision is natural in everyone. Real estate may be the largest single "buy" you will ever make, and therefore the largest decision you will make. It is for many people. The decision is perhaps the most important you will ever make that will involve you, your future, and money. It can very honestly be a frightening decision. "Yes, I will buy that property. Here's my check for $50,000." It is a decision few people were trained for. I know of no high school or college course that will prepare you for it.

It is important for you to know that everyone has this problem. Some people show the symptoms of indecision by procrastinating. "I'll do it . . . but tomorrow or later." A form of indecision is evident in people who have such neat, orderly lives that there is no room for change.

But wait a moment here. Indecision and procrastination are in fact forms of decision. Putting off a decision *is* a decision. "I'll decide tomorrow" is the same as saying "I have no answer today." If the question is, will you buy this property today, and you have been asked that question ten days running and you reply, "I'll let you know tomorrow, call me then," you have *decided* you will not buy today. Was that the decision you wanted to make?

The flaw in the competitive spirit can be mended. Fortunately, it isn't a break, only a small flaw. A product of an environment that hasn't given women the practice in making quick and decisive decisions. "Okay, men, out of the trenches and attack. On three."

How to Mend the Flaw

• Recognize that as a single woman you are apt to be overly cautious. This overcaution will lead you into indecision and procrastination, and in real estate that means you will miss the good buys that come to you and you won't sell at the opportune moment. Realizing that indecision is a natural human trait won't eliminate it from your habits, but it will help you look for those times when you put off decisions although you have all the facts needed to make up your mind. Watch how good salesmen aid you in the decision process by focusing your attention on the items you might need.

• Start making decisions. That's right. When asked for a decision, pause, think it over, and if you have the facts needed for a reasonable decision, make one. (Don't start out with buying real estate, however; work up to that one.)

You will find that making decisions without a lot of procrastination is better, even if you make a few bad decisions. A bad decision can come from the lack of a decision as well as the wrong timing of a good decision. And by making decisions you remove the nagging worry about having to make a decision that you have been putting off for days.

• Enjoy the excitement of making an important decision. That's right, it can be exciting. "Okay, I've examined all I need to, checked with all my advisers, and I'm ready to make my decision. Are you ready?" Successful business people have discovered that making important decisions is very exciting and, when they turn out to be good decisions, highly rewarding. The bad decisions are part of the pile, and no successful executive has a record of 100% good decisions. You won't either.

• Don't rationalize when you do procrastinate and lose out on an opportunity. "Well, Jack, I'm sorry to hear the property sold last night. I know you told me it might happen and, damn, I was going to call you and okay the deal, but I guess fate meant it to be this way" or "Jack, I tried to reach you last night to tell you I wanted to buy, but I lost your unlisted phone number. You should have called while I still had time to buy the property before the other person got it." Accept the fact that it was your hesitation that caused you to blow the deal and that you will have to act more quickly the next time. Opportunity waits for no one.

5. Overreliance on advisers. It is understandable that if you as a single woman feel you are being taken advantage of, caught in the "man's world" syndrome, lacking in the practice of making decisions that will shape your life, you may rely heavily on the advice of others. More often than not this overreliance (actually dependence) on the expertise of others will hold you back from your real potential.

Sally was a smart, well-paid interior designer for a large decorating firm in Miami. She made over $30,000 a year and had saved up about $45,000. She had a lawyer to handle her legal questions, an accountant to figure her income tax, and a financial adviser, a very nice guy who was into insurance. She didn't make a move without checking things out with them. Sally was forty-one when she bought her first real estate, a small home in Coconut Grove near Miami. Her financial adviser had told her not to; the accountant had nothing to say except that it wouldn't have much effect on her taxes; the lawyer told her she should play it safe.

Judy, on the other hand, was just thirty when she bought her first property, a four-unit apartment complex. She was a flight attendant for a major airline. She had a series of advisers who ran the gamut from lawyers and accountants to well-meaning friends. "Buy that run-down apartment complex, Judy? You must be out of your mind" was the kind of advice she got. But, like Sally, Judy was sick and tired of missing out on opportunities because her advisers were well-meaning, overcautious, and apparently not as confident of Judy's ability as Judy was. She bought the complex, spent some time and money (not much of either) fixing it up, and sold it at a big profit—which she put into another property.

Floanne is still living in a small apartment that her father bought for her. She has a good job as a head teller with one of the savings and loan associations in the area and has the time and the money as well as the ability to become a first-rate real estate investor. However, she has taken refuge behind her advisers and may never take a chance on anything, much less her own abilities. While she does own, it is the only property she will ever have unless she decides to make her move.

Experts are tools which the smart investor uses to his advantage. I have a number of experts in many areas of investing whom I frequently call on for ideas and advice. It will be necessary and prudent from time to time to consult such experts as you progress in investing. However, your reliance on the advice or dependence on the adviser should come only after you understand what an adviser's job should be.

Advisers are to give you the facts, both good and bad, so you are able to come to the most intelligent decision possible. Advisers are not advisers if they make your decisions for you. "Mr. Lawyer, you've looked over my plan to buy this office building. What do you advise?" "Miss Would-be-buyer, I don't think you should buy."

My experience with professional advisers has shown me that most of them (including real estate advisers) have a tendency to put themselves in your shoes. "If I were you I wouldn't buy this," or "If I were you I'd buy only if I could . . ." This empathy is nice but impossible. In the first place, they aren't you, and so are very safe in making a statement like that. Secondly, the achievement of your goals is what you should attain, and your goals are not their goals, so when someone says "If I were you . . ." what he means is "If it were me and I wanted *my* goal, then I'd do this . . ."

Advisers have a tendency to let the status quo remain and not make any changes that might upset the current situation. As most of us try to get the adviser to make the decision for us, they tend to be overly cautious.

Some advisers won't admit to a lack of knowledge in their subject, and to be safe will therefore advise against action. This is natural, yet will create a problem for the investor relying on her adviser if he really isn't knowledgeable on the matter at hand. If, for example, you were to ask a lawyer not well versed in real estate finance whether you should take back a wraparound mortgage in an upcoming real estate transaction, you might get a no simply because the lawyer may not be familiar with the technique and therefore may not want to get involved.

How to Find the Best Adviser for You

First you must realize that the family lawyer or accountant may not be the best person to talk to when it comes to investing in real estate.

A client of mine was selling her home. I showed her that the market range for the property was between $55,000 and $62,000. I reviewed with her the fact that the home needed several thousand dollars' worth of work (repairs, repainting) to get a price on the high side. I was told that the work would be done, and the property was listed slightly above the top amount because it might appeal to that one buyer who would pay just over the market; if not, the price could be lowered. The improvements were not made, however, and an offer of $55,000 came in following others lower than that. "Take this to my lawyer," I was told by the seller. The lawyer reviewed the contract and advised our mutual client not to accept $55,000. I spoke with the lawyer and discovered that he had never seen the property and had no idea of its condition or the market. Yet this lawyer is one of the finest tax lawyers in Fort Lauderdale.

You can find advisers who can give you the kind of advice that will benefit you. But you have to look around for them.

6 Key Questions to Ask Your Future Real Estate Adviser

1. Has the adviser ever owned the kind of real estate you are now thinking of buying or selling? His advice will have much more meaning if he has. Current ownership will be more helpful than past ownership, of course. The idea here is to have actual day-to-day involvement in the kind of property you want. Nothing is better than this kind of relationship. If the adviser has never owned the kind of real estate you are seeking, then ask why. It could have been he was acting on some faulty advice himself.

2. Has the adviser ever worked with the kind of real estate you are now thinking of buying or selling? It is possible that the advice you are seeking can come from someone who has worked in or with the type of real estate. It might be a lawyer who has closed many transactions on this type of property, or a manager of motels when you need to know something about management. An accountant for restaurants can tell you a lot about restaurant accounting, and so on. If the adviser hasn't owned the kind of property, then a close relationship through personal involvement is the next best thing, and in many cases may be more desirable than actual ownership.

3. Ask the adviser whom he would seek advice from. In short, ask the adviser whether he's qualified to give you advice on the problem you have. This is absolutely essential and is often overlooked. Yet the question is simple: "George, I don't know what to do about the situation I explained to you yesterday. I need to find someone who can give me some solid answers so I can make a sensible decision. Do you feel you can give me the kind of advice I need, or can you suggest someone else to me?"

See how simple this is. You don't have to hurt the feelings of a good and long-trusted friend who may not be qualified to field your specific problem. If he is qualified, then he will tell you now. If he isn't (and he will more than likely know this), then you've given him the opportunity to save face and in fact help you by suggesting someone who can help.

4. Ask the adviser if he understands your problem and your goal. Unless you are in direct communication on this you will never know if the adviser truly understands what it is you want from him. Much misdirected advice comes out of poor communication between the adviser and the client, and often it arises because the client did not level with the adviser. If you are seeking information the adviser should know why you need to know and how you plan to use the information. The data for data's sake can be obtained from experts and not advisers, if that is all you want. On the other hand, the adviser will adapt the factual data to your needs and your goals if he understands those needs and goals.

Whatever might have caused the communication gap is less important than the fact that the data you need might not be what you get.

A client of mine flew me to Europe at his expense to advise him on how to best obtain an American market in the development of a condominium complex in Greece. After a week in Athens I gave him my report, which was not optimistic as to the success of the project in U.S. sales.

A year later I learned that what he wanted to know was what he should put on the property. I asked him why he hired me to do a study for a condominium project. He said that he had been told (by his Greek lawyer) that a condo would go nicely there and that I was an expert on condo development.

My study a year earlier was very conclusive that a condo oriented to the U.S. market wouldn't do well at that time. So he did get information that served that need and that goal. However, his real needs and goals were different. I was able to review my earlier study, make a fast trip to Greece to update my statistics and market analysis, and come up with several suggestions on how the property could be best used. He finally got the advice he wanted, but it took a year longer and cost much more.

5. Ask the adviser for a reference (or two). Ask the adviser whom he has dealt with in the past, as a reference. You won't hurt his feelings unless he is an old friend or business associate. In that case you will have to rely on question three, above.

When you get a reference, call and be candid. Ask what the situation was so you can see whether it resembled your case. You might find that the adviser was very capable but his expertise isn't what you are looking for after all.

6. Ask about the fee for the advice you are seeking. Get that up front. Don't let the relationship build up without an understanding on what the fee is. First, a professional will invite discussions on his fee, as it makes him aware of your desire to have that part of the transaction out of the way. In many situations the exact fee may not be clear until there is a fuller understanding of what your needs and goals are, but you should know how much it will cost you to get to that point.

By the way, never feel you can't negotiate the fee. Some advisers set their fees by the PFA method. This scientific-sounding method, used by many lawyers and property managers, stands for "plucked from air." It is simply a fee selected at the time because it sounds right.

"Let me see, ah, yes, $5,000."

You can even shop fee prices if you want, but it is far more prudent to shop for the best advice and then pay a reasonable fee (after some negotiation if need be) to get that best advice.

The best dollar you pay will be for the best advice you get. The best advice you get will be the advice that lets you make up your mind quickly and with the confidence that you have enough facts and advice to decide, "Okay, here's what *I'm* going to do."

BUILD ON YOUR STRENGTHS

EVERYONE has something about her that makes her unique. Within this uniqueness is something that gives you a power—a strength—that can be put to use in everything you do.

These personal strengths shine in many facets of life for different people. The saleswoman has a dynamic enthusiasm or a personality that is warm and trusting, or some other attribute that makes her good at that job. The same is said for the athlete who has a physical talent that is used to its peak.

Investing is no different, and in the case of real estate there are many aspects of this field in which women are particularly adept. These strengths that I've noticed over the years of selling to women, both single and married, are not found in all women, of course, but many women have them. They are: patience, caution, decorative taste, stability in direction, seductiveness, and freedom from the male failure syndrome.

1. Patience. Sometimes I think I will go crazy waiting for a woman to make up her mind. There are times when even the simplest deal constantly gets off track, when all that is needed is calm and patience while the seller or buyer is thinking over the offer you have presented. These are times when patience will pay off.

Helen was eager to own the apartment building she made the offer on, but played it very cool. She had made her offer and was (as it turned out) willing to come up if she had to. She didn't want to give that impression, so she had told her broker (me) that the offer was not only a good one, it was her only one. She said this far more convincingly than any man I've ever dealt with. The sellers wanted to sell, and while they couldn't meet Helen's original offer, they countered with one of their own. The counter was for about 15% more than Helen had offered.

Helen looked at the counter and said she wanted to think about it over the weekend (this was Thursday).

On Monday she asked if the sellers would give her another five days to think it over, as her lawyer was out of town. (She didn't have a lawyer, I learned later on.) The sellers were on pins and needles by now, but what could they do if her lawyer was out of town, so they agreed.

She came back five days later and said she had not been able to get together with the lawyer but if they would accept her first offer she'd go ahead on the deal anyway. They did.

A prudent use of patience will work wonders in the game of negotiation. Your persistence in making offers and following up on them can make or break the deal. Fortunately, most deals are handled through a third party, the broker, and he is able to act as a buffer between the emotions of the buyer and the seller. This is a very necessary task, of course; however, at times it will be necessary for you to restrain the broker. If you are overeager, the broker can pick this up and also become overeager.

Patience mixed with good sense will pay off in any negotiations, other things being equal. Patience in this sense is the calm approach to the deal, understanding what you want, and then going about it in a steady, not overly anxious way. Being stubborn or ridiculous is not patience. "Tell them to take my deal or leave it" is not patience, as you have just pushed the other side to make a decision that may not be based on calm emotion. In the example offered above, Helen simply held up a decision, attributing her delay to a reasonable cause—the lawyer wasn't in town. Then she came back with a counter: "Take my first deal and I won't wait for my lawyer." It wasn't a demand that they take it or leave it. Knowing that the lawyer might kill the deal altogether was itself a motivating factor. Helen then used patience as one of her negotiating tools. "Look, gentlemen, I'm not busting down the door to buy this property. I'll even consider your counter if I can meet with my lawyer . . . but my original deal stands. Okay?"

2. Caution. Caution is like every good thing—too much and it's not so good anymore. But the lack of caution is disaster. Investing in real estate requires caution for the most expert, and especially for the newcomer.

Caution is simply not acting on anything until you have examined the alternatives and have the facts on which to base a decision. This is, of course, a path that everyone should follow, but that few investors truly understand, much less utilize. More often than not, too few alternatives are explored, too few facts examined.

3. Decorative taste. This interior decorating ability is not, of course, limited to women. Many men find themselves with this same talent, and when they put it to use along with the investment in real estate they profit from it. As a single woman looking into real estate for the first time, you may possess this seemingly inborn talent. If you do, then you should put it to use.

Decorating talent comes in handy when you are buying properties that are in need of fixing up. This "buy the dump and fix it up" form of investment can be most profitable. Many people work their way up the ladder of investment in this way. Shelley did exactly that.

At first it was Shelley and Norman. They were living together in a small apartment. They both had nice jobs and had saved up a few thousand dollars, which they put down on a run-down duplex outside of town. The deal was that Norman was to put up the down payment and Shelley was to pay for the materials to fix the place up.

It took a year for the duplex to be redone, and by then

Shelley and Norman had decided to part company. The property was sold at a nice profit.

Shelley has bought and sold over twenty properties in the past ten years, fixing them up and making big profits each time.

If you have this talent, look for property that needs the tender loving care you could put into it. Sometimes all it takes is a coat of paint.

I was looking at a small old house on a busy commercial street in Fort Lauderdale. It was occupied by two women who had lived in the property for over ten years and were now moving out to go back north. The owner of the property was ready to sell for $12,000.

I was looking at the property, trying to decide what to do with it. "Paint it, son," one of the women said. "We'd have done so years ago but the old skinflint who owned the building would have doubled our rent." It cost no more than $250 to paint the building, which I sold less than three months later at a profit of over $5,000 as the result of a simple suggestion from a single woman.

4. Stability in direction. Alas, this is sometimes called stubbornness. The woman is more defined in the direction she will stay in than the male. Possibly this is due to the earlier selection of a future career. Nonetheless, for whatever reason, the single woman who knows where she wants to go can usually be counted on to have more stick-to-it-iveness than the male.

This attribute can be utilized by the enterprising woman to hold her deals in line. This stability is seen in the patience I spoke of just a few pages earlier, and will enable the investor to be more persistent in attaining what she wants out of life.

The ability to stick to your guns is what I'm talking about. You've seen it in other women even if you haven't noticed it in yourself. It is stubbornness when the person doesn't have a strong goal or when the options available aren't known. Nonetheless, it is a female trait and should be taken advantage of.

• Don't stick to anything as a plan of action unless you feel you have all the facts you need to make a decision and have examined the alternatives.

• Keep your desired goal clearly in sight all the way.

• Use your natural stability to complement your other investment tools, such as patience and knowledge of the events that are developing.

• Never forget that flexibility is not the opposite of stability. You can change your mind, your plan, your goals, and should be prepared to do so whenever you decide it is in your best interest.

• Remember that sometimes your most worthy plan must be abandoned because of the problems that can be encountered due to other people along the way. There are times you are far better off biting your lip and letting something go, changing directions, and moving out in another path. People have left homelands and started new lives, better ones than could ever have been made with the "I'll stick it out" attitude.

5. Seductiveness. Take a look at the history of mankind and you will notice that woman's ability to bewitch has caused some rather interesting events. Male rulers throughout history have declared wars, built monuments, moved mountains, committed mass murder, and so on just because of a woman. (Usually a single one, at that.)

In our modern society the woman is a sex object in some people's eyes, capable of doing anything from selling cigars to automobiles just with her smile and attractive figure. Madison Avenue found out before *Playboy* the power of the female shape.

But we needn't think of the female purely in these terms. She is much more than anatomy or a smile.

Normally in our society children develop by being faced with, and overcoming, a series of challenges and competitions. These begin with a struggle to beat out other siblings for parental attention and love; later they are academic and social and sexual. It is a fact that a prime strategy for coping that nearly all females internalize at an early age is manipulation of others—especially male others—through seductiveness. All women in modern society know what I'm talking about and so do most men. Manipulation is something that girls learn faster than boys and are consciously aware of.

There are three ways which female seductiveness can be used to great advantage in dealing in real estate.

• Be feminine. I know that for some of you this is going to be a tough thing to do. If you are dealing with a male and you need to succeed in a transaction, then all you have to do is to win. It is not necessary to make sure the world knows a woman won.

I have seen countless deals made because the woman client did not try to act like a man, but instead made it very clear that she was a woman. "I'd be so ever grateful, Mr. Loan Officer, if you would take my loan application back to the loan committee and try again for pretty little ole me" is, of course, an exaggeration of what I'm talking about. The opposite is the single woman who comes on so strong with "I'm as good as any male, so why shouldn't I act like one, goddamn it!"

• Relax. Despite what a lot of single women think, the world is not out to take advantage of you. In fact, most of the people you deal with will go out of their way to be nice if you just relax and let the natural course of the events take place. Use your natural patience and stubbornness to ease you into the deal. Be sharp, be alert, and know where you want to go, but do it calmly.

Hysterics are not unknown and for some reason it is usually the female who falls prey to them. In investing they come from trying to move too fast, too soon. Get your foundation set before you move, then stay relaxed.

• Be secretive. There are times to "tell all," of course, but when investing in real estate you must learn to keep things to yourself. Your advisers must know all they need to know, but even then you needn't tell them everything. A woman's mind, like her body, is most attractive when there is something that isn't showing.

"I'd like to buy your home, Mr. Seller," she'd perhaps say, "I have some very interesting things I'd like to do to the home that I'd like to tell you about after we've come to terms. What do you say?"

Besides the alluring and bewitching factor of being secretive, you must remember that sometimes a single idea can mean the difference between your buying the property and making a profit and someone else doing the same thing. Your investment strategy should remain your own.

6. Freedom from the male failure syndrome. This is in part a counterbalance to the "man's world" syndrome, but I feel it is far more important as a solid strength than just a counter balance. Most single women aren't aware of its existence, much less how to take advantage of it.

To understand what I mean, let's examine the male failure syndrome first. In our society many men feel driven to achieve something extraordinary. There is an outrageous number of men in the over-thirty-five age group who seem to live with a sense that somehow they haven't measured up. It is almost as though it doesn't matter what they have achieved—it isn't enough.

This is, of course, a strong motivating force that will keep such a man moving his goals to a higher level year after year, simply because the success that is attained no longer feels like success.

Women so far have not been brought up to feel they must become the president of the United States, and often feel they are overachievers just by attaining more than their mothers did.

This is a very complicated situation that you needn't understand as long as you know that it exists. What you can do with it is rather remarkable.

Acknowledge its existence. It is evident in most men to some degree. The climbers, the hardworking never have enough of whatever it is they are working for; on the other hand, the down-and-out, negative-thinking men may have already given up because of it.

Realize that every time you deal with a man this emotion can be used to give you an edge. Get the edge by doing one of these three things:

• Feed the man's emotion by letting his aiding you in the quest for your goal be a success for him. "I know, Mr. Loan Officer, that *you* will succeed at the job you do so well and help me get the loan I need to buy" or "Mr. Seller, you have succeeded in convincing me to buy this home. I don't want to fail and let you down (and cause you to fail too), so if you would accept my offer . . ."

• Cut off the emotion by making lack of failure a substitute for success. This is done by playing the game where there must be some room for give and take. This give and take need not always assume the form of money. Remember Helen—she gave in in a way by agreeing not to wait for her lawyer.

• Adopt some of this emotion yourself. Realize that your own goals might be too low, that you are not setting your goals as high as you should.

3 Investment Strategies Every Single Woman Should Keep Secret from Her Lover

Since we are getting right down to the nitty-gritty of investing, it is a good idea to take a look at the investing problems that can arise from your relationship with a lover. There will be countless single women reading this chapter who are either living with a man or have a lover who shares a part of their life. There *are* things that they should keep from their lovers.

1. **Title to property.** Make sure that the title to the real estate you have bought is in your name alone. This means taking proper steps as advised by your lawyer to see that there is no future claim on that title by your lover.

2. **Your goals that don't involve your lover.** You will have some, and as long as your lover does not figure in them, they should be your goals and your secret.

3. **Your financial affairs.** If your lover started out as your financial adviser, I'd recommend you get a new financial adviser. Your affair might make your financial dealings a burden on the relationship.

8

Women + Marriage + Real Estate = Problems or Profit

Then Along Comes the Divorce

A few years back, the film *An Unmarried Woman* showed the story of a loving couple who broke up and got a divorce. He ran off with a younger woman; she soaked in her sorrow for a while. The story ended with the husband trying to get back with the former wife but she was now in love with someone else. Nice, but what about the house and the other real estate that this wonderful loving couple had before the divorce?

("Look, honey, you keep the house and I'll keep the office building because it has a huge mortgage on it . . ." he said.)

In the age of the uncontested divorce, the one the courts have made easy to get, there is often a rush to get out of a marriage rather than a planned approach to single life. Often one of the pair has lost interest in the other and the divorce seems more of an avoidance of a problem rather than a solving of the problem.

Do you know what lawyers tell their male clients?

I'm talking about long before the divorce, not just after the papers have been served. Whenever a male client confers with his lawyer and the conversation centers around investments such as real estate, the question of how title should be held enters into the picture. There are tax reasons for this, of course, but one reason (if not the most important one) is the thought, "If you got divorced, would you want this property held in such a way that she would have more claim on it?" After all, from an estate point of view the husband is better off putting more property into his wife's name right from the start. But lawyers know that divorce is a growing part of their business and there is no sense in giving the divorcée a head start on the property settlement by giving it to her before they are divorced.

I've even heard some lawyers explain away having put title in the husband's corporation as a tax savings angle when the main reason was to keep the prospective divorcée from having direct access to the property.

6 Things You Should Know and Do If You Are Married (Or Ever Will Be)

1. Who owns the home or apartment you live in? If the title is in your name, good for you. If it is in both your names, okay. If it is in his name because he owned it when you met him or before marriage, okay. If his corporation owns it and you and he lease it, there may be a sound reason which can be explained to you. If you don't know who owns it, find out.

2. Have a list of all the real estate your husband owns, whether or not your name is included in the title. List the date acquired, the price paid, how paid, where the money came from, and the mortgages on the property. Put in all the mortgage data, such as whom the mortgage is paid to, how often, how much, what the interest rate is, when it is due and payable. Know how taxes are paid; have the address of all property, the legal description, and knowledge of where the deed is. "Why in God's name do you want to know all of this?" he'll ask you. "Why, dear," you can begin, "someday when you sell this and make a fortune you will need this information for Uncle Sam. I just want to help you out . . . and besides, you might get run over by a garbage truck and . . ." Get involved in details.

There will be the occasional husband who won't tell his wife the above data. Try tact, then diplomacy, then perseverance. If all fails and divorce comes, rely on the legal deposition.

3. Is the family lawyer really his lawyer? Have a sit-down conference with the "family" lawyer who will represent your side, and ask his advice on how the growing family should handle its growing wealth. Ask if he feels you should seek out the advice of a tax expert or an estate planner.

4. Who rents your joint-income property? More than once in the history of real estate it was *his* girl friend. I've had several clients sell their nice apartment buildings because of troubles with the tenants that weren't troubles with the tenants at all. Keeping track of the tenants isn't the only thing you should know about the rental property, of course. In fact, if you keep the records of the leases, the income, expenses, and the like, you will know more about the goings on.

5. The pre-nuptial agreement—will you have one? There is a growing sentiment among lawyers that it is best for both parties entering into a marriage to have a marriage agreement spelling out what happens to the jointly owned properties or the properties to be obtained during this marriage. While most lawyers I've conferred with on this matter seem to agree that such an agreement is desirable for the wife as well as the husband, nearly all agree that it is unlikely that the vast majority of marriages will avail themselves of this kind of protection. These agreements are very hard to draft so that they take into consideration all potential contingencies and time elements. Marriages have a tendency to fall apart without prior notice and after short durations as well as after twenty or more years. So what do you do? Sit down with *your* lawyer before you get married and get some good advice. Remember, it must be your lawyer, not his.

6. Become integrated into the business dealings. You will find that if you take part in the investment part of the marriage you will become not only a more informed person with respect to the wealth of the marriage, but will be a far more interesting person within the marriage. This sentiment is an undercurrent of my dealings with many clients and was reinforced by many lawyers. The marriage that falters may do so for many reasons, but often the greatest cause is the lack of conversation between the couple. If the woman takes an active interest in the part of the marriage that improves its living standard, such as its investments, she can be in a prime position to praise her husband for the good job he is doing, or to take part of the blame if things go wrong.

Naturally, some women go off on their own path, and don't have much interest in what the husband is doing. There is nothing wrong with this, but these women will have less chance of being able to say, "That property is really half mine, you know, Your Honor."

When You Are Thrust into a Do-or-Don't Position

When the divorce comes along and everyone is at each other's throats, the emotion of the situation can be much more draining than people can imagine. Even after going through such an event many people find themselves getting married and going through it again for a second divorce. It takes the diehards of this world to become callous to this, and even the lawyer will become too closely connected to the proceedings to offer sound investment advice.

Often this is because the lawyer handling the case for the wife doesn't really know the wife's abilities and goals that well. This may be the first time she has ever had to use a lawyer, and her exposure to this kind of advice in these emotional moments can lead to the wrong kind of decision.

"Do you want the house or these apartment buildings?" This sort of thing is hard to decide unless you are knowledgeable about these investments. There is usually no real rush to make a decision on the spur of the moment, but frequently it is done that way.

If your divorce is tomorrow, it might be too late. You aren't going to become an expert in real estate overnight, I'm sorry to say. For some readers the news being imparted in this chapter is too late. But don't despair. You will be better equipped for the next time around.

Oh yes, you don't even need to be planning a divorce for this chapter to be important to you. In fact, if you follow the guides and suggestions here, the chances of a divorce will be reduced. It will be much too costly to your husband now that you know everything about everything, and you two will have so much in common that you won't be able to part company.

THANK GOODNESS REAL ESTATE IS SIMPLE!

The quicker you realize that investing in real estate is fun, exciting, and profitable, and can give you a future of comfort through the wealth you can build with it, the sooner you will approach the task of learning about the field. From a technical point of view, knowing how to buy real estate isn't that critical. Any really good real estate broker can give you insight into this aspect of real estate. Your lawyer and CPA can help you keep out of trouble in the legal sense. But only you can know if you want to risk your money, and in order for you to know what your risk is, you have to have an understanding of what the investment is, and its potential as well as its hazards.

Investing in real estate is a doer's game, so you must make active moves in this investment arena. It is a local game, and the home-towner has the advantages, but only as long as the home-towner is a doer. For the most part the local investor gets caught up in the grass looking greener on the other side of the county, country, or ocean. Knowing that your pot of gold is more than likely right in your own back yard is to your advantage if you use it.

The simplicity of investing for a profit in real estate shouldn't cause you to become reckless, however. That, too, is easy and simple and can happen if you don't follow the prudent buying suggestions outlined in this book. Even then, circumstances can come up and snatch away from you what you thought was a prime profit which you had already started to spend long before the deal to buy had closed. Don't forget the saying, "Don't count your chickens before they've hatched." In real estate, don't count your profits before the closing is held, the check is cashed, and the taxes are paid.

Aside from that, the novice in real estate investing need only have dedication and the ability to learn to have the basic tools. Beyond that, the capital to begin with or the time to substitute for capital gets you rolling.

5 Things a Married Woman Should Do to Prepare for Real Estate Investing

I will make the assumption that your marriage will involve real estate. If it is a question of rental, where the marriage seeks its living quarters in the rental market, your advance knowledge gained from this book will show you that renting is not beneficial in most cases, and that you can afford to spend more in ownership and have it cost less at the end of the year. Also, I will assume for a moment that as the marriage progresses you and your husband will become more and more involved in investing in real estate because you will have the added knowledge that will help him accept this form of investing, and you, too, will be more comfortable in real estate.

With this in mind then, there are five things I feel all married women can and should do if they wish to prepare themselves for real estate investing.

1. Reread this book. There are things that you more than likely glossed over the first time, techniques and methods which will be important for you to know and understand more fully. By going over some of these things again you will become aware of specific interests you might have in areas you will want to learn more about. You should follow up this book with more material on those subjects.

2. Become an expert on your own back yard. I've said it a thousand times so far, I think. Your pot of gold is right in your own back yard. To be more specific about where your back yard is, look at a map of your home town area.

Draw a series of circles around your home that indicate how far you can go in all directions in fifteen minutes, then thirty minutes, then forty-five minutes. Your prime area will be the first circle, and then the second, and then the third.

Concentrate on the first circle only, unless there is some specific reason to go to the second or third areas. Do not go beyond the third circle unless you are willing or planning to move from your present home into another area. If that is the case, draw the circles around the area you are planning to move to, and start becoming expert in that area as soon as you conveniently can.

You will become an expert on these areas by becoming aware of the marketplace: what is going on, what is selling, who wants to sell and for how much. You don't have to keep copious records, but become familiar with what is happening.

Know the rental market, too. I've mentioned this before, and it is very important for you to know what is being charged and what the tenants are getting for the rent they pay. When you go to buy income property it will be very helpful for you to know this information. Only by knowing the market will you understand and be able to improve the property you have just bought, or know if a property on the market for sale *can* be improved.

3. Learn how to improve property. You don't have to become a carpenter, but knowing the difference between why a run-down property sells for $20 per square foot and a slightly fixed-up property just like it sells for $30 per square foot gives you a fantastic edge.

The simplest and often most controllable way to improve a property falls into what I call the two P's—plants and paint. Landscaping will do wonders for any property, and if you are looking at a buildup of value over three to five years, you can get maximum return from invested capital through a landscaping program. In this way small plants are given time to mature into a value many times their cost. Paint is more immediate, as are more mature plants, which pay off in enhancing a property quickly. If you aren't inclined to be artistic in either plants or paint, look around for literature or classes on these subjects. Most adult education programs have courses which are related to both of these subjects (not how to paint a house, but color, design, decoration, etc.).

4. Learn how to sell real estate. Recognize that the key to making a profit in real estate isn't buying the real estate but selling it. I've seen prime investments become unprofitable to the owners because the property wasn't sold. Not that the property wasn't salable, only that it wasn't sold. There is a science to selling real estate. Many real estate brokers know the techniques which will move your property within the time you want at a price which will produce a profit for you. The other alternatives—to profit through exchanging, building to suit, and so on—are also options that you may know about or not, but you will truly be a success in real estate investing only if you know how and when to sell the property you bought.

In a typical marriage, the husband has more time to devote to the buying end than to the selling end. This is where you can come in handy. All the stages that follow the purchase of an investment parcel or building or property must be directed to the concept of selling that property. Even if you have no immediate thought of selling the property, you must anticipate that there will come a day when you will no longer have the benefits out of that property that something else would produce, and a sale or exchange or other disposition may become the prudent thing to do.

Look around again at the adult education classes in your area. Classes in becoming a real estate salesman will be informative for you even if you have no plans for getting into the profession in that sense. Your ability to deal with these professionals, which is the subject of Chapter 22, is improved when you know the ins and outs of what they have to do to make a living.

Local junior colleges and the like have classes in real estate marketing. While they might be complicated, you don't need to get an A in the class to get some meat out of the course.

There are countless real estate journals that give the up-to-date creative things going on as well as the conditions of the money market. These can generally be found in your local library or through real estate offices.

5. **Become a doer.** Do things in the field that will show you how to become more knowledgeable about real estate and investing in it. Get involved with your family investments and participate in them as much as possible. So far this chapter has

been slanted toward the woman who gets a divorce or may get one someday. You may feel sure that couldn't be you, but what if your husband does get run over by a garbage truck tomorrow? You are now thrust into a similar situation, possibly with even longer-lasting emotional ties to the property. Don't wait until the last moment to say, "Now what was that we owned?" Real estate sales statistics are full of good buys coming from divorces and also deaths. Don't let your property be one of those statistics simply because you were too involved in other things.

Real estate is the divorcée's or widow's cup of tea as an investment. Remember all the good and positive things I've said about why singles should own real estate. That goes for newly single people too. The only difference here is that the married woman has the edge on the forever single because, for a time at least, there are two people working toward what should be a common goal. As tough as it might be, those two people can combine earnings and sacrifices to build up some wealth. This wealth is not to be taken lightly no matter what the size of the bank account it can generate or the credit it throws off. If, while married, you work in the directions I have suggested, after the divorce or after a death, your future will be brighter.

9

Should You Rent or Buy?

IT IS TRUE, unfortunately, that many people rent real estate when they should own it. Most people are capable of owning real estate instead of paying their hard-earned money to someone else in the form of rent. The reason many people are in this situation is simply that they don't know what they can afford.

The high cost of ownership isn't that high. It is relative, of course, but the chances are that as a single you are renting right now and can maneuver yourself into a buying position without making a change in your earning capacity. On top of this, the odds are that one of the reasons you haven't become an owner is because you are having a tough enough time meeting the rent, let alone what some feel are costs that come with owning real estate.

Okay, I'll grant you that sometimes it is tough to make the ends meet, but unless you see just how much you can afford you won't know just how powerful you really are. Just how much can you afford when it comes to paying the ownership cost?

In setting the stage to determine just how much you can afford, I have developed a checklist for you. This "How Much Will It Really Cost to Own?" checklist will surprise most of you as to the reality of owning real estate and just how much clout you have in owning. Keep in mind, of course, that the term *cost* is relative and is based on the other factors that make up your financial environment. The idea is for you to recognize that the money you pay in rent is lost forever. You will never get anything except an *instant* benefit from rent, as rent is a temporary investment.

Before the checklist can be properly utilized it will be necessary to establish several factors. These are facts easily obtained from charts and tables that I have provided for you in the various sections of this book. Some are tables that won't change from year to year, while others, such as the tax rates, are subject to change. I have given you a simplified tax rate chart (Table 11) in this chapter for the purpose of determining the answers to the cases. The full tax charts for 1979 are given in the Appendix (Table C)

TABLE 11.

INCOME TAX RATE SCHEDULES, 1979

For singles

TAXABLE INCOME	PAY THIS TAX	% OF TOTAL TAXABLE INCOME	NEXT $1 EARNED TAXED AT
$ 5,000	$ 422	8.44	18%
10,000	1,357	13.57	21
15,000	2,605	17.36	30
20,000	4,177	20.08	34
25,000	5,952	23.80	39
30,000	7,962	26.54	44
35,000	10,207	29.16	49
40,000	12,657	31.16	49
50,000	18,067	36.13	55
60,000	23,943	39.09	63
70,000	30,243	43.20	63

For married persons filing jointly (and certain surviving spouses)

TAXABLE INCOME	PAY THIS TAX	% OF TOTAL TAXABLE INCOME	NEXT $1 EARNED TAXED AT
$ 5,000	$ 224	4.48	14%
10,000	1,062	10.62	18
15,000	2,055	13.70	21
20,000	3,225	16.13	28
25,000	4,633	18.53	32
30,000	6,238	20.79	37
35,000	8,088	23.10	37
40,000	10,226	25.56	43
50,000	15,072	30.14	49
60,000	19,678	32.79	54
70,000	25,078	35.82	54

so you can see how they would appear in the updated version obtainable from the Internal Revenue Service. When using the checklist in real life make sure you utilize the current tax rate for that year.

The mortgage amortization schedules found in the Appendix (Tables A and B) are never out of date and can be used with assurance that if you are using the correct table you are getting the proper information.

The mortgage amortization tables are in two forms. Table A will give you the constant rate for mortgages which are payable monthly. The constant rate is always an annual rate, however, and the debt service for any mortgage which has monthly payments is found by going to the pertinent interest column and reading across the column to the term of the mortgage. You can see that the 10% interest mortgage will have a 10.53% (rounded) constant if the term of the mortgage is thirty years. Let's say the mortgage amount is $46,400; the annual debt service is found by multiplying the amount of the mortgage by the constant percent: $46,400 × 10.53% = $4,885.92 annual debt service. The monthly payment is that annual amount divided by 12, or $407.16.

Table B is the same except that the results would give you the amount of annual payments. Instead of dividing by 12 to get the monthly payments, you would simply use the annual payment. Notice that the 10% annual payment for a mortgage of thirty years (Table B) would have a constant payment rate of 10.68%. This is greater than the mortgage with monthly payments simply because payments made on a monthly basis have a pay-down of principal over the year that didn't occur in the annual payment schedule. In the latter, reduction didn't occur until the end of each year when the single payment was made.

Income Tax: The Hidden Partner and the Toll It Takes

Income tax is the percentage of what you make that goes to your partner, Uncle Sam. Singles have a bigger tax bite taken from their earnings than married people do, because of families' ability to utilize deductions, particularly when only one spouse works, so you as a single have more to win by developing some tax shelter. To fully understand tax shelter, and in particular how owning pays over renting, look at the simplified income tax schedules in Table 11.

This table gives you a direct comparison of the income tax paid by singles with that paid by married persons filing jointly. You can see the break the married guy gets that the single doesn't.

The table shows taxable incomes (not the amount you earned but the amount on which you would be taxed) and the amount of income tax you'd pay in each situation. Note the column "% of Total Taxable Income." This shows the actual percent of the total tax in relation to the total taxable income.

The last column, at the right, shows the percent of tax you'd pay on the very next dollar you would earn which would be taxable. This rate is higher than the percent of total income and climbs rapidly. This is the top bracket, which you might hear the fat cats talk about from time to time. Paying tax at the top-bracket rate is more painful than in lower percentages.

Because the percentage of tax in the top bracket may have some intermediate stages not shown in this simplified chart, you may want to get a more accurate idea by using the current tax rate applicable to the current year as published by the IRS.

The whole idea behind the tax shelter concept is that any reduction of your taxable income that can be accomplished will come off the top-bracket rate and not the overall rate shown in the third column. If you can convert nondeductible payments for your normal living expenses into tax shelter (deductible) expenses, then you can get Uncle Sam to pay part of that expense. This is so because your income tax would be less at the end of the year by the amount of the top bracket times the amount of the expenditure. For example, if you had a taxable income of $25,000, using the table you would pay $5,925 in income tax. However, if $5,000 of the money you spent was relabeled from regular expenses to tax-deductible expenses, then your taxable income would have been reduced to $20,000. (Keep in mind you still have the same real income.)

At $20,000 you would pay a tax of only $4,177. Now watch carefully what is happening. If all you did was relabel the expenditure (not increase it or reduce it or anything else) and it became deductible, then instead of paying $5,925 in tax you paid only $4,177—a savings to you at the end of the year of over $1,700.

This form of tax shelter is the most basic of all, and often the most misunderstood. However, you need not become a tax expert to take advantage of the benefits available to you in owning real estate. Using tax shelters is the best way to keep what you have, and one of the best tax shelters in real estate is the simple ability to relabel current expenses.

Owning Real Estate Is a Combination of Economic Events

Unlike renting, owning has several factors occurring at the same time. In Chapter 3 I described the six magic factors of real estate: equity buildup, appreciation, tax shelter, cash flow, inflation fighter, and emotion. Each of these factors will have an impact on your eventual financial structure, and all factors must be considered in the ultimate determination of renting over owning. From a purely economic standpoint, it is easy to ascertain the short-range impact of owning by examining equity buildup and tax shelter.

Take a look at the checklist.

"How Much Will It Really Cost to Own?"

Section A

1. Monthly rent payment	$ ________
2. Annual rent	________
3. Other rent-related costs for year	________
4. Total rent expense for year	$ ________

Select a property you might consider buying in your area. It should be priced between 9 and 15 times line 4.

Section B

5.	Total price of property selected for analysis	$ ________
6.	Down payment	________
7.	Balance to be financed	$ ________

Section C

8.	Annual debt service	$ ________
9.	Annual real estate tax on property	________
10.	Annual insurance on property	________
11.	Annual maintenance of property	________
12.	Total ownership payments for year	$ ________

Section D

13.	First year's interest payment on mortgage	$ ________
14.	Real estate tax for year	________
15.	Total lines 13 and 14	________
16.	Applicable income tax rate	________ %
17.	Direct income tax deductions, if any	$ ________
18.	Adjustment of actual payments made	________
19.	Total tax credits	$ ________

Section E

20.	Actual annual ownership cost (out-of-pocket)	________
21.	Adjusted actual monthly ownership cost	$ ________

How to Fill Out the Checklist

Section A

Line 1. The amount of your monthly rent payment, which includes tax (if any) but not payments for utilities, repairs, or other non-landlord costs.

Line 2. Your annual rent. Multiply line 1 times 12 to arrive at this amount.

Line 3. Other rent-related costs. If you have annual expenses which are directly related to your rent, such as tips to the doorman, valet parking, elevator tax, and the like, include it here. Put down the total for the year.

Line 4. A total of lines 2 and 3.

Section B

Line 5. In each of several examples you will want to select the estimated price of the property you feel you can afford. This should be in the range of

9 to 15 times the amount of rent you are currently comfortable with. Start at one end of the scale and adjust up or down until you find the bottom-line cost that you can actually handle in ownership.

Line 6. The down payment you can come up with is a purely subjective matter, and the more honestly you answer this question the more accurate the answers you get at the bottom line will be. This is a test you can't afford to fudge. Because ownership is more than just permanent rent, you should stretch yourself into this down payment situation. Don't spend all your savings, of course, but try to go at least 20% of line 5 if possible.

Line 7. The balance to be financed will clearly be line 5 less line 6. This amount of money will be the net financing needed to close the deal. If the lender and the seller are the same person, then you won't have to calculate additional financing to cover the cost of the borrowed money. If you are obtaining your loan from a savings and loan association or other institutional lender, then you will be faced with the prospect of having added cost to the purchase in the form of mortgage points. These points and other out-of-pocket charges are placed on the deal by the lender.

Section C

Line 8. The annual debt service on the amount of money you need to borrow is the total annual payment needed to meet the obligation of the financing. This can be found using Table A in the Appendix. Find the mortgage term and interest rate general to your area by first contacting one or more savings and loans in the area and asking what they are charging on loans of the approximate amount you may need. After you have located that interest rate, read across the column to the term of years to locate the constant annual percent, which represents the rate which when multiplied by the amount of the mortgage will give you the annual debt service.

For example, on page 138 you will see one checklist worked out. The total on line 7 was $46,400. The interest rate available was assumed to be 10% for thirty years. The 10% interest column for thirty years showed 10.53% (rounded) as the constant rate. To find the annual debt service, multiply $46,400 by 10.53%. The answer, $4,885.92, goes on line 8.

Line 9. The annual real estate tax on the property can usually be estimated. Either use the existing tax for the past year on similar property or try to get an idea of the tax applicable to similarly priced properties in the market area where you would like to buy. The area is most important because taxes will differ greatly from town to town and state to state.

Line 10. The annual insurance on the property will be entered on this line. It is included because it is a requirement of nearly all lenders and is a cost not similar to insurance for a renter. You will only include insurance cost that is casualty coverage—fire, windstorm, flood, vandals, etc.—not liability or other coverage of personal property. While you may take out such extra coverage, this would be similar to the "rent" insurance you might have had to cover your own goods inside the apartment or home you rented. The concept of this checklist is to show you the closest picture of ownership cost in relation to rent cost.

Line 11. The annual maintenance of the property is the most important cost you need to calculate, because it can be devastating if overlooked or improperly estimated. To arrive at the maintenance cost of the property you plan to buy, take 1% of the price of the property; add any fixed maintenance fee charged each year against the property (in many condos and co-ops and retirement areas there is a fixed or varying charge each month against the property, which must be calculated here); if the property is over ten years old, take an additional ½% of line 5; add lines 1, 2, and 3.

Line 12. Add lines 8, 9, 10, and 11.

Section D

Line 13. The first year's interest payment on the mortgage can be calculated to the exact penny by using an amortization table, but if one is not available you can utilize the same constant table you used to establish the annual debt service on line 8. Look at the amortization table again. You see the constant rate at 10% for thirty years is 10.53%. When you multiplied that rate by the mortgage amount, you got the annual debt service in the example. In the example on page 135 the annual debt service was $4,885.92. Some of that amount was principal and some interest. The interest portion would be deductible from your income tax. To find it, look at the annual constant rate for the previous (29th) year. It is 10.59%. The formula to follow is:

$$\text{Mortgage amount} = \frac{\text{Annual debt service}}{\text{Constant rate}}$$

or in this event:

$$\text{Mortgage amount} = \frac{\$4{,}885.92}{0.1059}$$

This will give you the amount of principal still owed at the end of the first year—in this example, $46,137.11.

Mortgage balance at start of year	$46,400.00
Less mortgage balance at end of year	46,137.11
Total principal portion of the debt service	$ 262.89

Total payment on debt (from line 8)	4,885.92
Less principal portion	262.89
Total interest paid for the year	$ 4,623.03

A shortcut to arrive at the amount of interest would have been to simply take 10% of the gross amount of the loan. This would have given you $4,640 for the year and would have been sufficient in this example. However, in larger amounts or in shorter year terms (or combinations of the two), errors of magnitude could result.

Line 14. Real estate tax has already been found on line 9.

Line 15. Add lines 13 and 14.

Line 16. For this exercise, the tax rate applicable to your income is found by using the simplified tax table I've given you. When computing to actually make a decision, be sure that you are using a current table, obtainable from IRS or any accountant. Always make sure you use the top-bracket percent which is applicable to the income you no longer have to report.

To estimate how much of your expenses Uncle Sam pays for you:

a. Estimate your taxable income for the year (use last year's amount unless you anticipate an increase this year). In Charles's case, this is $25,000.

b. Reduce the above amount by the tax shelter shown in the checklist on line 15 ($5,105.06). Charles's new taxable income is $19,895 (rounded to $20,000).

c. Check the tax table I've provided. Look in the far right column. What is the rate the next $1 would be taxed at above the amount shown as new taxable income? The chart shows a 34% rate on a single's tax over $20,000 of taxable income (but under $25,000).

d. Savings are found by multiplying rate times shelter: 34% × $5,105.06 = $1,735.72.

Line 17. Direct income tax deductions, if any, would occur when there was an approved IRS deduction from tax for something related to the purchase of the property. A portion of the down payment might have been applied (for tax reasons) to solar heat or insulation and direct credit to tax obtained. In the example, no such credit is obtained.

Line 18. Adjustments for the tax shelter are made by multiplying the total tax shelter (line 15) by the tax rate on line 16.

Line 19. The total tax credits would be the total of lines 17 and 18.

Line 20. The actual annual ownership cost is the total real after-tax dollars you spend. Mind you, you have actually written out checks totaling more than this. The adjustment would come by the payment of less income tax for the year. The total ownership cost is simply line 12, which is the actual payments you have made over the year, less the amount of tax you don't have to pay now, as shown on line 19.

Line 21. The adjusted monthly ownership cost is found by dividing the annual amount (line 20) by 12.

The "How Much Will It Really Cost to Own?" checklist filled out by Charles

Section A

1. Monthly rent payment	$ 426.40
2. Annual rent	5,116.80
3. Other rent-related costs for year	196.00
4. Total rent expense for year	$ 5,312.80

Section B

5. Total price of property selected for analysis	$58,000.00
6. Down payment	11,600.00
7. Balance to be financed	$46,400.00

Section C

8. Annual debt service	$ 4,885.92
9. Annual real estate tax on property	482.00
10. Annual insurance on property	225.00
11. Annual maintenance of property	580.00
12. Total ownership payments for year	$ 6,172.92

Section D

13. First year's interest payment on mortgage	$ 4,623.06
14. Real estate tax for year	482.00
15. Total lines 13 and 14	5,105.06
16. Applicable income tax rate	34%
17. Direct income tax deductions, if any	$ 0.00
18. Adjustment of actual payments made	1,735.72
19. Total tax credits (Line 17 + Line 18)	$ 1,735.72

Section E

20. Actual annual ownership cost 4,437.20
21. Adjusted actual monthly ownership cost $ 369.77

A comparison of costs, adjusted for after-tax dollars, shows $5,312.80 in annual rent versus $4,437.20 to own—a savings of $875.60 per year for the owner.

How Charles Filled Out His Checklist

Charles has a good job and a nice apartment. He lives a normal singles life and is wondering just what is going on in the ownership world. Charles is tired of being one of the other guys, paying his landlord's way and building up other people's fortunes and not his own.

He pays $410 per month rent plus tax on that rent of another $16.40 per month, making his total rent $426.40 per month, or $5,116.80 per year (lines 1 and 2).

He pays other expenses which are related to the rental, such as tips to the doorman and house lights, which come to $196.00 per year (line 3). (Other expenses for utilities and the like have to do with occupation of the place and will occur in ownership just as in rent, and so are not included.) Charles has a total rent expense for the year of $5,312.80 (line 4).

In his first attempt at the chart Charles multiplied the annual rent times 11 ($5,312.80 × 11 = $58,440) and rounded it down to an even $58,000 to make the calculations a bit easier.

The down payment was set at 20% of the purchase price, a standard payment in conventional financing markets. Thus, $11,600 down was put on line 6. This left $46,400 remaining to be financed. Let's assume that Charles had done what you would do and called one of two savings and loan associations in the area and asked them what the current deal was on financing this type of real estate. The horrible real estate mortgage market had improved over the past year and Charles was able to get a thirty-year loan at 10% interest. That payment would be $4,885.92 per year.

Charles then went down the list and put in the real estate

tax of $482, insurance of $225, and maintenance on the property of $580.

By now Charles could see that on line 12 he had a total ownership payment for the year of $6,172.92.

At this point he might be inclined to stop. This is nearly a thousand dollars more each year than he is paying in rent, and he has $11,600 working for him earning some interest in a savings account. But he went on.

In Section D he began to establish his tax credits. He added up his mortgage interest (line 13) and real estate tax (line 14), giving him a total of $5,105.06 in tax credits (line 15).

Using the method shown in the instructions, he found his taxable income was approximately $25,000. With the reduction of the taxable income by the amount of the tax credits on line 15, he saw that his "next dollar rate" above the $20,000 level was taxed at 34%. He therefore put 34% on line 16.

He skipped line 17 and went on to the adjustment of the actual ownership cost by finding out what part of the tax shelter on line 15 was actually paid by Uncle Sam (through the reduction of Charles's income tax at the end of the year).

By shifting $5,105.06 in expenses from a nondeductible category to a deductible one, Charles would pay $1,735.72 *less* in income tax. He has made the same money, spent the same amount of money, but he now owes Uncle Sam less. This is seen in the reduction of the actual ownership cost in line 20 when this credit is made.

Charles paid out $5,312.80 in after-tax money to rent. His ownership in after-tax money cost him only $4,437.20. For Charles the pure and simple dollar criterion showed that he was better off owning than renting.

Mind you, this example does not take into account the other benefits that have occurred. On top of the advantage in the actual payments each month (after year-end adjustment) Charles will have a monthly savings payment in the form of a mortgage reduction. This equity buildup occurs until the mortgage is paid off. Rent has no such advantage.

I haven't made any room for adjustment on the $11,600

that Charles had to take out of savings to put down. Some analysts will insist that Charles now has a loss of income because of that expenditure. However, I feel that Charles has simply moved the investment from a savings account earning a meager interest rate into a solid investment that is going up in value faster than his interest from the savings account would accrue.

The Multiplier Effect of Appreciation

This is one of those secret items that makes real estate so good for the investor. Real estate goes up in value, and often at a rate faster than that available in the money investment market. Let's use a 10% per year increase in value, and to make the case for the money investments (bonds, savings accounts, and the like) seem more attractive, let's say you might be able to get 12% on your money in a prime cash deposit or CD.

	Money Invested	Real Estate Owned
Total holdings	\$11,600	\$58,000
Rate earned	12%	10%
Amount earned	\$1,392	\$ 5,800

The \$11,600 put into the real estate gave you a holding of \$58,000 worth of property. The fact you owed \$46,400 isn't a factor here, because you are going to pay that off out of what you would have been paying to someone else anyway. The increase of value in the property was based on the entire beginning value. You would earn \$5,800 against \$1,392. An additional bonus (as if you need any more convincing) is the fact that you must pay tax at earned-income rates on the interest from the savings and loan, while the appreciation of real estate continues to build at compound rates until you are ready to sell. And when you do sell you will be taxed at the capital gains rates instead of earned-income rate, and that can be one hell of a break.

Not everyone is ready to buy just because they see the advantages in ownership. There is more to ownership than just being able to meet the payments. You must be prudent in choosing your investment. Nearly all real estate is going up in value, but some won't and some will. The properties that will be the best investments will be those you find after following the simple rules of selection. There are four rules:

1. **Buy in a location that you know and understand.**

2. **If you are going to use the property, don't be afraid to bite off a bit more than you think you can chew.**

3. **Keep some financial reserve to cover your ownership cost in the event of emergency** (three to four months of cost is a minimum).

4. **Don't analyze a deal to death.** You'll miss out on the deal.

This last bit of advice isn't meant to do away with analysis. The problem with overdone analysis is simply the fact that what generally happens is you begin to look too far into the future. Advance thinking is okay to a point and then once that point is past all accuracy begins to deteriorate. That makes long-range projections nothing more than guesswork in most cases. The short haul is the only haul as far as I'm concerned. If it doesn't look good within the first two years of your projection, then a carry-out beyond that is too risky, as the projection will be full of holes.

Remember the greatest investment tip: "If you like it and can afford it, then buy it."

10

The Single and the Single-Family House

THERE IS a grass-roots movement back to ownership of private homes, and the number of singles presently buying their first home is a marvel that has caught many real estate analysts by surprise. But not me. In fact, I'm disappointed only that it took so long for the buying public to realize that being single is the proper status to make your first real estate buy. And what could be more fitting than to buy your home first?

This gets back to some of the things I've already mentioned, such as your shelter should be the first place you look to when you are deciding where you should start your real estate portfolio. That's not all the story, of course. You need to begin each transaction with your eyes wide open and a tight hand on your pocketful of money. There are advantages and disadvantages in nearly anything. As the purchase of a home may be the first real estate transaction for most people, there is the fear of the unknown that must be dealt with. Thus this chapter.

Everything you will ever buy in your future career of investing in real estate should be because you selected one item over something else. You may not have made the pick from a wide selection, but you should have looked at every potential option available to you, within reason. Therefore, when you are considering a home you will be able to decide if you want a single-family home or a duplex (a two-family) or other form of small apartment or a co-op or condo. Then again, you might choose a farm or something else. Each of these selections has its advantages. Below you will see six advantages in ownership of a single-family home. Not all of these advantages need fit your situation, and certainly if none of them do, then that is apt to be because you should look to another form of real estate for your purchase . . . or not buy at all.

6 Advantages to Owning a Single-Family Home

1. **Your home is your castle.** There is something about this philosophy that does wonders for its adherents. "I own this" is something that anyone who owns real estate can say, but the house owner makes it his home. This point, however, is a very personal one, and should be the element that breaks a tie if another form of real estate (say, a duplex) is in the running for your dollars.

2. **A home is your private domain.** Or nearly so, it seems. But one thing for sure, the home is more private than any building that has party walls and apartments upstairs above you with the all-night party. For many people the quest for privacy will make the single-family home the only way to go. The more privacy, by the way, the more potential you have in future resale. Now keep in mind that privacy is a relative thing. If all the homes in the area are very secluded on five acres of land, then the amount of privacy you have to offer (in a potential resale) may not be unique. If there is something special about the way your back yard was landscaped, then you may capitalize on privacy you created to the tune of big profits.

3. **A home can be a showplace.** All you readers living out in the smoggy skies of Beverly Hills know what I'm talking about. This might seem contrary to the second advantage of privacy, but for many folks a showplace is absolutely necessary. I know several architects, for example, who designed their own homes to display their talent, several actors who bought homes in prominent locations so the sightseers could find them, and many

friends and clients interested in having a monument to their lifestyle. To my mind, buying a home because it is a showplace is not as profitable as *making* a home a showplace.

4. High loan acceptability. A home can usually be bought with a low down payment and the balance financed through one of several lenders. If you are a veteran you may qualify for 100% financing. If you are not, and can qualify for an FHA loan, then you can get in for as little as 5% down.

Sellers of homes often hold financing, and this fact alone can help you buy something in a time when lenders aren't free with their money or their interest rates.

The ability to borrow lots of money on a home can be a great safety valve as you grow into that home you have bought. The home increases in value, and so does the amount of loan potential. Later on I'll show you some of the creative buying and financing techniques that can pyramid your wealth to higher and higher levels by using the seller's motivation to your best advantage.

5. Single-family homes in good neighborhoods can be a fantastic investment for the future. You've heard it a thousand times, real estate is governed by three things: location, location, and location. The point is, the location of what you buy is crucial to its future. If the area goes downhill then the real estate will go down with it. On the other hand, if you have done your homework and checked out the area and know what is going on, not only now but planned for the future, then your investment in single-family homes can increase your equity to very high levels. For example, I built a home in Fort Lauderdale and the total cost for the lot and home was $33,000. Seven years later it sold for $78,000 and two years after that for $98,000, and then once more twelve years after it was originally built it sold for $147,000. Another home, bought by a client of mine for $19,000, sold five years later for $62,000. In each case a combination of location and prudent investing gave the investors solid profits on their purchases.

6. Tax relief in single-family homes. The concept of private ownership and the need to have a shelter over your head is the basis for the tax relief that accompanies personal residences. Naturally, this concept holds true for single-family homes as well as your owned apartment, but there seems to be a more dramatic tax relief in the single-family homes. High profits in many resales are buffered by tax relief. These tax-relief items come in several packages. The first is the ability to "move up" from one home to another without having to pay a capital gains tax on the sale of the first. This is a solid way to increase your wealth without having to pay tax, provided you comply with the rules governing this purchase. The new home must be your principal residence, must be purchased within eighteen months of the sale of the first, and (to get full benefit of the tax-savings portion of the law) must be more expensive than the first.

If you bought a home for $30,000 and five years later sold it for $130,000, the $100,000 gain would not be taxed if you bought another home within eighteen months that was worth as much as or more than the property you just sold.

Senior property owners get breaks on taxes as well, and this goes all the way down to property taxes in the local area. A call to the tax assessor or collector in your county will give you the special tax breaks available to you (if any).

From time to time Uncle Sam offers tax-relief credits for certain improvements to your home. These might be in the form of improvements for insulation and energy conservation. Each such tax break will allow you to invest money on which you will someday have a profit returned to you, while Uncle Sam pays part of the improvement expense.

The rights of property ownership are at their strongest when it comes to the single-family home. It is here that you can see and feel the pride of ownership and the benefits that go along with that ownership.

These six advantages of ownership of the single-family home may apply to you or not. The other side of the coin, however, is very real and must also be examined. The disadvantages of ownership of a single-family home can be a very personal thing; one person's poison might be another's fertilizer. Nonetheless, there are some distinct drawbacks in ownership of single-family homes.

5 Drawbacks

1. **The single-family home can be a static property.** Static because sometimes it doesn't seem to go anywhere fast. Static because it can be an economic drain when compared with other forms of real estate investment.

There is no question that the single-family home can be favorably compared with the alternative of renting in many cases. The opportunity to buy at a low down payment and convert your rent into equity is real and valuable. On the other hand, many singles need income and the best real estate for you to buy may not be the single-family home but something that is able to provide income as well as shelter. The appreciation in the best areas of town and the finer residential homes can be excellent, but the steady input of extra income into your bank account might be a greater advantage to you at this time of your life.

2. **A single has something going for him that may be inconsistent with the single-family home.** I talked about this back in the examination of the single's advantages in investing in real estate. Time is the great equalizer when it comes to investment in real estate. If you accept the premise that nearly everything is going up in value and that all you have to do is find out what is going up before something else and invest in the early bloomer, then you will have it made. Sounds easy, right? Sorry, it isn't so easy.

When it comes to the single-family home, most singles don't seem to want the responsibility of that kind of property. It's like buying a car that isn't stylish enough or dressing in clothes that aren't your style.

This "the single-family home isn't for me" attitude is a very real thing and should be examined carefully. If you have a solid reason for not investing in a home, then acknowledge it and look for an alternative form of real estate to invest in. On the other hand, if you are overly cautious toward the single-family home because you don't see yourself in that kind of living environment, you need to take a deeper look at your own attitude about buying real estate.

Single-family homes do require attention to detail. Your ability to devote time to produce an income and profit may be more suited to buying income-producing property. This need not eliminate the single-family home, of course, as it is possible that by taking in a partner or someone to share the "rent" you pay you can have some of both worlds.

3. The single-family home may not be within your reach. This can be both geographic and economic. Your job might require you to live in the center of town, and that may blow the idea of a single-family home. Even if you don't have to live close to your job, travel time and expense should be considered. The economics of home ownership must be taken into account as well as the problems of ownership. Miscalculations in planning your expenses can be a primary reason for economic problems after ownership, and the best way to overcome that is by careful examination of the other alternatives to your investment. While the amount of cash put down to buy may not be that crucial, as you can buy with a low down payment, the total payment structure might be less attractive to you than other alternatives.

4. Homes are a special problem to the absentee owner. If you buy a home for the income you might get from renting it, you have more than likely made a mistake. It is rare for a single-family home to produce income commensurate with its real value. If you buy for appreciation and then are transferred to another town, you may be faced with the prospect of having to sell at a time not opportune to the market. Of course, some homes in some areas may become good rentals, but for the most part this is not the case. Some alternatives, such as duplexes and apartment buildings are, by their nature designed to be oriented to the income they produce. The single-family home has other advantages than its economic rental potential.

5. The single-family home provides no depreciation to help you build your wealth. This tax shelter, the kind that comes from depreciation of a capital asset, is that paper loss that enables millionaires to pay little or no taxes. You can do the same, but not by owning an expensive home. Apartment buildings provide the most tax shelter. The fact is this: Single-family homes offer those six advantages I've shown you, and if those are more important than these five disadvantages, then the single-family home is for you all the way.

Buy and Fix Up

Despite these disadvantages, some areas of the country are ripe for what I call "refurbishmentations"—a long word that means buy a run-down house and fix it up for big profit.

If your personal advantages lie in the ability to work with your hands in the building trades or interior decorating, then this form of investment work could be the way for you to go. Take a look around the country. In such cities as Savannah, Charleston, Houston, St. Louis, Salt Lake City, Los Angeles, Miami, Fort Lauderdale, New York, Chicago, Portland, and almost anywhere you go you will find areas of town that were down and nearly out and are in the stages of being brought back to life.

I don't mean the ghettos of the cities, either. In fact, I'd suggest you leave the ghettos for the other guy, and invest in areas that are on the fringes of the prime, or in older neighborhoods that will provide you with the right price structure. Buy in a location which is in need of upgrading.

Form a Partnership and Make a Business of Providing Your Own Shelter and Profit

I've seen it happen many times, and it is a great way to build your fortune. You start with one home, or townhouse, and go from there. If you plan to do this, it is important that you answer these three key questions.

1. Are you personally able to do much of the work yourself? Answer no to this one and I'd suggest you stop and go no further. Sure it is possible to bankroll someone else in this kind of venture and come out ahead, but if you haven't had experience in any of the areas of remodeling and decorating, then leave this one to those who have. The idea is to make a job for your own profit. If you do this on the side—that is, fix up your own property and then sell it down the road—you will convert your earned-income time into capital-gains income, and these dollars are more powerful than the kind you earn at a nine-to-five job because capital-gains earnings are taxed lower than wage earnings.

2. Can your partner do an equal share of the work? If you are planning on having a partner who can't meet the number 1 key requirement, then you will be in trouble from the first moment. Of course, partnerships in this imbalanced form of relationship do work from time to time, but I'd not recommend you start out that way. Look around and I will promise you that you can find someone ideal for the task.

3. Will you have time to devote to the start of this new job? If you don't want to give up your good-paying job for the moment and hope to do this on the side, then take stock of your time. If you can only put in a few hours over the weekend while your partner can put in double or triple that amount of time, you are headed for disaster. You can make this go only if you put time into it. The real estate market for rejuvenated properties is very strong in many areas, and more than likely you will find that there is great potential in your own back yard. Take advantage of that only if you can devote the time to fixing up the properties.

How Can You Be Sure You Have Found a Good Buy?

THERE ARE many factors that go into the concept of a good buy. After all, what you want in a property isn't necessarily what I want. Nonetheless, in the concept of an investment it is easier to be objective about a property and to examine each home from one standard to see if it measures up.

The Single-Family Prepurchase Checklist

1. *The Neighborhood*

A. What does the price picture of the homes in the neighborhood look like over the past ten years? Have your realtor check four or five homes of similar size, going back ten years. If the prices have not maintained a steady rise during this time, find out why. If the reason has not been rectified, then continued and sizable appreciation may not continue.

B. What are the plans for the area? Check with the city and other governing bodies to see if there are roads planned which will change the complexion of the area, or civic construction projects which will change the area in a way positive or negative to its value. These long-range plans are available to you if you take the time to find out.

C. What are the current restrictions and how do they affect the future value? You might find that one home directly across the street from another will not have the same restrictions (deed restrictions, city or country, home owners' associations, etc.), and the lack of imposed restrictions can make the area better or worse. One example that comes to mind was a beautiful home on a golf course. You'd think it would continue to rise in value; however, a home directly across the street had no restrictions on things such as parking boats in the drive, having dogs in kennel pens, etc. The home on the golf course was nice, but its value was lessened by lax restrictions on use across the street.

D. Is the neighborhood a place for you? The buy might be right, the place nice, but the neighbors all against you. It can happen, you know. A retirement area might not be the place for a single to buy, even though the terms are good. The social aspect of buying where you want to be comfortable is important. Your market may be narrowed when you go to sell, if for no other reason.

Check out the neighborhood by spending some time there. A quick drive through isn't enough. Visit the place at all times of the day and night. Drive through and if possible walk the area (have some proof that your reason for wandering around isn't to case the joint). Much can be discovered on Saturday morning that wasn't evident Thursday at noon.

2. *The Property*

A. Is it what you want? Or are you in such a hurry you don't need to be particular? It is important for you to recognize that time is on your side if you take advantage of that time by moving ahead in the culmination of each task directed toward a clearly seen goal. Don't buy unless what you are buying serves your goal. Don't worry too much if it isn't the goal itself as long as it helps you get there. For example, you might buy a condo that you may be able to exchange a few years later for the home you wanted in the first place but couldn't afford.

B. Does the property offer room for appreciation above the norm? Take a look at the values of similar property in the market area. If everything (similar property) is selling in the $100,000 range (plus or minus 5%) and your property has benefits above average, then you have a good potential. On the other hand, if you are buying at the top of the market and your property is just average or below average in comparison to the market, you've chosen the wrong property. Buying the most expensive property on the block is something to avoid if appreciation is what you are after.

Keep in mind that properties go up for some of the strangest reasons. Often being on one street or another can make a big difference. Of course, knowing how these trends affect the values will give you an edge. Over a longer range, look at an area and the properties available and take a look at the kinds of properties that are selling 50% above the price you are now considering. If you can buy the same kind of real estate as that but at a lower price, by going to older parts of town or farther out of town, then you are acquiring real estate that is going up in value in the near future.

C. Have the property inspected. Even if there is a condition in the agreement that the seller will deliver you a property with everything working, you still need to have an independent inspection of the major (even the minor) parts of the house. It is probable you will need more than one inspection to cover the different items. These inspections will include things such as the roof, plumbing, electrical, air, and heating systems. Often these can be made by one company specializing in such inspections. Expect a written report on the condition and estimated cost to bring the property up to snuff. It is a good idea to have a provision in your agreement allowing you to withdraw from your offer if the repairs would cost more than a predetermined percentage of the price. This option to withdraw can be a negotiating tool in bringing the value down to cover the amount you will have to spend to repair the property, or at worst allow you to get out of a bad deal.

Many standard-form contracts for the purchase of real estate have clauses for these inspections, and generally limit the cost which the seller must pay for the repair of the property.

3. *The Terms*

A. Do you have a deal that you can handle financially? The last thing you want to do is get into a buy that will eat away at your reserves and starve you out while you are trying to await a profit. Keep in mind, however, that you can afford to pay more than rent, due to the tax credits and the help in making those payments which you will get from Uncle Sam. Yet the help from Uncle Sam won't come until the following year. The "eat" of your financial bankroll in the meanwhile might be more than you can handle. Watch the dollars-and-cents part of all transactions carefully.
B. Is there a future profit allowed in the terms you have negotiated? This is often the easiest way to assure you can have a profit in what you buy. The terms of your transaction can benefit or hamper a resale later on. You need to have favorable terms, of course, for a profit to show its face around the corner. Profit, in the terms you negotiate, is often easy to see in retrospect. For example, take a look at Lucy's deal where she bought a duplex for $55,000. She put $15,000 down and owed $40,000. She bought this property back when the marketplace for conventional financing was 9% per year. The seller didn't want to be paid off in cash so he held the first mortgage of $40,000 and took 8½% interest on a long-term pay-out of twenty-five years. Today that 8½% mortgage rate looks dirt cheap, and has actually increased the value of the equity because of that fact. If Lucy went to sell the duplex today she might be able to get 12% or more interest on a mortgage she would hold. Her original mortgage ($40,000 at 8½% for twenty-five years) had a payment of $322 per month. If she sold the property at the same price she paid for it ($55,000) and held a wraparound mortgage of $40,000 at 12% for twenty-five years, she would collect nearly $422 per month. Out of that amount she would pay the first-mortgage payment of $322. She would be left with $100 per month for the duration of the mortgage. That $100 would total $30,000 over the term. Of course, it's likely Lucy would sell the duplex at a higher amount than what she paid, but this illustrates that the terms alone would have put $100 per month for twenty-five years into her pocket.

If the investment is an income-producing property, this leverage up over future terms can be very important. As with the duplex deal shown above, only more so, the advantage you can reap in making good terms now and selling those terms later will put big dollars into your pockets.

The opposite, of course, will work against you. If Lucy had taken out a 12% mortgage and the interest rate in the general market went down (and the mortgage couldn't be paid off without a stiff penalty, which is the usual case), the value of the property would have suffered.

C. Can the terms be passed on? This is the catch the lenders want to slip in—that is, that their loans at today's rate and terms may not be used as speculation for the owner. So watch this. Most savings and loans will push you into a loan that doesn't allow for a transfer of the property without some kind of adjustment in the terms of the loan. These adjustments might be minor or substantial, and as you don't know what they might be in advance of your future deal, you might find your sale being held up because of this provision.

In my opinion, the loan made by the savings and loan association is against the property and what happens to the ownership shouldn't affect the loan. Some state courts are considering this matter, and hopefully it will be settled. Take a good look at the laws in your state, and make sure you have the most recent laws, as this is one area that is in constant flux.

Your ability to pass on the financing should be insisted on right down to the moment of decision as to whether to buy that property.

If you are torn between two properties that are more or less equal and you know you are going to turn the property around for a profit (or hope to, at least) in a few years, then go with the property that has the best terms that can be passed on to the next buyer.

How to Increase Your Equity in a Hurry

BUYING real estate makes this easy because you can simply say your equity is increased. Got that? Simply say your equity is greater, because it will be 99% of the time.

Here's how it works. Frank bought a lot for an investment. He had deep in the back of his mind the thought that he could always build a small office building on the commercial site if nothing else happened. He contracted to buy in March of the year, putting up $5,000 in an interest-earning account with the broker (this can be done now in most states—if not in yours, your lawyer can tell you how to use interest-earning accounts to protect the yield you might otherwise lose on that deposit). The transaction called for Frank to make several soil inspections of the lot to be sure there was no bottomless pit lurking under the topsoil. Also, he wanted to be satisfied as to local building restrictions before completing the transaction.

Frank wrote in these steps not so much because he was concerned with these potential problems—he had checked them out before deciding to buy—but because delay increases appreciation. Appreciation generally requires one element only: time. All other things being equal, the longest time will create the greatest appreciation. As long as the cost to hold doesn't eat up the appreciation, time works for the investor.

Once Frank notified the seller that all the inspections and checking were approved, the deal went forward to the next step: the closing of title. This was still sixty days off—more time bought.

In fact, it was nearly seven months after the first contract was signed that the closing took place—seven months of appreciation that accrued to Frank and not the seller. The day the closing took place Frank was able to say, "The property is now worth more than I paid for it." And Frank was probably right.

If property was going up at a rate of 12% per year, Frank would have had a 7% rise in value during those seven months. The price of the lot was $100,000 and called for $20,000 down, with the seller holding the balance over a sufficient term for Frank to handle. The 7% increase in value meant that at the closing the property was worth $107,000 and Frank's equity was $27,000. This was an instant increase of equity by 35% of the original $20,000 and occurred with no real risk to Frank.

Value is relative to what is offered, of course. In looking at property values it is important to remember that what you want isn't necessarily what you will get. On the other hand, if you are prudent you can let time become your ally and win out in the majority of investments.

Sometimes you have to help time along and do something positive to increase value. Lou has gone through several fortunes, the first one taken away by the Nazis, the second by the Russians. He lives in Florida now and is working on his third fortune. His motto is "Buy it right, then plush it up for a quick sale."

This "plush it up" concept is often the easiest way to help time along in raising the value of your property. When you are looking for properties that you want to tackle in this way it is important that you find sound properties that are in good resale areas. The fact the properties might be somewhat run-down is working for you in that the price should reflect their condition. Also working for you is the fact that most top-of-the-market buyers want properties that are already in good shape, that don't need a lot of work to be made livable. This is where you come in with your paintbrush and hammer and saw.

Don't get carried away with plushing it up, though. You want to take a property that doesn't show its potential and turn it around by bringing out the positive factors through repair or beautification. But you don't want to go whole hog in this or you will risk limiting two things: your market and your profit.

I'll admit that there are many people in the business of taking homes and moving in and doing a number on them that won't quit. They completely redo the property, turning a dog into a glittering model home. But this is not where the fast bucks are, and a full remodeling job is damn risky.

Instead look for properties that need landscaping, paint, a small but impressive change of look that can be done by adding a wooden fence or putting a door on an open carport. Things like that.

The one most impressive thing you can do to increase the value of any residential property is to make sure the entranceway is clean, fresh, and the newest-looking part of the property. Sometimes this means nothing more than a refinished front door, or a new mailbox, or some steppingstones and plants along the walk.

You don't have to repaint a whole building when just the trim needs to be changed or redone. Look at the surface first, because that is the one part that turns on or off 80% of all buyers.

11 Quick and Cheap Things You Can Do to Instantly Increase Value of a Used Property

1. Clean it up. Often a yard has a trashy look to it. This makes a very negative first impression.

2. Have the landscape cut and trimmed. A run-down house

will usually have a neglected yard. Get it back into shape as quickly as possible. A good cutting will make even the worst yard look better.

3. Review and fix general cosmetic items on the exterior. If there is anything broken that can be seen from the outside, get it fixed. Don't cover up a problem, as that will only cause you more expense later on, but do take care of those items that are obvious. Remove all negative appearances.

4. Give the entrance a once-over to make it the most impressive part of the exterior. Paint the door, paint trim around the door, clean up the walkway, and if necessary put in new landscaping along the walk. This is the most important part of whatever you are going to do. Make it count.

5. Paint the exterior only if paint will improve the appear- The fact that the property could use a coat of paint is not a reason to paint. That is a luxury you can approach when the more crucial items are taken care of. Sometimes a good cleaning will freshen up a dull exterior to the point where painting can be put off for a while.

6. Clean the interior from top to bottom. Do this before you attempt any major remodeling. If carpets must be replaced, decide on this prior to the cleaning, as the carpets should be removed first. Sometimes you find beautiful floors (hardwood, tile, marble) under soiled carpets—like finding a Leonardo in an attic.

7. If there is any animal smell, attack it instantly. There are chemicals at your nearest hardware store that will help. A fresh clean smell is money in the bank.

8. Paint the interior where needed. Use neutral colors unless you are planning to furnish the interior and need decorator colors to match your furniture.

9. Replace the refrigerator with a more modern one. Nothing will turn off a prospective buyer like an old refrigerator. A newer model (it doesn't have to be brand-new, only nearly so) will freshen up the whole kitchen.

10. Keep it clean until it sells. This is a secret that developers learned a long time ago. Everything should look carefully attended to on a daily basis. (The yard can be left to grow unless you are turning over the property right away.) The more care you demonstrate, the higher the offers will be.

11. Continue to upgrade. If you are living in the property, map out a schedule of things you can do while continuing to live there. If you don't know how long that tenure will be, then go from project to project but try to develop a long-range goal (one you might not reach if someone comes along and offers you a deal you can't refuse).

Of all the things you can do, the most productive over the long haul will be landscaping. Plants take time to grow. If you start with small, inexpensive plants, in a few years you will have turned an investment of tens of dollars into thousands of dollars. The most important part of landscaping is that you can develop something that cannot be bought. There is a limit to the size of many plants sold out of nurseries. I have a hedge around my home in Fort Lauderdale that simply could not be obtained in any landscapery, yet each plant cost me just a few dollars five years ago.

This list could go on and on, but the idea is to give you some of the solid instantaneous points toward the positive end of the buyer's "I like it so I'll buy it" scale.

When You Should Sell

There are three ideal times to sell a single-family home. Paradoxically, the best time is *not* when you can get the most money for it. I'll explain why in a second, but first let's look at the times to sell:

- You sell when you get the price you started out to get and there is no good reason to change that goal.
- You sell when you are ready to move on (up or down) in your investment strategy. You make the decision on this and don't let someone come and buy you out until you are ready. A rash sale will only put your next investment off. If you can, however, don't turn an offer down cold. Take stock of the situation and try to see if you can take advantage of an offer that might

come in out of the blue. Remember that flexibility is the key to your ultimate success.

• You sell when there is a dramatic shift in the market and you determine that the market is going to turn against the type of property you currently have. Keep in mind that some market shifts are temporary and you might be able to ride out the storm. But don't hold on unless you can see a silver lining in the dark clouds of the storm. A dramatic shift is not always easy to anticipate. It can come because of a new roadway, a community development that will add traffic and reduce the value of an otherwise tranquil neighborhood, or a vast multitude of other causes. When you see it coming, it may not pay to stay and fight it out.

So Are You Going to Buy a Single-Family Home, or What?

It is safe to say that single people make up the largest untapped market for single-family homes. The real estate industry is just beginning to cater to the single buyer, and some of the age-old techniques of marketing real estate need to be changed and altered to suit you and entice you into owning.

This is happening, of course, and soon you will see more and more developers offering singles a way of ownership that has not been available before. Singles' communities may be the wave of the future, just as adult and retirement communities have been waves of the past and present.

One thing is for certain. Single-family homes will be sought after, not because they are the American dream but because they are good business. If you can afford rent and don't wish to expand your investment capability through the other options in this book, then single-family properties can be a way for you to build your fortune.

11

One Single + One Single = Magic in a Duplex

THE SMALLEST of all apartment buildings is the duplex. This property is really a combination of two single-family living units in one structure. The duplex comes in many forms and designs, of course, just like the single-family home. Every city has them, and for the single the duplex is an excellent choice for the first investment in real estate.

The current trend of singles buying duplexes should continue. That doesn't mean you need to follow that lead, but let's take a good look at duplexes and see why this kind of real estate is appealing to single buyers.

• **Duplexes produce income.** This is one of the most interesting parts of the duplex. If you are buying with the idea of living in one of the living units, then you have another unit to rent out. This extra income can help carry the extra cost that the duplex might have over a single-family home you were considering buying. The income you get from the other guy who has to pay you each month has made you a landlord and has started you off as an investor in real estate. You are no longer looking at your purchase as just shelter—indeed, you have invested capital that will return a dividend.

• **Duplexes produce tax shelter.** In keeping up with the fat cats, it's a good idea to play their game when it comes to taxes.

The part of the duplex that you live in isn't a tax shelter unless you are able to depreciate part of that as an office, but the other unit is purely investment property and you will be able to get the benefits of the tax shelter that is generated by the depreciation of that portion of the total investment.

For example, if you buy a $50,000 duplex and the units are equal in size and value, you can divide the investment down the middle from the tax point of view—$25,000 of the total is investment, and at the same time the other half is a residence. Of the investment you need to deduct one-half of the land value, as there is no tax shelter there. If the lot under the duplex was worth $12,000 and you deducted $6,000 from the investment portion of the purchase, you would have $19,000 which could be depreciated. Depending on the method of depreciation you used, you would get a rebate off your year-end taxes which would shelter that portion of the income the duplex generated.

• **The duplex can be a double condo.** The duplex is in reality two homes nailed together, or, perhaps better stated, a very small apartment house.

• **Two singles each owning half a duplex.** When you can't find a reasonably priced apartment or home, you might find that half a duplex is not only ideal but well within your price range. A half-duplex has all the advantages of the single-family home, giving up only a little privacy. With this in mind, you might want to consider buying a duplex with a partner or co-owner who will take the other unit for his own use.

This can be done in several legal ways, and I'd suggest you confer with a good real estate lawyer to see which is best for you in your state. Examine the options of ownership in the entire property (both units) and separation of the two units so that each of you owns one. It would be possible for you to form a corporation and have a mini co-op, for example, with the articles of the cooperative spelling out the mutually decided rules of operation and the common expenses and liabilities. Whatever method you decide on should come from a frank discussion with your lawyer. Laws governing ownership and interaction with partnerships and corporations are not uniform across the country.

The important thing is to keep this option in mind when you are trying to decide what you want to do. A duplex can be a good source for apartments and may compete favorably with condos and co-ops in your area.

I would also include triplexes in this discussion. Many times this three-unit type of property is found in the same areas as the duplexes. One word of caution with the triplex, however, that you must pay close attention to. Many triplexes are built in duplex zoning. That is to say, there is a zoning violation that one day may be enforced.

These zoning violations may have occurred when the property was built. What frequently happens is that a duplex is constructed with the owner's unit larger than the rental unit. Somewhere down the road an owner may have taken the larger unit and divided it into two units. The "once duplex" now is in violation of the zoning, but unless someone complains it might go unnoticed for years. That is, until you come along, then zap—a fine, and an order to turn it back into a duplex.

Don't ever rely on what a property appears to be. Check the current zoning and find out if the current use complies with the existing zoning. This applies to all real estate, of course, and never should be underestimated. The duration of previous use can be misleading, too, as sometime a zoning changes and the old user was given a "grandfathering" of use. But that use may not carry over to you, the new owner.

6 Advantages to Owning Duplexes

1. Income producing. While you may not get rich off the income from one side of a duplex (or both sides if you live elsewhere), the income will pay all or most of the expenses and debt service of the property and perhaps throw off some spending money to boot. Remember, cash flow is just one of several advantages in owning real estate. Income property that has a zero cash flow can be a good investment depending on the other factors, such as paying off a heavy second mortgage out of the income. The equity buildup in such transactions may offset the lack of cash flow. Never get caught in the trap of judging all income property as good or bad because of the cash flow. Keep in mind that most investments (stocks, gold, jewels, art, antiques, etc.) are not sold or bought because of the income they produce, but rather because of the appreciation that comes to them. These static investments, unlike much real estate, can't even help pay for themselves.

2. Appreciation. Any income property will go up in value if the income can be increased. I'm talking about real income, the bottom line. Contrary to common belief, it isn't necessary to increase rents to increase the bottom line. Another solution is to decrease expenses, and it is here that a keen eye for details comes in. If you are able to do some or all of the costly items that the previous owner had to farm out, such as repairs, lawn maintenance, and painting, then you can save the cash expenditure and put that lost money in your pocket. Of course, this depends on your having the time to do these things. Duplexes are a sound investment in this respect, however, as the amount of repairs is generally less than larger apartment complexes, and if you are living in one side you have control over the majority of problems that come up.

3. Provide shelter plus. The plus, of course, is partially the income. But there is more to it. The idea of picking who lives next to you is nice from several aspects. Security is one, comfort another. Because the duplex has the advantage of being an ideal place for partnership buying, it might be possible for you to do what Brad McKay did.

Brad and his school chum Eric bought a nice duplex about one-quarter mile from the beach in Lauderdale By The Sea. They fixed up one unit and rented it out in the winter season to some of the snowbirds from up north. They got, in three to four months, more rent than they would have if they had rented it on an annual basis. During the winter season Brad and Eric doubled up in the other unit.

As soon as the season was over they would each take a unit for themselves, living a more private life for eight to nine months a year. The income was divided between them, and it paid nearly the entire mortgage payment on the whole duplex. With only a little inconvenience for several months a year, Brad and Eric had worked out what amounted to living nearly free.

4. Good supply-and-demand ratio for investment. The duplex is a "lost" zoning. It is not a single-family property and not exactly an apartment building. It is a two-family unit and is zoned exactly that way in most communities. Of course, often you can build the duplex in a higher-density zoning, and sometimes you will find the duplex is built on a lot that is zoned for four or more units. Hidden value goes to the owner who puts that to work by adding more units to the property. For the most part you will find there is little new duplex zoning being developed by the land planners of America. This means when you find a duplex you have found a scarce commodity which isn't being re-created in vast supply. This works for the investor, as the demand need not be great for the values to go up.

5. Often found in conditions ideal for remodeling. Because the duplex seems to be a fading commodity (caused by the lack of new duplexes being built due to a lack of zoning), it isn't hard to find duplexes in nearly every community which are older and in need of plushing up. If the duplex fits these key factors shown below, then you should seriously consider its potential as your next investment.

- The area is older but on the fringe of a good part of town and is on the verge of rejuvenation.
- You wouldn't mind living in the area yourself.
- Neither side of the duplex has tenants who can't be removed within a few months (ideal if you can get in right away).
- Current rent is below what a tenant would pay if the property was fixed up a little.
- The building is sound and no major repairs are needed.
- You calculate that you can do the majority of the work yourself within one month.
- The price and terms will allow you to service the debt out of rent from one side.

6. Wide market on resale. The duplex is an excellent product to sell and if you have worked on yours and fixed it up you should find no difficulty in selling it later at a profit. Besides singles buying duplexes, almost anyone becomes a market for this kind of property. If the condo market is really hot in your area, the division of the units into condos isn't a bad idea and can produce quick profits.

Investing in any kind of real estate requires you to look at who your ultimate buyers will be. With the duplex you have the edge over many other kinds of real estate.

Okay, six good advantages that make duplexes an interesting way to invest in real estate. My advice to most singles is to look at the duplex as a place to live and generate income at the same time. It is not going to be an income source on which you can retire, but if you are holding down a good job and need to get your act together by converting your rent into equity, then this is a good way to do that by letting the other guy carry part of your load.

3 Major Drawbacks

1. High vacancy factor. It is possible to have a high vacancy factor in renting. Even in a tight rental market you will have turnover of tenants. They move for one reason or another (perhaps they bought this book and have decided to stop being one of the other guys). When they move you can have a vacant apartment for a while. The duration of the while will depend on many factors. What is the condition of the unit? Do you have to paint or do other repairs to the unit before you can rent it out again? Do you have the time now to do even the most minor of repairs? Vacancy factors can hurt, and it is simple mathematics. If you have a hundred units and have ten units vacant each month on the average, you have a 10% vacancy factor. This eats into income for sure, but it isn't that bad overall, and some analysts will figure a 5% to 10% vacancy factor as a normal operation.

If you have two units and you live in one and the other is vacant for one month and one week, you have a 10% vacancy factor right off the bat. If you are left with some damage that takes you a month or two to get fixed before you can rent again and then it takes another month to rent out, you have a 20% vacancy factor.

2. In between. It's an in-between animal—not a house, not an apartment building. The argument goes like this: "If you want a house then buy one; if you want apartments then don't stop with two units." There is no question that this argument is both real and justified. For many of you the amount of cash needed to buy the duplex is sufficient to buy a four- or five-unit apartment complex. Of course, you may not have all the advantages of the duplex with the apartment complex, but then that's a matter of finding what you want. This disadvantage is purely a matter of taste, but taste is another word for what you like, and don't let anyone tell you what you should like.

3. Not maximum producers. Duplexes don't produce the maximum return on capital. From the economic viewpoint, the duplex is not meant to be the maximum income producer. Like its cousin the single-family home (which if lived in may not produce any apparent income), the duplex is designed to provide a home for its owner—only the duplex goes one step further and with the rental income from one side it will help carry itself. Yet on the dollars invested you will find other forms of investments produce higher cash flow.

How You Can Tell If You Have Picked a Good Duplex to Buy

It's time to think dollars and cents from a landlord's point of view. With the single-family home it isn't necessary to pay that much attention to the rental market and what you can do to rent the property you have just bought. With the duplex or any other income property this becomes crucial. Value, both the present value and the future value of any income property, is greatly determined by the amount of income it will produce. That aspect of the duplex is what you must examine prior to its purchase. You will pick your best investments among all duplexes in your area out of those that will do the best in the rental market in producing a return on your investment. That doesn't mean the duplex that can be rented for the most money, but simply the duplex which will give you the most return for your invested money. If you can buy two duplexes each for the same amount of cash down, then the one that generates the maximum cash rent should have the edge. Yet if you can make a buy at half the cash on another duplex and obtain a higher yield, that property could have the edge. The return on your investment is often misunderstood, so this is a good place to examine the mystery of cash flow.

The Cash Flow Analysis

Remember before we start this: Cash flow is only one part of the total picture in real estate. If the cash flow of one property is less than that of another, that may not be an indication that it is the lesser of the two properties. However, if all things are equal except the cash flow, then you can have a clear determination.

Cash flow analysis is important for other reasons. It will show you what you are making on your investment and will help you see where you need to make changes to improve your investment return and thereby increase the value.

A simple cash flow analysis would look like Table 12. The numbers used in the calculation are based on a duplex with both sides rented. Each tenant pays $600 per month in rent. One side is vacant for one month. The mortgage is an $80,000 balance at 10% over 25 years that pays out at $726.67 per month principal and interest.

You can see that of the total income possible which could have been collected ($14,400), only $13,800 was collected because of the one-month vacancy. The operating expenses total $2,940. These are the actual out-of-pocket expenses paid during the year. It is important that you take a look at expense number 8. I put management in with no dollar amount, as the owner of the duplex was managing it himself. In reality, some amount of money should have been put here if for no other reason than to show the owner what he should have been paid for his own time. The invested capital is not his time, and all real estate investors who spend time on their investments should take stock of that time spent so they can establish a proper respect for the expense

TABLE 12.

Total rents possible		$14,400
Less vacancy (real or projected–never 0)		600
Rents collected		$13,800
Operating expenses		
1. Accounting	$175	
2. Advertising	25	
3. Insurance	350	
4. Electricity (outside only)	290	
5. Water	185	
6. Trash collection	160	
7. Sewage collection	185	
8. Management (self-managed?)	0	
9. Real estate tax	820	
10. Repairs and maintenance	350	
11. Supplies	50	
12. Yard expenses (self plus)	200	
13. Other	150	
		2,940
Net operating income		$10,860
Annual debt service		8,720
Cash flow (pre–income tax)		$ 2,140

of that time. Never take time off from your $25-per-hour job to fix something that would cost $10 per hour to have fixed.

Take note that there are two other expenses yet to be considered: depreciation and interest on the mortgage. In the pre-income tax cash flow analysis, neither of these expenses is calculated in the operating expenses, as they are not a function of the actual expenses on the property.

The "interest paid" is a part of the debt service (therefore a function of the money borrowed) and has been deducted from the N.O.I. to arrive at the pre–tax cash flow.

The pre–tax cash flow is simply a number at this point, but in real terms it is the amount of cash that the property throws off over the year.

Continuing with the analysis, let's pick up with the cash flow:

Cash flow	$2,140.00
Equity paid on debt (the amount of principal paid against the mortgage owned)	799.28
Gross cash benefits (you had the equity portion and then put it in the bank by paying down on the mortgage)	$2,939.28
Less depreciation expense (estimated here)	2,872.00
Taxable income	$ 67.28

Let me explain quickly that this is an investment that has sufficient tax shelter to hide nearly all the income from it. The owner would pay tax on only $67.28.

The principal paid on the debt was found by using Table A in the Appendix. As the mortgage was a twenty-five-year mortgage at 10%, go to Table A and find the 24th year in the 10% column. The constant rate there is 11.01% (rounded). Divide this constant percent into the annual debt service ($8,720 ÷ 0.1101 = $79,200.72). The $79,200.72 is the balance at the end of the year. As the beginning was $80,000, simple subtraction will give you the amount of principal paid that year ($80,000 – $79,200.72 = $799.28).

The depreciation would easily be as much shown ($2,872) and could have been substantially more depending on the goals of the owner. Let's continue.

Taxable income	$67.28	
Tax to be paid	33.64[a]	
Pre-tax cash flow		$2,140.00
Less tax paid		33.64
Bottom line after-tax cash flow		$2,106.36

[a] Assume the owner to be in a 50% bracket: $67.28 × 50% = $33.64.

In a review of this investment it is important for you to recognize that if you are in a 50% tax bracket, this bottom line would be the result of your having earned $4,212.71 in regular earnings. For example, if you had invested $42,127.20 in a savings account earning 10% per year, you would have ended up with the same bottom-line after-tax return as above.

On the other hand, this duplex showing not only cash flow but equity buildup, appreciation, tax shelter, and the inflation hedge could have been acquired with less than the $42,127.20 cash out of the savings account.

Look over this analysis of the cash flow. You will see that much more than cash flow is analyzed, and the format will be used later on with the larger, more complicated income properties.

A Good Investment Takes Effort

THE EFFORT need not be solely yours. You can't be expected to know everything about the real estate market in the areas where you want to buy. Professional realtors will come in handy here, so use their services. They will be invaluable to you in helping you find the real good buys in the neighborhood.

Be as candid with the realtor as you can. Don't lead the real estate agent down the wrong path by giving him the wrong goals to work for. If you have only $5,000 cash to work with (along with your tons of determination), then be sure to tell him this. Nothing is more frustrating to real estate agents than working to find $200,000 properties for a client who should be looking at $50,000 properties.

You must put some brainpower to work if you plan to make it in the buy-and-fix-it-up end of real estate. You are the single most important factor in this game. Know your limitations—physical, geographical, economical—and work within them.

The real key in investing is knowing as much as you can about your own goals, the alternatives, the options, and your limitations. From this you will be able to act on those good buys when they come around.

Making the Investment Better

This is where the effort really occurs most of the time. I say "most of the time" because there will be times when you seem to fall into a real winner without really trying. When that happens, don't let it go to your head; just as many people fall into a hole as easily.

Duplexes can be treated much like homes in the quick-increase-in-value area. You will be able to increase values simply by saying so in almost any kind of real estate. This doesn't mean that someone will pay you that increased price, but if you are being a prudent buyer following the suggestions in this book you will be ahead of the other guy.

Of course, when it comes to improving the entrance and the front door, you have double the effort, so keep that in mind. And something else—because this is a rental-income property, you can instantly increase the value by improving the bottom line.

4 Ways to Enhance the Bottom Line in Income Properties

1. Increase the rent. Sounds easy, doesn't it? Just think—if you can increase the rent on each side of a duplex by just $50 per month, you will have an additional $1,200 per year in income. With nothing else changed you will have increased the value by a multiple of anywhere from 7 to 10 times that amount. This possible $12,000 additional value is real and can come back to you in a quick sale by such a small thing as raising rent.

In fact, many of the income properties you look at will be viewed with the idea of doing just this simple thing. Here's a quick test for you:

Which duplex would you buy: a) The one with rent higher than the market (and short or no leases)? b) The one with rent below the market (and short or no leases)?

If you chose b), you're correct. I always recommend that a young person buy income property that has room for improvement. If you fix it up to a point where it is doing the maximum, then you can sell it to a more passive investor who wants the income without the problems of getting the property into prime condition.

Watch out for properties under rent scale with long-term tenants. Any income property with tenants who are paying rent too low for the current market must be discounted to account for that, unless the real potential is worth waiting for. In the larger commercial properties there can be great differences between the rent being paid and the rent which could be collected. Often the sellers can't hold out over those last three or so years until the leases expire and they can roll over the property into higher-paying tenants. In duplexes this will occur, but on a far more diminutive scale.

Read all the leases and watch out for the standard but different contract. Be careful of the standard-looking lease that isn't standard. If the owner has two (or more) leases that look identical and have blanks filled in, don't just read the blanks to see if there is any difference between the leases. Many lawyers use a technique of "similar but different" lease forms in negotiations with landlords. While it is not a common practice, it is an interesting technique and produces effective results in some negotiations. Here's how it works:

The owner of the building (duplex or whatever) writes the lease for the prospective tenant. The lease might be a standard-looking form or a standard lease drawn by the owner's lawyer. Usually blanks are filled in to make this lease different from the other leases the property owner has in the building or has used over the years.

The tenant might then have the lease completely redrawn, making small but important changes in the terms of the lease, sometimes changing only a few words. The standard lease used by the owner might have said, "This lease will expire on July 1, 1986, and will not be renewable." The redrawn lease might say, "This lease shall not expire on July 1, 1986, and will be renewable on the same terms."

The property owner going over the lease, not realizing it was redrawn, might sign a lease contrary to his intent. You, in buying a property, might overlook these changes in the same manner. Read everything twice.

Increasing rent is the best way, of course, to increase the value because it gives you additional yield if you are able to decrease expenses.

2. Decrease operating expenses. While this method can be highly effective in some situations, it is usually the least successful way to increase the bottom line. Operating expenses, unfortunately, have a way of continuing to go up no matter what you do. However, sometimes you find a property that has grossly overstated expenses and you can do something about reducing them. If this reduction occurs, then even with an increase in the income you will have increased the bottom line, and with that, an increase in the value of the property.

The larger the property, the more room there is to work. This is so because there is more area to cut expenses. In a duplex and other small properties with only a few units to share the load of the operating expenses, there is a limit to the amount of reduction you can expect to make. However, every dollar will increase value by $7 to $10, so each cent does count.

Be careful of the trade-off between your time and someone else's. I've said a lot about your doing much of the work. This is fine and can pay off for you in cash in your pocket instead of some highly paid workman's. However, there is an economic breaking point where your own limitations can work against you. I'm talking about time limitations as well as ability. If there is a job that needs to be done and having it done right away is more important than the extra dollars you would pay an expert to handle it, then you should never hesitate to make the decision to have someone else do the work.

I've seen many property owners try to take on a repair job on their own property and end up having to call in a professional to put something back together at much more expense than would have occurred if the pro had been given the green light at the outset.

At the same time, I've seen the weekender (the guy who has

a few hours each weekend to work on his income property) leave work early, taking time off from a good-paying job, to attend to some nitpicking thing like a toilet that's not working. That's a matter of priorities in your own head, of course, but keep in mind the whole picture. It is fine to do as much of the work as you can within the proper economic strata. Don't take off from a $25-per-hour job to handle something you can get done by paying someone else $10 per hour. Even that $15 to your advantage makes sense.

3. Restructure the debt service. This is the third element that can be tackled in the quest to increase the bottom line and the value. The amount of debt service paid on the property is, of course, a full deduction from the net operating income. If you can effect a more satisfactory constant rate payment on the balance owed, you will reduce the actual payment and increase the cash flow.

This is not as difficult as it might appear at first. If you are looking at a duplex you have selected out of several for your investment portfolio and you are reasonably sure of the lowest price you can get the property for, then you need to work on the terms to bring the overall constant payment down (not necessarily the amount of the mortgage).

Let's say, for example, that the duplex with a current N.O.I. of $8,950 is available for sale at $80,000. There is an existing first mortgage of $30,000 which has twenty-two years to go at 9%. This is possible because it would be an older mortgage, perhaps one put on in the mid-'70s. The total of twelve monthly payments on this mortgage would be $3,135. (Look in Table A at 9% for twenty-two years and see the constant rate of 10.45% [rounded]. This multiplied by the amount owed gives you the annual payment: $30,000 × 0.1045 = $3,135.) The seller has indicated he would accept $16,000 cash down and would hold some kind of "short" financing. It is not uncommon for a seller to approach a sale in this manner. The idea of a short mortgage given back to the seller isn't bad, but it would probably kill the cash flow in this property. If the deal were structured with an eight-year short mortgage at 11%, here is what the deal would look like:

Price	$80,000	
Cash down	16,000	
Balance	$64,000	
Existing first mortgage		$30,000
Second mortgage held by seller (8 years at 11% is an annual payment of $5,620)		34,000
Total to be serviced		$64,000

Now let's look at the cash flow analysis on this deal so far:

Net operating income (operating expenses already deducted)		$8,950
Less debt service		
First-mortgage payment	$3,135[a]	
Second-mortgage payment	6,409[b]	
		9,544
Pre-tax cash flow		($ 594)

[a] Principal of $480.22 plus interest of $2,654.78.
[b] Principal of $2,812.65 plus interest of $3,596.35.

The parentheses around the pre-tax cash flow indicate a negative. In this transaction you could expect a minus cash flow to occur. This would continue until you were able to make some other change in the economic nature of this property by increasing income or decreasing other operating expenses to offset the loss.

What you would want to do is structure this transaction so you could develop some positive leverage in the financing. Leverage is the effect you can get out of financing. In the above transaction the effect of the financing is to the negative side. You would get a better return on your capital (if you had enough) to pay all cash. In that event you would have over an 11% cash flow yield (11% of $80,000 is $8,800, and that is less than the N.O.I.). Instead, under the present investment plan you have a negative yield on the $16,000 invested. This is caused by the high constant on the combined effect of the two mortgages.

There are several creative ways to reduce the overall debt service payment in this transaction; I'll show you two. As you read this book you will gain insight into other creative methods that could have been used. Each creative financing method you use will have a different effect on the total picture. The more options you have available to you, the better your edge against risk.

The Interest-Only Mortgage

Suppose you had offered the seller the same price, the same down payment as in the earlier example, but instead of the mortgage being an eight-year pay-out (amortized at 11%), you offered this:

The second mortgage would be interest-only for the seven years at 11% with a principal payment at the end of the seven years (or before) in the amount of the outstanding principal. This would mean you didn't have to pay principal at all during the seven years, but you could if you wanted to at any time during the seven years.

Here's how the cash flow would look now:

Net operating income		$8,950
Less debt service		
Payment on first mortgage	$3,135[a]	
Payment on second mortgage	3,740[b]	6,875
Cash flow		$2,075

[a] Principal of $480 plus interest of $2,654.78.
[b] Interest-only at 11%: principal of $0 plus interest of $3,740.

In this situation the cash flow has jumped from a negative $594 to a positive $2,075. On the invested $16,000 the cash flow yield is now about 13%. Not bad for a simple creative idea.

Of course, there will be one heck of a bite at the end of the seventh year if the principal is not paid down in the meantime. One option for the buyer is to keep the interest-only payment right up until the fifth or sixth year and then refinance the two mortgages into one new first mortgage. This is a viable option but the investor runs the risk of a very tight money market at that time. The positive side of that argument is the time between now and then would give the investor a chance to improve the income picture of the property. With the increased value due to increased income, the property would support even more financing than would be needed to retire the existing two mortgages. The extra cash becomes a form of yield that is tax-free.

Another option would be to pay down the balance owed little by little each year, from the increased rents, until the seventh year, to reduce the bite by whatever amount you can. Hopefully, through increased income you could maintain a healthy yield as well as reduce the future balloon payment. (Balloon mortgages are explained in Chapter 20.)

The Wraparound Mortgage

In this technique you would offer the seller one mortgage with one payment instead of assuming the existing first and taking on a second. This technique, called the wraparound mortgage, is a very useful tool and is described in great detail later in Chapter 20. Its function as used here is to reduce the overall constant payment of two or more mortgages without reducing the principal amount owed.

For example, you have a total of $64,000 in debt to be handled in this transaction. If you were to look at the total $64,000 as one mortgage—say, at 10% interest—and establish a normal amortization on this mortgage amount for thirty years, you would have a payout of $6,739 per year on that $64,000. This would make your cash flow picture look like the following:

Net operating income	$8,950
Less debt service	6,739[a]
Cash flow	$2,211

[a] Principal of $364.50 plus interest of $6,374.50.

The seller would continue to make the payments on the first mortgage out of the mortgage payment you made on the wraparound, and he would then pocket the balance. At the end of the twenty-second year he would keep the full payment you make to him for the remaining eight years.

Often the seller can be enticed into taking a wraparound because of the many advantages it will have to him when compared to a normal second mortgage. Frequently, however, the seller will insist on a balloon at the end of the existing financing (in this example, at the end of twenty-two years). That would present no real problem, as it is unlikely you will own the property at that time, and even if you did, refinancing would present no difficulty.

4. Increase the tax shelter to suit your situation. There is a fourth way to increase the bottom line and that is through the tax shelter aspects. Each property you examine will have a depreciation schedule that can be used to create the shelter you may need. You can speed up and slow down (within some restrictions) the rate at which you use up this shelter. Some properties will be more oriented to tax shelter in the early years than others. This advance depreciation, which might be obtained, can aid you in paying for improvements needed in the early years by allowing Uncle Sam to become a partner in the expenses.

You need to remember that the depreciation (tax shelter) a seller has taken for the past year is not the amount you will have to take. Indeed, he is depreciating from a lower basis than you will use.

Your accountant will help you set up the most favorable depreciation schedule for your set of pre-tax circumstances. It is entirely possible that because of the amounts of depreciation available from one property or another, you can obtain more beneficial shelter from one property than the other. This factor becomes another criterion in helping you decide which property to buy.

The first three methods of increasing the bottom line were applied in the pre–cash flow area. This aspect, the tax shelter method, is going to be between you and your accountant. In the smaller properties it may not be too crucial, but let's see what might have happened.

In this duplex assume that both sides are rented furnished. As you are buying furniture and fixtures along with the building, you will find the furniture and fixtures can be depreciated over a much shorter life than the building. If there is $6,000 in estimated value of furniture and it is already several years old, it may be possible to have $1,000 or more depreciation each year for six years on that portion of the deal alone. I've provided a brief cash flow and tax analysis of the three formats of buying this property (Table 13).

In each case the value of the duplex is $80,000, with land value estimated at $20,000, furniture and fixtures at $6,000, and building at $54,000. Assume six years depreciation on the furniture and fixtures and thirty years on the building. Also, let's put you in a 50% tax bracket. Total depreciation to be used in each example will be $2,800 per year (good for the first six years).

TABLE 13.

	First Deal	Interest-Only Mortgage	Wraparound Mortgage
N.O.I	$8,950.00	$8,950.00	$8,950.00
Less debt service	−9,544.00	−6,875.00	−6,739.00
Cash flow	($ 594.00)	$2,075.00	$2,211.00
Plus principal paid	3,292.87	480.00 (1st only)	364.50
Gross cash benefits	$2,698.87	$2,555.00	$2,575.50
Less depreciation	−2,800.00	−2,800.00	−2,800.00
Taxable income	($ 101.13)	($ 245.00)	($ 224.50)
Tax or credits	+$ 50.56	+$ 122.50	+$ 112.25
Cash flow	(594.00)	$2,075.00	$2,211.00
Tax or credits	+ 50.56	+ 122.50	+ 112.25
Bottom line: after-tax	$(543.44)	$2,197.50	$2,323.25
Cash in your pocket	−3%	+13.7%	+14.5%

In a review of the cash flow analysis you will note the yield after tax went from a negative 3% all the way to a positive 14.5% on the invested $16,000.

In each example the tax shelter remained the same for this deal. It would have been possible for the amounts of the depreciation to be increased by using an accelerated form of depreciation, thereby changing the bottom line in each. Tax shelter, however, will diminish quickly if you use accelerated methods. In the method used, unless there would be additional capital expenditures to increase the depreciable assets, within six years the depreciation would drop from $2,800 per year to $1,800 per year.

MAKE IT WORK BY KNOWING THE OPTIONS

A GENERAL will have a better chance of winning a battle if he knows just what he can expect from the units in his command. It is even more helpful if he has a good idea of what the enemy is going to do. It is the same in investing in real estate. You are the general in command of your own destiny. The men under your command are your assets and the options that you have available to you (both economic and personal). You can learn much about the way the adversary will go from the history of the area and the economic trends that affect the kind of real estate you want to buy. Do your homework and you will make it big.

12

Small Apartment Buildings

SOMETIME way down the road investors will look back on the history of real estate investing and say, "Why, my god, the whole shift to small apartment buildings started right back in 1981."

This shift they will be talking about wasn't a sudden movement. The trend to investing in small apartment buildings is something that began prior to 1981, and unlike gold, which jumped from $500 per ounce to over $600 per ounce in January 1980, small apartments slowly eased into the limelight.

The best advice I could give to singles would be to look to the small apartment building as the prime springboard for advancement into the world of the wealthy. It will be through the collection of as many other guys as you can amass that your bottom line will steadily grow and your wealth will be assured. To assemble a collection of other guys you need to have things for them to rent. To make the most money in "things people rent," the first step is to have what people *must* rent. That, for a great number of people, is their apartment. Since many people must rent, why not let it be from you?

It's as simple as this: If you have what people need and want and must have, then they will rent it from you if they can't buy it. And let's face it—many people don't know (because they haven't read this book) that it is easy to own, so they rent.

First let's see what I mean by a small apartment building. To me, anything that is larger than a duplex and as large as you can handle without the need for a management team is a small apartment building. It should be obvious that in similar rent brackets, the smaller the apartment building the smaller the purchase price. So the idea is to start with small complexes and work up to larger apartment buildings.

The rental market is a direct recipient of the great rise in prices in the single-home market. Each year since the middle sixties the price of homes climbed higher and higher at a steady but reasonable rate. Then the seventies hit and the price for homes took off like a rocket. By the end of the seventies, with a new decade ahead, the home buyer was looking at the highest borrowing rates the United States has seen since the Civil War reconstruction years, and home costs were quickly closing out millions of potential buyers.

Interest rates of 13% to 18% have broken through the usury barriers in many states. A loan at the low end of these high rates on a twenty-seven-year term made a mortgage of $60,000 cost $232,146 over the twenty-seven years. For this investor to stay even with his investment, assuming there was no other cost to that property (maintenance, taxes, etc.), he would have to sell at about one quarter of a million dollars above his down payment just to break even (if he paid off the mortgage with his own money).

The results of this bad news is that some people, not aware of other opportunities or options, choose to rent. The number of these people is steadily increasing, and that is good news to the owners of apartment buildings.

In some cultures young single people work and save and when they have enough money to buy (without a mortgage) they buy. This can save a lot of money. In fact, if you were to put into a good-yield certificate of deposit the amount of money each year it would take to pay on the $60,000 mortgage I mentioned, it would take about six years for it to accumulate to $60,000.

Now, true to the form of a real estate investor, I wouldn't think of trying to convert all tenants into becoming owners. Where would I find people to fill my apartments? On the other hand, it is okay for you to know this secret: Buy something that has that big $60,000 high-paying mortgage—only don't make any of the mortgage payments. It doesn't matter how much you owe as long as you don't make the payment. Let the other guys make the mortgage payments for you.

8 Advantages of Owning a Small Apartment Building

1. An increased collection of the other guys. With the duplex you have only two units to collect the other guys with, and if you are living in one, that cuts down your other-guy traps to one. All you have to do to double that is buy a triplex. Get a fourplex and you have tripled your catching power, and you still have a place to live.

2. With more than one unit to rent out you can create a desirable environment. I have a small apartment building that has not had an unpaid vacancy in over five years. This four-unit building, which I built and lived in for several years, seems to stay filled and with a waiting list. The reason isn't that I'm a great property manager (I'm not), but that I stick to one market for my tenants: singles. I don't mean that I have turned this four-unit building into one of those hot sex dens of a singles' apartment complex (that's hard to do with only four units). And besides, I have had tenants ranging from their seventies to early twenties at the same time.

What happens is this: If you pick the right market to rent to, the tenants will produce more tenants when they leave.

Your environment doesn't have to be singles. If your small apartment building is near a school, then you might specialize in renting to schoolteachers. Stick to your market and once you are rented up you will more than likely stay that way. This ability to create a desirable environment is unique to the small apartment building. Once you get up into the larger complexes, the need to fill up the buildings tends to diminish the desirable environment and increases the need for "frills" to cater to the diverse needs of the tenants.

3. You have better control over the vacancy factor. This is partially because of your ability to create the desirable environment you want, and also because you are dealing with a size of building that will allow you the time to give each apartment and each tenant some personal attention. This keeps tenants in your building longer and makes them want to help you get a replacement when they leave.

4. Expenses reach an ideal level with the small apartment. I'm anticipating that you are planning on doing many of the "little" things around the building yourself. If this is the case, you will find that a duplex is only a little less work than a four-unit. It is possible to take care of twenty-five units or more if you can set aside an hour or so each day and don't mind giving up a couple of weekends each month to handle some of the larger duties. An ideal size for you will depend on you, of course, and your "free" time. You might do very nicely with five or eight units and bomb out on twelve.

Your move into small apartments will depend on your economic ability to some degree as well as your own ability to save on outside expenses.

The level of expenses, when seen in a "time" aspect, does not increase proportionate to the number of units you have to rent. Instead, the increase is gradual, lagging behind the number of units.

When you reach the saturation point for your available time, you have attained the maximum output you can handle. How that will relate to the number of units isn't possible for me to say, but the first-time buyer not prepared to give up his job would be advised to start with a building of under ten units.

5. Good loans are available for the purchase of small apartments. This is true for the smaller of the small apartments and this is important for the single trying to work up the ladder. If you can get into your first small apartment building easily, then you can buy another, and soon you have a large complex.

Government-insured loans, such as the FHA program, can be gotten on four-unit buildings, which will enable buyers to get in with low down payments. The conventional loan market favors the small apartment house buyer, especially when the buyer is going to live in one of the units. Lenders know the value of the on-the-site manager also being the owner. The lender knows that the job will be filled with an interested person who won't mind the modest salary.

Income properties are viewed by the lenders on the basis of how well they can produce cash to pay the loan. If the income and expense projections are positive in favor of the investor, then the lender is going to come out okay too.

6. They can be good condo conversions. Like the duplex, anything that can be divided into apartments and sold can be a condominium. If you buy the apartment as a rental you can make the conversion yourself later on down the road and make the best of all worlds work for you. Keep in mind, however. that there are some necessary things for you to do when you convert your own apartment into a condo. The things I'm referring to are legal and involve the laws of your state as well as the Internal Revenue Code. When you get to the stage where you want to consider an actual condo conversion, you will need to consult a good real estate lawyer to go over the requirements so you don't get hit with excessive earned-income tax. Condo conversions can be taxed as a capital gain, at a lower rate, if you are careful and follow your lawyer's advice.

The small apartment building with a pleasant environment can generally be easily converted to condos. The smallness is no handicap and can be a great advantage in the marketing. Many people would rather live in an apartment in a nice, less institutional atmosphere than in a sprawling complex of thousands of people (and thousands of people's problems).

7. They don't tie you to them with a chain. This might be the very best advantage to owning a small apartment building in comparison to a large apartment building. The smallness of the units enables you to keep the personal touch and allows you to get away from time to time without things falling apart. This is because you will have more control over what is going on, of course, but it is more than that. The larger complexes need someone around all the time. The resident manager might be you, and that can mean trouble in the larger units, where you can't be as selective in your tenants, or you lose control for other reasons.

You don't want to be tied down to any real estate investment all the time—it isn't healthy for you or, in the long run, for your pocketbook.

8. **Rents are on the way up.** This is true for all apartments as a general rule, but I'd expect that the smaller units that pay careful attention to the creation of an environment to attract good tenants will fare better in the rental market.

This means you can expect to increase your rental income substantially over the next few years, and if you hold down expenses it will mean substantial value jumps. If you can increase your rents by $50 per month above expense increases per unit, that will mean close to a $6,000 increase for each unit. This dramatic event is that multiplier effect showing its face again, whereby $600 in annual rental increase ($50 × 12 months = $600) will raise the value of the property from 7 to 10 times the amount of the rental increase.

There you have it—the eight best arguments I can think of for why the small apartment building is a good investment for the single investor. It doesn't make any difference what age you are, either, as long as you can devote time and ability to looking after the property. Senior singles, by the way, would find this form of investment ideal. Again we would see the advantage of creating your own environment that would suit *your* life-style and accumulate the kinds of people that *you* want to be around.

Now the bad news.

5 Headaches in Owning Small Apartment Buildings

1. **Inexperience in dealing as a landlord.** Handling people in critical situations is an art that not everyone has. Indeed, you might have known a landlord who was such a bastard that neither you nor anyone else in the building could get along with him.

Unfortunately, there aren't too many courses in schools today that teach how to be a good landlord. But everyone has to start somewhere. You may find that getting up in the middle of the night to fix a leak in someone's sink isn't your cup of tea. You may not have to do this, but handling the situation is what you do have to do.

2. The personal touch has its drawbacks, too. Everyone can become close friends and like one big family. Only you are the owner still, and they still pay you rent. Then one of them doesn't pay you rent . . .

You have a confrontation that has been generated by one of the advantages of small apartments. You have to be firm with someone who has been with the building for a long time. You are running a business, and that means keeping the rents in par with the market. That means you will want to raise your rents from time to time.

"Oh, Mr. Cummings, I've been here for so long I feel just like one of the family. I just love everyone here. I couldn't bear having to move out, but if you increase my rent $50 I just won't be able to stay. Can't you please let me stay on at the old rent?" If she was already $70 under the current market, what would you say?

3. You may not be able to run completely free. While you're not chained down to the small units, you aren't a free-and-easy bird either. This is because you may not have enough income or units to warrant having a manager other than yourself.

For many singles this isn't that much of a drawback, but if you are apt to be transferred or travel a lot, that can be a handicap to your owning property that requires a close look on it to keep it in line (both income- and expense-wise). There are advantages for you in other kinds of real estate if this drawback is more than you can take.

4. Larger investments are now going to take more cash. This is a relative point, of course, but in most cases the more units you want to buy, the greater the cash down.

Jeff was able to convince the owner of a six-unit complex to sell for only 5% down. He then bought (riding on a crest of good luck) a motel for nothing down. His luck ran out and he found himself overextended and out of cash. He lost the motel and had to sell the six units.

I want to impress upon you that often it is better to own just six units and build up your solid equity than to dash out and stretch yourself to the limit. If you can't afford fifteen units, then drop down until you find a property that will fit your abilities.

5. There may not be a good supply of the small apartments in your area. Remember what happens with the supply-and-demand rule when the supply dries up. The supply isn't how many small apartments there are in your area, but how many are for sale. If there are just a few, then the prices might be what we call future prices.

The future price is generally a price the owner will put on a property, saying, "I know it isn't worth this now, but in a year or two it will be . . . so you have to pay that now if you want the unit."

The fact the owner is right about the increase in value doesn't make the buy a good one. What you will have to examine is whether you want to gamble on being able to sell the tenth-year future price five years after you bought the property.

How to Find a Good Apartment Buy

Most prime investments are found in your back yard. That goes for almost anywhere in the world where there is a stable government and a wide distribution of the country's wealth. "The grass is greener on the other side of the fence" is more rationalization than fact.

Of course, that doesn't mean there aren't some areas of the world that are super hot in investment capacity. But are you ready to rush down to Rio or São Paulo just because they are super hot—or to Fort Lauderdale because other investors have made a bundle here in Florida?

For every rags-to-riches story, someone will come up with, "Why, I could have bought that property ten years ago at one-fifth the price."

What happens is that we tend to see the puppy grow faster when we see it only once a month than when we watch it ten times a day. Canadians who have been coming down to Florida each winter are more amazed about the growth of South Florida than many residents who have lived here for fifty years. The old-timers often don't take advantage of their own back yard because of two elements :

1. They can't see the growth because so many people have gotten in the way.

2. They remember the price of the land when it was peanuts, and now that it is gold they just can't see how anyone would be so crazy as to buy it.

You need to take off your blindfold and look close to home for your investment. The chances are your gold mine is right in your own back yard.

What Makes a Good Buy a Good Buy?

Remember the six magic factors of investing in real estate: equity buildup, appreciation, tax shelter, cash flow, inflation fighter, and emotion. You don't have to have six ideal situations to have a good investment. In fact, as you compare different properties you will more than likely find a different balance of these factors in separate investments.

There is generally a trade-off between these factors, so you might have excellent cash flow but poor equity buildup or appreciation. Another property might have high tax shelter but no cash flow and zero equity buildup. Each of these properties might be an excellent investment for the buyer who needs what the property has to offer.

It is the total picture that you need to look at. Your own situation must be seen in the light of the property.

Caution on Overpaying!

This is probably the one element in the deal that might make a property a bad buy. You see, every property will have a buyer at a price or at terms that make the total picture look good for that investor.

To aid you in the quest for an income property, I have provided two guides. The first is for the investor looking for a good start in the real estate market, someone who can spend some time to improve a property in need of tender loving care. The second guide is for the investor who is more set in his life and is ready to settle down and reap the benefits of past years of life as a bachelor or as a newly single with cash in the bank.

FOR THE NEW INVESTOR

• **Know the neighborhood.** Remember, location is the most important single factor to success in real estate. If you aren't sure the neighborhood is good, then look elsewhere. Be cautious of areas where the majority of tenants work in one industrial plant or commercial business that has a shaky future.

• **Know the rental market.** You need to check around and see what is renting and on what terms. Compare the conditions of the competition to see what is offered for how much.

• **Watch the trends.** Is there a potential upswing? What is going on in the feeder market: home construction and industry in the area? As homes go up in price, apartment rents do the same.

• **Look for the maximum number of units you feel you can handle.** Remember all the reasons for this. Your comfort-level is the key.

• **Plan to move into the units yourself.** You can't fix up a property quickly if you have to travel across town just to do an afternoon of work. You need as much control over the units as possible.

• **Check the building out from top to bottom.** You need good sound construction that doesn't need a major construction job just to fix the problems.

• **Watch the leases.** You don't want to get trapped with tenants who are paying next to nothing and will continue to do so for the next twenty years.

• **Look at the total picture.** You will get great advice from your bartender, your hairdresser, and your best friend. "If I were you . . ." they will tell you. Remember that they will advise you from the bottom of their hearts, and their situation may not be yours.

For the Senior Single

• **The numbers.** What is happening with the building? Has the maintenance been kept up? Are the rents at or neat the market value for this kind of property? Is there a positive cash flow? Will the property give you a good and sufficient (for you) bottom line on your investment? If the answers are yes or can be made to be yes with a little work and effort, then move on to the next item.

• **Will the property take care of itself?** Or is there sufficient income to carry professional management and have a yes to the questions asked above?

You want to make a passive investment and you should not have to work to have that return. Keep in mind that to get this cash flow and good bottom line you may not see as much appreciation as you would in other investments. This is your trade-off.

• **Can you handle the deal?** Have you looked at the down side? Will your investment be sufficient to carry both you and the property if things should shift downward? You don't want to buy on the narrow edge between break-even and doom, because doom will get you. Be more conservative and follow the advice of your accountant and lawyer when it comes to how the property fits your total picture. But *you* make the important decisions about buying. Don't let your advisers (any of them) do that for you if you can help it.

• **Are you satisfied that you have examined the other options open to you?** Simply put, have you looked around enough to be sure you won't kick yourself later for being hasty? I'm not advocating overanalysis, only prudence. You are now willing and able to buy the creampuff because that is what suits your style, and when it comes to creampuffs you can afford to be picky.

• **Do you have other baskets?** Other places to put some of your eggs, that sort of basket. When it comes to real estate and the comfort years, it is a good idea to have some diversity of holdings. When you are starting out that diversity might have to wait, but in the later years that diversity is not only prudent but smart.

Those five items are comprehensive and probably seem rather simple and somewhat obvious. Unfortunately, one or more of the five items are often not taken into account, and the results can be even more unfortunate. But you are now armed and your future of buying apartment buildings can be that much more secure.

Buying real estate is half of the profit game, however, and selling is only sometimes the other half. There is a beautiful way to build wealth in real estate that works with the law rather than against it.

DON'T SELL—EXCHANGE!

IF you have something that has outgrown its usefulness or benefit to you, then the first idea most people have is to sell what they have. If you have been playing the real estate game correctly, selling will more than likely work against you. Don't sell—exchange for something bigger, better, or more productive for you. Later on I'll get into exchanges in more detail. But it is important here that you see another of the secrets of building wealth in real estate.

The 1031 Wealth Machine

Section 1031 is what it is all about. This is the section of the Internal Revenue Code that governs what are often known as tax-free exchanges. The exchanges aren't necessarily always without tax, and from a technical point of view they aren't tax-free anyway. But from the practical viewpoint they can be.

What the code says is: "No gain or loss shall be recognized if real estate held for productive use in trade or business or *for investment* is exchanged solely for property of a like kind to be held either for productive use in trade or business or *for investment*." What this means is that it will be possible for you to own an investment that has one hell of an appreciated value, but instead of selling and having to pay tax, you exchange.

Let's set the stage: You bought a small apartment building of ten units for $150,000 and worked like a demon for a few years with a paintbrush and a green thumb and good decorating ideas to create a beautiful environment with high-paying tenants. In short, a mini gold mine. Its present value due to your hard work and the trends of the times is $300,000.

As you bought the property with $30,000 down and have put $10,000 of your own cash into the property, owing $120,000, you stand to make a profit of $140,000 over and above your $40,000 cash invested.

If you sold for cash and reinvested that cash, here's what the deal would look like:

Price of property sold		$300,000
Original cost	$150,000	
Additional cash invested in capital improvements	10,000	
		160,000
Profit		$140,000[a]
Exclusion for capital gain	−$84,000[b]	
Gain to be added to taxable income	$56,000	

[a] Without allowing for depreciation, which would reduce the adjusted cost and increase the profit. Assume all profit is capital gain.
[b] 60% of profit.

If you had $56,000 added to your taxable income in any given year, it would most likely throw you into one of the highest income brackets. In this example, assume it does just that to the rate of 63% of the full amount: Tax liability on the gain is $35,000. You would pay $35,000 tax. Now keep in mind that we haven't calculated any depreciation on this property, which would have increased profit and also tax at this level.

How about cash available for reinvestment?

Price on sale	$300,000
Less mortgages	120,000
Gross proceeds from sale	$180,000
Less tax liability	35,000
Total cash available for reinvestment	$145,000

This cash available for reinvestment is about 20% less than you would have had to reinvest if you had exchanged your equity into another property, as the tax of $35,000 would not have been applied at this time.

The like-for-like requirement isn't the problem that many people think it is. Although the IRC 1031 refers to a like-property exchange, this doesn't mean identical property, so while you can make an exchange of a farm for a farm, an apartment building for an apartment building, or vacant land for vacant land, it doesn't have to be that way. For the most part, as long as the intent of ownership meets the requirement of investment or productive use in trade or business, you can exchange for another property to be held in investment or productive use in trade or business.

To get the benefits of the exchange, you cannot exchange a property not held for investment or productive use in trade or business. This other kind of property would include residential property (your residence) or property which you own for the primary purpose of sale. This inventory of property for sale occurs if you are a dealer or developer in the business of moving property as a commodity or product. Developers and dealers can, however, establish property which they own for investment (hold for appreciation and later sale rather than immediate sale) and get the same benefits of the 1031 exchanges as everyone else.

There are many things the exchange can do for you as another option available to your program of building your wealth. It will become one more marketing technique for you to use in the disposition of property that has no problem of excessive tax, and can be used as an adjunct to a for-sale plan.

It is not unusual for a transaction involving an exchange of property to go through three or more steps before you end up with a property acceptable to you. The three-way and four-way legs of these transactions are complicated if you are not accustomed to the workings of exchanges, and nearly always are the work of the exchange broker (a realtor who does a lot of exchanges).

Assume for a moment that you have that $300,000 apartment building and you want to exchange it for a resort hotel in Fort Lauderdale. Your equity in the property is $180,000 (plus commissions, as the $300,000 is a net-to-you amount). Using a rule of thumb of your equity being a 20% down payment, you could end up with a maximum property value of $900,000 (20% of that is your $180,000 equity). However, finding a $900,000 hotel whose owner would take your apartment building will take much too much time, and in the meanwhile cause you to miss out on some properties ideal for your needs.

Thus the extra legs come in. You want a hotel. I find a hotel you want. The owner of the hotel will not take your apartment building. If he will only take cash down, then I must find a buyer for your apartment to make the deal work. In that event, the buyer of the apartments comes in and makes it work by taking the apartments, paying cash (which goes to the hotel owner), and you end up with the hotel, the buyer gets the apartments, and the owner of the hotel gets his cash.

On the other hand, the owner of the hotel might want to exchange his equity for a farm in Kentucky. Now I've got to find that. When I do, I go through the same steps, still perhaps needing a buyer for the apartments to provide cash—but perhaps finding a farmer willing to take the apartments.

These legs take time, but not as much as you might think. There is a comprehensive system of brokers in the United States who deal in exchanges, and they have instant access to many properties ready, willing, and able to fit right into the exchange. Often the broker himself becomes one of the legs.

Exchange Your Way Out of the Dog

"I'll give you two of my cats for three of your dogs." This is sometimes how it goes. There are two things at play here:

1. Some people own something that is good, but not for them.

2. Any exchange that improves your position is an effective exchange.

Following this philosophy, making deals isn't so tough. When you find yourself owning something that just isn't working out for you for one reason or another, don't get discouraged about the property. Your worst dog will seem like a jewel to someone else. For that person to unload one of his dogs on you may be just fine. Remember, beauty isn't always in the eye of the beholder.

13

Larger Apartment Complexes (Where the Big, Smart Money Is)

THE LARGER APARTMENT COMPLEX, one that has from fifty units up to hundreds or even thousands of units, is not a place for the beginner in the real estate investing game.

4 Factors That Attract Big Money to Large Apartment Complexes

1. Tax shelter. This has got to be the number one reason institutional investors seek out apartment buildings for their investment portfolios. This is because the large apartment complex offers a greater and more effective tax shelter than most other forms of real estate. If the property falls into categories such as government-approved, low-cost housing, subsidy housing, or certain renewal programs as allowed by the government, then above-normal tax credits can be obtained.

The public limited-partnership deals love apartment complexes because the tax credits and tax shelter mean the money needed to put down on and fix up the complex can be obtained by offering limited partners a tax shelter deal.

These tax shelter deals are very common and some are good for some investors. The trick to investing in tax shelters is the good old Catch-22! To make a lot of money from tax shelters you need to make a lot of money from somewhere else so that you are in a high tax bracket. Because you are in a high tax bracket, Uncle Sam will be paying a greater portion of your investment (perhaps all) and you will make more money. This gets back to the fact that sometimes the rich do get richer because they are rich to start with. Keep this trick in mind so when you get really rich you can do the same thing.

Getting rich, however, doesn't mean you have to start out rich. Just because residential units do have a favored tax shelter status for the super rich, that doesn't mean you can't take advantage of that too. In fact, a solid and well-organized plan to start with small apartment buildings and work your way up the hill to your very own large apartment complex can work. It has, a thousand times over. Also remember that all residential units of any category have the same tax advantages; however, the larger complexes have more advantages to spread around.

2. The management system. The management of large apartment complexes is a profession in itself that requires great dedication to the property and to the tenants, as well as to the owner of the complex. The big smart money likes the idea of this central management concept because in theory a well-run management organization can handle more and larger complexes without increasing the total management expense by the same proportion as other expenses. For example, a team of ten professionals can take on another large complex with only a fraction of the additional load of work that an individual owner of that same additional complex can, because of computerization of payroll and general accounting as well as the other aspects of apartment control. Writing leases, examining rent rolls, updating leases that are rolling over, sending out rent notices, and the like are all part of the central management duties which can be computerized, and that makes sense (in theory) for the big smart money.

Also, there is another advantage that has to do with the management system. When a big project is bought by a public company through a limited-partnership tax shelter deal, the management team is usually separate from the deal. That is, the limited partnership hires the management team.

Management teams will usually get paid right down until the last penny of income is used up. I've even read prospectuses on limited-partnership offerings where the management team was owned and operated by the same person who was forming the limited partnership. I point this out as a potential disadvantage for investors going into those kinds of deals. Such built-in management where the right hand hires the left hand is not healthy, so avoid it if you can.

3. Combined buying power. The more units you own, the more you have to buy to supply, clean up, fix up, refurbish, paint, and on and on. This creates an enormous headache on one hand, but in theory it provides an opportunity to buy in volume and save. This combined buying power works not only for the items needed in the operation of a larger complex but the services as well. An in-house maintenance team, for example, takes care of the daily items that the small apartment owner might have to contract out as needed.

4. Condo conversion potential. Beginning with the waning years of the '70s and moving into the '80s, conversion of rental complexes to condominium apartments made believers out of the smart money that large apartment units were the way to go.

This single element, the ability to convert to a condo, can make the rental apartment an excellent investment. It is likely that a rental apartment building will sell based on its "rental economic value." Some rules of thumb on this would indicate the value of rental apartments (as rental apartments) to be 6 to 8 times the N.O.I. As condos, however, this same building could be worth ten to fifteen times the N.O.I. As long as the complex can be bought on a value base near the rental value and later sold on a higher basis, the investment can make a great deal of profit for the investor.

Conversions can be expensive, as there is often considerable legal work to be done. Then there is a matter of tenants who need to be removed (they often become the primary buyers, though), and the plushing up that often accompanies the conversion. There is a considerable cost in condo conversions, but despite this the profit side of the economics of condo conversions can be well worth the effort.

There is nothing that says you have to be big or for that matter smart to cash in on the big apartment building. Once you have gotten your feet wet with a smaller building or feel you have the experience of dealing with larger complexes, you can make your move.

The big difference between the small unit and the big unit isn't necessarily the same for everyone. To me, a building that can no longer be handled by you alone is a building that needs a management team. If the building's income won't support this management team, then you have found the cutoff between the small apartment complex and the large complex (for you). A move upward into more units would then establish the size that both needs the management team and throws off sufficient income to support it. This might be thirty units or sixty units, but it will be a complex that needs this management approach.

Having management opens up the opportunity for you to branch out into other areas of investing. Once you have income property sufficient to pay for management, your time is freed to follow other areas of interest. You might want to start over with a new buildup of small apartment buildings, now utilizing the management capabilities of the team you have set up for your newly purchased apartment complex.

Making this step, however, is getting ahead of the game. First you have to make the decision to do this: find a complex, decide it is a good buy, make the buy, set up your team, and start making a profit. All this takes time and some proficiency.

Getting into Larger Apartment Complexes

The first step is to ascertain if you are ready both mentally and physically for the move into the larger complex. It will mean more responsibility, greater obligations, worry, as well as profit and the potential freeing of your time. This is a step you are going to have to make by taking careful consideration of everything you are learning from this book. By the time you finish this book you will be much more capable of making that kind of determination than you are at this moment.

Mental and physical considerations are just the start. There is the economics to be looked at. Can you handle the larger investment? Will there be a money reserve to fall back on, if needed? Sometimes the best of plans don't work out as you want.

The economics of buying apartment buildings, small or large, is much the same. The more picky you are about what it is and where it is, the greater the percentage of cash you are apt to have to put down. If you don't have much cash reserve, you need to look at some of the other options open to you.

Remember, it isn't the amount of cash down that you need. With creative financing, you will have more opportunity to buy with a lower percentage down. But you will have a larger mortgage, larger payments, and more things to go wrong!

BUYING WITH LIMITED READY CASH

Low-Down-Payment Seller-Held Financing

THERE are many ways to approach this kind of transaction and I'll cover only a couple of ways here. As you go through this book you will see how the seller's motivation to sell can be used to help finance the sale.

One such method is to offer a combination of refinancing to generate some cash to the seller in addition to the cash you have plus his holding some secondary financing. For example, you want to buy a fifty-unit complex at $1,500,000 and it has a small existing loan of $300,000. Offer: To pay off the existing loan, pay the seller $1,000,000 cash if he will hold an unsecured note or a second mortgage against the property in the amount of $200,000.

Now this looks like it has taken a lot of your cash, right? Wrong. You went to the lenders (savings and loans or insurance companies would be good) and borrowed 80% of the purchase price. Out of this $1,200,000 you paid off the loan. That leaves you with $900,000, to which you add your own cash of $100,000.

Give this to the seller. He holds a small (for this deal) second mortgage of $200,000.

You would have some other costs, of course, such as the mortgage cost and legal fees, but not bad. If the seller could be convinced to hold a larger second, you might get in for nothing down (out of your own pocket).

Sometimes the seller doesn't need a lot of cash down and can be enticed into the deal with a wraparound mortgage. This form of financing (covered in detail in Chapter 20) can save the seller some real big tax money if his situation needs this technique, and your investment in the complex might be with a limited amount of cash. In some cases the capital you need to generate can be borrowed using another of your properties as collateral.

Pyramid Your Way into the Larger Units

This is an interesting way to "buy" units. In this technique you will use equity from other units or property to trade into the property. The pyramid is a very effective way to entice the seller to hold more paper (second or third mortgages) on the property.

In this situation (using the example of the $1,500,000 property) you could offer the seller $500,000 cash, the taking over of his existing financing, and a second mortgage on other land or property you have. This is sometimes called the "grass is greener on the other side of the property line" deal. It is not at all uncommon for the seller to look more favorably on the second property as security on the mortgage than he does on the property he is selling.

Here's how this deal looks to you:

You go and refinance the property and get a first mortgage in the amount of $1,200,000. You have to pay off the existing first mortgage of $300,000 and give the seller $500,000. From the cash angle you end up with $400,000. Of course, you would have some loan costs and closing costs, so let's deduct $75,000. Cash in-the-pocket to you: $325,000. The balance of the deal is the second mortgage you gave the seller. What you have ended up with in this exaggerated (but not unrealistic) deal is the property *and* cash.

You could, if necessary, improve the deal for the seller and still end up at the same place by agreeing to cross-collateralize the mortgage you are giving him (on that other property) by adding as additional security the apartment building you are buying. This means the seller would have the right to go against not only the second property, if you defaulted, but the apartments as well. This is another technique using the blanket mortgage (see Chapter 20) and is useful in decreasing the amount of cash you pay to the seller. Sellers use it with equal finesse in locking up the buyer's other assets to add security to the transaction.

Land Lease

Many clients will wrongly shy away from any deal that doesn't include ownership of the land. The fact of the matter is, it is all a matter of economics. If you own the right to use the land in the form of a lease, and that right is for as long as you will need the land plus enough time to enable you to sell that right, then it boils down to dollars and cents. Ownership or leasehold is economics.

Fact 1: Land is not a tax shelter item. You can't depreciate it, so it is just invested capital that goes nowhere from the tax point of view.

Fact 2: The value of the right to use often is more attractive than ownership.

Here's how it works: On this same deal with the $1,500,000 units, you broke the deal down to two segments. The first was the purchase of the building and other improvements. A value of $1,000,000 was established for that. The purchase terms could be handled in any way agreeable, including those methods shown previously by adjusting the price to this new lower amount. In this case assume you simply paid $1,000,000 cash to the seller.

The second part of the deal is the land-lease portion. You agree to lease the land for ninty-nine years at a set annual rental of $50,000. This rent might have some increases over the years to take care of inflation for the seller. The lease could even allow you to purchase the land sometime down the road if you wanted to (it's a good idea to have this provision). The best term for you to include would be a subordination provision whereby the seller agrees to permit you to place a first mortgage on the property. With this subordination provision you can go to any lender doing business on that kind of property and make a loan just as though you owned the property. Even without the subordination some lenders will loan on that same basis provided the lease term goes ten years beyond the term of the mortgage. You could borrow the $1,000,000 on this deal and be in the property with nothing invested. (And you thought only small run-down properties could be bought with zero cash down!)

Convert Earned Income to a Capital Gain (The Ultimate Goal)

There are the intermediate goals: the tax shelter, the tax-free income that comes out of the property. But ultimately, somewhere down the road, unless you exchange the property, you will benefit from the conversion of earned income into a lower-taxed capital gains income.

As you own a property you are sheltering certain amounts of earned income through its tax shelter. In the meantime this property is increasing in value to the point where, when you do sell, all the tax shelter you have taken will ultimately be part of the "profit of the sale" and will be taxed as the capital gain. This assumes two things: First, you are not a dealer, and secondly, you have taken into account the proper depreciation methods and any accelerated depreciation adjusted for the earned-income recap.

A dealer in real estate is someone who buys and sells as a business (not an agent in buying and selling) or does a sufficient amount of buying and selling so that IRS determines that the investor is really making this his business. Being a dealer in real estate is not the way for the small investor to go, and you want to avoid making one deal after another. Usually you don't have to fear this classification, as most investors find it more profitable to hold on to their investments awhile and get the maximum benefits out of the tax shelter.

The recap of depreciation is basically the way the IRS gets

to adjust your accelerated depreciation schedules if you sell the property prior to the elimination of the effect of the recap. In short, any depreciation which is in excess of a straight-line depreciation taken in the first 100 months of ownership (8⅓ years) is subject to a full return. This excess depreciation that sheltered income over the years is now returned to you the year of the sale as additional earned income.

Beyond the first 100 months you are faced with a phaseout of this penalty over another 100 months, until it disappears altogether 200 months from the time you started (since 1975) the depreciation.

The effect of this recap of excessive depreciation is simply to add earned income to your transaction in the year of the sale. This can be most unwanted income. You are now to be taxed for income you took excessive shelter against earlier in the ownership. In essence, you are taxed on money you spent some years ago.

Planning will help avoid these problems, and it may be possible to anticipate such an event and absorb any losses you might have in other property that same year.

Let me show you how this conversion of earned income to capital gains income works and makes the deal worthwhile.

You purchase an apartment building for $1,500,000. The down payment is $300,000 cash out-of-pocket. The allocation between land and buildings is: land, $400,000; buildings, $1,100,000.

Assume for a moment that your accountant suggests you set up a straight-line depreciation on a life of thirty-five years over the total depreciable value. This would be much less than other options available to you, such as the 125% or the 150%, or sum-of-the-years digits, or component depreciation.

In any event, the straight-line over thirty-five years would give you a depreciation of $31,428.57 each year. In ten years this sum would have totaled $314,285.70.

If you had been in the 50% tax bracket this depreciation deduction (an expense, but you didn't write a check to pay it—just a paper deduction) would have sheltered earned income in that same amount. Thus, you would have saved the tax on that amount of earned income.

Total savings over the ten years in taxes would be $157,142.85.

If you sold for the same price you paid (thus no appreciation to be considered) you would have a gain that looks like this:

Price sold at		$1,500,000.00
Price paid	$1,500,000.00	
Depreciation	314,285.70	
		$1,185,714.30
Profit on the sale		$ 314,285.70
Tax saved due to shelter		$157,142.85
Less tax on the profit from the sale		
Profit	$314,285.70	
Exclude 60%	188,571.42	
Portion taxed	$125,714.28	
Amount of tax (50% rate)		62,857.14
Profit		$ 94,285.71

The result: Because you converted $314,285.70 of earned income into capital gains income, you benefited greatly.

In any normal deal you wouldn't have sold the property for the same price you paid ten years earlier. So on top of the tax shelter, you will see an appreciation added to that capital gains benefit.

This aspect of real estate, by the way, works on any kind of real estate that is depreciable.

Depreciation and its tax counterpart, the tax shelter, will run out, however, and this aspect makes even the best property available to be purchased. This occurs because the new buyer starts his depreciation all over from the moment he closes on the property with a new set of numbers. You might have run the book value of the property down to zero, whereas he can begin once more at the full price he pays after allocation between land and buildings.

A look at the ownership records of the apartment buildings

in your area will show you who has owned the buildings for a tenure of from five to twelve years. Depending on their specific method of depreciation, the best time for them to sell, if tax shelter is important to them and the other advantages of that specific property are not that overwhelming, would be within that five to twelve years.

It is possible to increase your depreciation base by adding to the depreciation each time by the capital amount spent. That may not be enough, however, to reverse a declining shelter when you may have a need for just that.

Have Your Cake and Get Another One Just Like It

MANY apartment owners (hotel owners, office building owners, etc.) make the decision to sell in this situation and buy something else. This probably is the wrong decision, and they may soften the blow and gain on the reinvestment potential by using the exchange that has already been illustrated. The exchange may get them into another property, and if it is more valuable, the increased value would add to the depreciation for the future years.

Yet there is another way whereby you could keep what you have and add to the depreciation schedule: Simply get another apartment building to provide the shelter you have lost.

What if you don't have the cash? Not to worry. Take the land under the first complex, separate it from your package, and exchange it as a down payment on the second apartment building.

You didn't get any tax shelter out of the land anyway, so as long as you have the use of it and the lease-back is reasonable, you shouldn't care. You don't have to give up what has been a gold mine just because your accountant is screaming at you to do that.

Oh, and don't worry if the seller of the second apartment building doesn't want to take your land. Some hotshot exchange broker will make a three- or four-leg deal and get everyone what they wanted.

What about the bad-news side of large apartment complexes?

1. **Dependent on a broader market.** If you have five hundred units to rent out, you can't be as picky about your tenants as in the small complex. And if the market goes lower, you could be in trouble.

2. **The alligator called management.** The theory of big central management works only some of the time. Many limited partnerships falter on this one element. It's the old story of people doing business with people.

3. **Rent control.** It is a growing desire everywhere, and it must be watched. The biggest hazard is in small communities where a sizable percent of the population (20% or more) rents. These people will turn out en masse and vote on a city ordinance calling for rent control.

4. **Condo-conversion regulations.** Much the same as rent control. These laws are designed to stop or slow down condo conversions of rentals. The idea is to protect the rights of the tenant (but what about the apartment building owner?).

5. **Taxes.** Property taxes are a way for cities to get back at the apartment owner. So far taxes are not very tough on apartment complexes, but if rent control hits, watch out.

Five bad-news items that simply mean you have to be on your toes. But when you're that way you are already able to see above the rest of the guys.

14

Making a Killing In Condos

To invest in condominiums you must know and understand what a condo is and how it differs from its near neighbor the co-op.

A condominium, or condo for short, is a vertical subdivision. The land developer takes a plot of acreage and divides it into lots (subdivisions); the condo developer takes the airspace over the land and puts a building there. Each part of the space that is taken up by an apartment is a portion of that vertical subdivision.

When you buy a condo you buy that space and the right to use, with the other owners, the common parts of the space that connect the apartments to the ground. A percentage of ownership of these common areas is established, but you own your unit outright. This outright ownership is important because you can borrow on it, mortgage it, and dispose of it relatively freely.

A cooperative, or co-op, is much the same except that the co-op is owned by all its owners in common. You own a percent of the total and have the exclusive use of your own apartment, but you may not be able to get an individual mortgage on the property, and may even owe a percent of the total existing mortgage and any new mortgages on the structure.

There are other legal distinctions between the co-op and the condo, but these are the major important differences. Looking at them, you can't tell one building from another; bricks and mortar don't care if they are condos or co-ops.

Another of the little-known secrets of investing in real estate and making big bucks is this: Anytime you can get someone to sell you something where you pay today's price for something in the future, take advantage of it.

Tie Up Tomorrow's Value Today

Take a look at what happens in the typical condominium development. The builder decides to construct a condo, finds the land, gets his plans, gets his loan, then gets the sales program under way. Let's stop at this point for a moment. Many lenders who finance condo projects like to see some advance sales prior to a major commencement of the actual building program. These advance sales tell the lender that the market is there for the apartments the developer was promising all the time, and the lender relaxes. A relaxed lender is the best kind to have.

With a certain percentage of advance sales under his belt, the developer can up the price of the predevelopment sale and start construction of the project. Prices are apt to continue to go up along the way, as a large project development may take a year or longer. It is during this delay between the first sale and the closing, when the units are completed, that the smart investor can make his big bucks. If he is prudent, that is.

One investor I know, a senior bachelor, put down a deposit of $1,000 on a new oceanfront condominium that was announced in the Fort Lauderdale area. This deposit was just to hold his reservation on the unit he selected. The developers had announced that they expected to advance the reservations to the contract stage within six months.

There was a slight delay, so he had seven months in which to make another decision: try to sell his contract or put up the second deposit of $4,000.

He put up the second deposit and thus far was in good shape even though he now had $5,000 on deposit. Under the terms of the contract, the deposit was fully refundable until he had had the opportunity to review the declaration of condominium (a legal document, filed with the state, that creates the condo entity). This document wasn't due for another four or five months. By the way, by the time my friend had to put up the $4,000 second deposit, all the units in this condo had been optioned on a similar basis. There was no opportunity for anyone else to get what amounted to a first shot at these units, and the selling agents were taking what amounted to second options on the units (in some cases third and fourth options).

The value of these types of units had been going up prior to the investment and continued to do so. With something that is guaranteed to be in short supply (oceanfront units), the upward trend of the market was assured. (Just wait until one of those things gets washed away into the surf in a hurricane . . .)

By the time the declaration of condominium came around, my friend had already been offered $50,000 for his contract. In the end he sold his option for $74,500. All this on a deposit of $5,000 in total.

Eric, a young gad-about-town, had made more money in condos than you'd ever expect looking at him. He seems just too damn carefree to be such a shrewd businessman. But he knows the condo market and has gone from one building to another, buying in and then moving one unit after another. Sometimes he actually moves into a unit, closing on it himself at the presale price he got by being first in line. He fixes up what is often very cold white walls and gray concrete floor and after a year or so sells for a bundle.

The Condo Law in Your State May Be on Your Side

If any of you are stockbrokers or deal in the options market, you know the value of having a lock on something that might go up in value. You are even better off if the law gives you the right to get your money back after a time if you decide you don't want the option after all. In many states the law says exactly that, and you aren't fully committed until you have been given time to examine and approve the legal documents that establish the condominium. This document may have different names in different states, so when you are dealing with a potential buy, ask lots of questions about this aspect.

The laws are there to protect the buyer because in the past

many condo sales promotions offered lots of benefits that looked like they had to be worth the price . . . only they were never built, or if built, were less than they were supposed to be.

The 5 Steps to Speculating in Condos

Here the idea is to make a prudent investment in a condo that will stand a better than average chance to appreciate to the point where your contract to buy will be at a price substantially less than what you can sell that contract for. In short, make a profit on your deposit.

1. Select properties because they are in a favorable situation with the supply and demand for the market area. This is the touchy part. If the demand is very high that is good, but if the supply is even greater at the same time, you want to shy away from that kind of unit if you are looking for quick appreciation.

The ideal is growing demand and decreasing supply. Don't look just in the locale of the property to satisfy yourself on the supply-and-demand market, either. Keep in mind that if you are looking at a ski area, the market for these unique properties is much broader than just Vail, of Snowmass, or wherever you are looking. If Vail is hotter than a firecracker while every other ski area is peaking out, then watch out because Vail might be next. (I don't really think so, however.) You don't know what the market is in the supply-and-demand aspect just by looking around. You need to get some professional help on this or become a pro yourself. Visit a broker and have him show you some units in the same category as the ones you are anticipating buying. You can pick his brain, and perhaps you will discover you have picked the wrong market and make a switch.

2. Be an early-bird. You want to both catch the prices before they have jumped up and have the first selection of the best units. Any building will have a certain percentage of units that will bring a higher price, sustain a stronger market, and appreciate faster than other units in that same building.

3. Read the sales documents very carefully. Even if you

have decided on the first place you see, it is a good idea to see what the competition's sales documents have to offer and how they differ. Have your lawyer take a final look before you buy. Watch out for and avoid:

• The developer who has full and free use of your deposit money.

• A floating sales price. The price will rise as the market tightens up, and there goes your potential profit. This is the developer trying to narrow down his buyers to people who intend to live in the building.

• Highly *un*restrictive rules and restrictions in the condo documents. A complex that is too loose in its rules and regulations —that doesn't maintain a desirable environment—may not be a good resale.

• Restrictions that limit your resale. A sales agreement may say you can't resell the contract at all, or you can sell but only with written approval of the developer (if you notify them sixty days before a full moon comes on a Saturday).

• Other restrictions that are fine for some units but not so good for others: limitations on leasing, on pets, on children, on nude blondes—you know, tough things that might blow your intended resale. The current problem in resale of many units is the owners' association's right to approve your buyer. Most condos and co-ops have some version of this rule. It may not be in the declaration of condominium but in the ownership rules and regulations voted in later. Make sure you understand just how restrictive it is.

4. Know where you stand in your state with respect to your deposit. If you can get it back up until the time you have to approve the condo documents, you can risk more than you might otherwise.

5. Look for units that have an environment suitable to a growing market. It should be clear that a condo complex that has an identifiable market—oriented to tennis, retirement, skiing, and so forth—will be more clearly defined in its orientation to the supply-and-demand side of things. Also, and most basically—if the environment is nice it will be in more demand!

Cut Your Risk by Being Ready, Willing and Able to Buy
Being able to buy if you have to or if the market looks so good that it hasn't peaked out will make your days much easier and your nights more restful. You wouldn't want to sell gold at $400 per ounce just before it was on its way to $700 per ounce, would you? Sometimes the condo market is just that way. Everything seems to bust open at the same time, and if you have picked your market carefully then the chances are you will have this happen.

The Best Way to Speculate

Following the five steps I've just given you, put some money down on an apartment. Cut your risk by being able to actually buy the unit. There can be no doubt that you will remove much of the risk by following these five steps and by being ready, willing, and able to buy. But there is still speculation in this form of investment, and you need to have the speculator's attitude to be successful.

There is a big difference between the investor and the speculator; not all investors are willing to speculate. Speculation comes in when there is *not* an absolute or more than highly probable result which can be anticipated. When it comes to real estate, not everything can be predicted.

You invest in something that follows a trend, that has everything going for it except the mixture of the person and the property. An investor buys an apartment building because he feels he can improve its management or increase its return by conversion to condos. A speculator buys the apartment building because he feels sure the state is going to build new government offices across the street. The investor buys farmland because it can be leased out and one day divided into ranchettes. The speculator buys it because his homework tells him that the new highway system about to be built in the area is going to bust open the land values and he'll make a mint. Therefore, I define investors and speculators as follows:

Investors are people who don't want to risk their capital, so they only buy property (and things) that are going to go up in value or throw off solid proven benefits.

Speculators are investors who realize that no one really knows for sure what will go up in value over the long run or will throw off solid proven benefits, but do their homework to remove as much risk as they can, and attempt to buy low and sell high.

Of course, speculators have generally learned one thing more (if not, they will someday): that not everything you buy will go up in value, or go up fast enough to keep ahead of inflation or costs or a combination of both. The sad fact is some real estate eats you up while you wait for it to go up in value.

To develop some of the speculator's attitude, realize that chance is for the crap table, not for investing in real estate. Nothing magical is going to happen to pull your rear out of the fire unless *you* help it happen. Believe and trust in your own abilities.

Don't be lulled into complacency by trends. These systematic movements that seem like they will go on forever don't, and often just when you needed them to go on the most. History follows ups and downs, and knowing that doesn't make it any easier if you have bought during an up and have to sell at the down. Look at the long range of past trends. That is more indicative of what can occur than the recent past.

Be careful of overanalysis. This is usually filled with crystal-ball stuff. "Why, son, ten years from now according to my projections you will be rich. Listen to me, son, *rich*." I've heard it all and can tell you from experience that to project beyond a few years is to forget Iran and all the sudden events that shape our lives. Speculators have long since learned that analysis of a property right down to the nitty-gritty usually loses the deal anyway, because if the property was really good some dumb buyer from overseas bought it out of luck (or is luck really just being at the right place at the right time and knowing it?).

Accept the fact that all real estate has a certain amount of risk attached to it. You can narrow your risk by following the guides in this book and knowing the options open to you, yet you will never eliminate it. You can have current events against you and get caught with something that eats more money than you care to or can feed it. Speculators know that hoping it will go up, wishing it will go up, even praying it will go up isn't always going to help.

Speculators know that sometimes the biggest risk of all is never taking a chance.

Just Another Option

Putting all this together, condos may not be the maximum investment when a property meets these ideals. The investor-speculator, getting off the ground and moving out of the need for shelter, may look at condo speculation as a fairly safe way to risk time and money.

If you can tie the ability to speculate with the need for shelter, then, as I've mentioned before, you cut to the bone the risk factor.

In many areas of the country the condo is more than a way of life—it is the majority way of life. In Florida, California, and other Sunbelt areas where the need to produce a lot of views from a limited space is compelling; the condo has become king. Apartment values have taken escalator rides to the sky and in many cases look like they will continue to do just that.

Apartments that sold for $45,000 only a few years ago are now over $150,000. The $95,000 apartment is pushing a quarter of a million, and the bottom side of the scale—the $15,000 condo —is now the $45,000 unit.

I remind you that the person who says today, "I'll never buy one of these . . . why, look how much they have climbed in price . . . who'd buy at that price?" will look back on today some years in the future and say, "I remember back in the early eighties when I could have bought that property at a fraction of what it would bring today." Buying condos or anything else for appreciation is the way of the '70s and '80s, so don't overlook the potential.

The condo *is* a viable property and has many advantages for many investors.

15

Time-Sharing—How to Get a Villa in the Mountains, a Home by the Sea, and a Condo in Acapulco

TIME-SHARING is relatively new to the United States, although it has been around Europe for many years. It basically is a marketing technique for selling holiday-style second homes. Instead of buying a second home and owning it outright for all twelve months of the year, you buy only two weeks or so for your annual holiday.

The concept is great, and by itself not something you would want to shy away from if it suits your pocketbook and the facility is where you would like to go. Come to think of it, you don't even have to like the place, due to a twist that most developers of time-share units are able to offer.

The exchange capability of the time-share programs is highly sophisticated, as there are several international clearinghouses for the swapping of time. Interval Inc. and Resort Condominiums International (RCI) are two such clearinghouses and they work much the same to provide the owners of time-share units a way to swap-around-the-world. Their exchange systems are set up by the developers of the time-share apartment complexes as an added and well-worth-the-cost benefit. There are some restrictions in the exchange, but the number of time-share programs being developed around the world has assured the owner of a unit that there is a likely chance of being able to go to one of his first three choices when he wishes.

The time-share unit has become a product to buy not just because of its location but because of its connection to many locations. As the exchange system expands and more time-share units are developed in more and varied locations around the world, it would seem to me that the value of any unit within the system will increase in value.

The cost to join the program is surely going to go up, just as the cost to buy a newly developed unit anywhere goes up with rising building costs.

Let's take a look at some of the typical time-share projects around the world. They include exotic places like Acapulco, Mexico, and most of the Caribbean Islands from St. Thomas in the U.S. Virgins to Grenada to places in Europe and Asia. The purely resort spots have time-share condos mixed in with the more conventional condominiums, but the time-shares are gaining.

Most of the successful facilities are based on the hotel concept, with the complex designed and operated much as a deluxe resort hotel would be. This is because the time-share is a living place for holidays. People are coming and going at a very high rate of occupancy all year round, and the only kind of facility that functions well in these conditions is the hotel.

Look at your favorite ski resort and I bet you will find time-shares already there, or just about to be. In places like Vail and Snowmass you will find that for a two-week stay apartments sell for $10,000 and up.

Now $10,000 isn't bad for a second home in a classy place like Vail, but when you realize the developer is selling this same unit to as many as twenty-seven owners, each having two weeks at different times over the year, that is a grand total of $270,000 for that apartment. That same apartment might bring $125,000 or so if it were bought outright in another complex. Despite the markup, however, the time-share can be a great bargain.

• You don't have the upkeep cost for the eleven and one-half months you don't use it.

• You pay only one twenty-eighth of the taxes.

• You don't even have to go to the same place each year to benefit.

• You are guaranteed a place to stay without having to pay the climbing hotel rates.

This last factor is growing in its importance to the holiday traveler. Hotel rates are shooting out of sight all over the world. It has gotten to the point where the cheapest place in the world for comparable accommodations is the United States.

Europe is already priced beyond most "reasonable" means and continues to go up. South America has astounded even the most veteran traveler, as the room rates in hotels from Argentina to Venezuela have been doubling on a regular basis.

With the time-share unit you are above all that. Your unit goes up right along with the rest of them in the comparable swapping arrangements that Interval or RCI can make for your approved unit.

Okay, so this is a product that sounds good, has all the trends working for it. It meets what I call the maximum test for things to invest in:

1. Is it a property that people will buy?
2. Is it a property that many people can afford to buy?
3. Is it a property that people can get immediate benefit from?
4. Is it a property that is not adversely affected by increased supply?
5. Is it a property that has positive upward trends?
6. Is it a property that has a wide market appeal that many people will recognize and take advantage of?

In my opinion the time-share answers all these questions with a loud and resounding yes.

As this is the case, it is something that you will want to consider as an interesting investment that puts you into a second home plus other benefits at a very reasonable cost.

Still, create a good thing and someone is bound to mess it up along the way, trying to get a bit too much of the pie for himself. So it is with time-shares. Not everything labeled time-share is going to be a good *buy*.

The 3 Elements in Time-share Projects

1. The developer. This is either an advantage or a disadvantage, depending on his track record and attitude about the project. Here's what happens: The time-share is really a financing method of developing resort hotel complexes. This is basically how the programs were first developed in Europe, and it works very well as a creative form of financing. The reason for this is that simply by owning your own unit (even if it's just for two weeks), you and the other owners like you keep the facility nearly full all year round. You will pay the taxes, the maintenance, and your own maid service in your annual "dues." When you aren't there the management often has the right (with your contractual approval) to rent out your unit and collect a portion of that rent for themselves. When you are at the facility you will eat in its restaurants and drink in its bars (if there are any), so the operator of this facility is going to make money hand over fist.

In other words, it makes economic sense for the owner of a hotel to sell his "rooms" as time-share units at a small profit in order to get the operation's profits over the succeeding years. Many time-share projects in Europe were sold on this basis, and the developers have the "attitude of hoteliers" and are into time-sharing not as a hit-and-run business, but over the long haul, when they will make their money by giving good service and keeping the management contracts. These are the best facilities to invest in, but unfortunately they are hard to find in the "best" size of under two hundred rooms. Any resort facility is an environment, and when they get too big they are, in my opinion, a less attractive environment. The best time-share units would be those developed by hotel operators (a conversion of an existing hotel by the already successful hotel operator, not a newcomer) in a facility of moderate size for the area.

The less attractive developers you will come across are the condominium developers who have seen the fantastic markup possible in the time-share field and are flocking into time-shares, relying on their past experience in building condos.

This experience can be good when it comes to building and marketing a fine product. However, the attitude about marketing condos isn't what makes time-shares good. The condo builder builds and sells out and moves on. He doesn't have the long haul in mind when he builds. In fact, he wants to get out of the building before the owners' association has a chance to organize and take him to task on every item that goes wrong. This causes some condo developers to view the time-share as just another condominium project and look to a management company to take over the day-to-day operations once they have made their condo profits.

This combination is the usual one and sometimes works out okay, but it is full of potential problems. The vast differences between the attitudes of these developers will be the major criterion you will look for in deciding if the developer is the one you want to buy from. Here are three areas you want to look into:

• How many time-share projects has this developer actually built, converted, or sold? Be wary of answers like this: "Our team is well experienced in the time-share field. We are associated with Resort Condominiums International," and as you can see from his brochure, there are over *x* hundred projects in the world. You've just been told this is the developer's first time-share project.

• What other condo buildings has the developer built? Get the addresses and dates built. If there are any around you can go to see, do that. If you can meet a resident, ask him about the building. Is it sound, were there any problems with the developer? That sort of thing. This often will be most revealing. If there aren't any around, call a realtor in the town where they were built and ask him his opinion. You may or may not get much information this way, but it is better than trying to guess what to do next.

• Who is the management? And best of all, what is the connection between the management and the developer? If there is no connection, then you must look very hard at the makeup of the management team. Have they operated time-shares before? What kind of hotels have they operated? Time-share properties are not like normal hotels. The operation doesn't have to devote as much time and energy to the same kind of promotions as does the non-time-share facility, as the time-share has its own ability to provide guests.

2. The project. Some developers are more entrepreneurial and they move into a prime resort area with the "get rich fast" idea of using a time-share as the way to go. They will take an option on an existing hotel that may have enjoyed a good reputation in the town, and often agree to pay the owner of the hotel a premium price for the facility. The catch to the transaction is that the owner has to give the developer an option for a duration of time in order to get the time-share sales program into swing.

A few less-than-prudent hotel owners have agreed to subordinate their title to these developers, and sales programs have actually begun on some units only to go down the drain when the market just wouldn't bear the price the developer was asking. A few units might have been sold and now the hotel owner gets his property back with a messed-up title. And you—well, you might have been one of the few people who bought a unit in a time-share that didn't make it off the ground.

There is the grandiose developer who bites off more than he can chew by doing a hotel or time-share project that is just so big that marketing problems eat the deal full of holes. If the facility has five hundred rooms and they are to be sold in two-week increments, then the salesmen need to sell fourteen thousand units. That is a lot under the best conditions, and few developers have met with success in this area.

Since the project *is* the main reason you may be attracted to that particular time-share facility, it should provide an environment that suits your comfort level. There is no need or benefit to you in buying a holiday time-share unit in a facility that caters to tennis if you can't stand tennis. You should invest in a time-share unit because you plan to get some active use out of the unit or the exchange program. Shop around until you find the kind of unit you want to own.

Remember, if the exchange programs falter and go out of business, you will be left with your own time-space in the facility you purchased. You won't be able to rationalize away the aspect that you bought into just any facility to get into the exchange program.

3. The method of ownership . . . or lack of ownership. There are several different forms of time-share, and it is important for you to recognize some of the most-used kinds of "ownership." Keep in mind that each of the following forms can vary, depending on the state or country where the unit is located. Each form will have some advantages over the others, the main trade-off usually being the price for the unit. Despite this, I feel the best of all kinds of ownership for a time-share unit will be the condominium ownership of a time interval.

Time-Interval Condo

This form of time-share ownership is much the same as a condo except that instead of owning the unit outright for the full twelve months, you have a subdivided time within the year. This time is set down in specific terms as to exact days of the year, with the beginning and ending dates shown for the first twenty or so years. As the ownership is outright for that time, a formula is devised to carry forward the ownership time forever.

This name, time-interval condo, is not uniform, so you may find the same situation being called something else. In this and the other forms the name it's called isn't important. What is happening is, however.

As with a condominium, you have rights of ownership and mortgage ability that will not be the same in the other forms.

You own forever, so to speak, but since buildings may eventually be torn down for other kinds of construction, you or your estate may someday benefit in some way from the redevelopment of the site.

Leasehold Time-share

The ownership you get in this form of time-share is a leasehold right to the unit. This term may be for ten years, twenty, thirty, or any period of time. It gives you absolute right to that unit within the terms of the lease.

The value of the leasehold ownership will greatly diminish as you approach the end term of the lease, and unlike the condo version, your investment may wane rapidly rather than increase. The trade-off here is usually that the sales price for the leasehold form is less. The seller will have another go at selling the units when the first batch of leases run out.

The biggest hazard of this kind of ownership is that you don't own the property, only the right (with the limitations of the lease) to be there. The actual ownership of the real estate belongs to someone else. It might be the seller, and if that's the case, then your problems aren't monumental. However, it is likely that the developer (the seller) doesn't own the real estate either. He might have entered into a deal with the owner of a facility to turn it into a time-share and start selling these leasehold increments of time. You buy, and shortly thereafter, through no fault of yours, the deal goes under. In small print in your leasehold agreement there may be some provision that "your rights are subordinated to the fee simple owner." This or other wording may limit your rights to that of the deal the developer made with the owner. This may mean you have paid your money but don't have anything to show for it if the deal goes under.

The big advantage of the leasehold is its lower cost and limited time span. Sometimes it is more reasonable (for some buyers) to look to a short period of ten years or so, in order to lock in their holiday rental cost. The leasehold time-share can do that.

Cooperative, or Corporate, Time-Share

This form of time-share takes the same approach to holiday time increments as the cooperative does to selling year-round units. It is a corporation, or in some areas a limited-partnership form of ownership, whereby you buy a share in the development. Your share entitles you to the time use of one of the units.

This kind of ownership is widely used in Europe and has many advantages if the developer is looking to expand and own more than one operation. A club will operate nicely in this kind of ownership, and there are many such clubs around Europe that have two or more facilities in holiday areas. You own a share of stock, or limited-partnership interest, and this is relatively easy to sell if the need arises, based, of course, on the value it has because of the facilities involved and the times of the year available.

The disadvantage is that your rights of ownership are limited and your future appreciation is acutely related to the ability of the operator to provide an environment that will be in demand.

Buying into this kind of unit is risky unless the facility and the operation are well under way, or you have a lot of confidence in the track record of the developer and operator. If you do, then it's a nice way to buy stock.

LOOK AT THE FRINGE BENEFITS

ALL time-share units should offer one method of exchange or another. If you are looking at units you will find that besides the international exchange ability they will offer other fringe benefits. These may include: travel club and discount travel; travel insurance; discount auto rental; swap of time in the same unit for different time; rental pool of outside rental income to offset expenses; maid service; food provisions in advance of your arrival; private facilities for members only; full resort-hotel-type facilities; golf course privileges; discount rent for extra time at facility (space available).

Don't be shy about asking what the operator will do for you and the other owners when and after you buy. See if these fringe benefits are actually in your contract, and not in the management's package. As management changes, you might find the fringe benefits disappear.

What Time of Year?

Obviously, the time of year you cannot get away should be eliminated. This isn't always easy, and the selection of two weeks or so should be given the most leeway possible. In the exchange programs you are not fully limited to time, however, and that will aid in giving you some flexibility.

Look very closely at buying time in the off season, which will cost much less than the in season. Remember that the off season in places like South Florida (summer) is the peak season in Switzerland. The exchange of units works to your advantage. Besides, the experienced traveler has long since discovered that travel in season is more expensive and often not as enjoyable as in the less crowded times of the year.

Time-share Your Own Deal

If you can't find what you really want in a time-share, or feel you should be on the inside of the deal, making every cent count the most, then why not do your own private time-share? All it takes is the desire to put something together, and if you follow the suggestions I'll give you you should be able to make some money while having a lot of fun.

Assume for a moment that you, a resident of Fort Lauderdale, want to get a nice place in the mountains of North Carolina. That would give you a retreat not more than one day's drive or a few hours by air from your seaside residence. The cost of a home or apartment is just above (or a lot above) your budget, so you decide to go the time-share route, as you realize you wouldn't use the place enough to warrant year-round ownership. But the offerings in the area in the public time-share programs are just not your cup of tea for one reason or another, or you can't find any time-share facilities in the area where you want to be. But you do find some nice homes that would suit your needs just right—except for the price.

Let's set the stage: You find a three-bedroom home on a beautiful lot overlooking a valley. The home might be a few years old and still have a decent mortgage at moderate interest rates. It is furnished comfortably, but for your purpose you feel it should have some new furniture.

Price of the home as is is $65,000. You calculate you would spend another $10,000 on furniture and closing costs. You can buy the home for $20,000 down, so when you add the furniture and other costs you will need $30,000 cash to buy the facility and have exactly what you want.

You don't have to put up a cent of this. All you have to do is find eleven other people to put up $3,000 each to buy one month in this facility. That would give you the $30,000 cash you need to make the deal plus some other cash for reserve. You would have your one month at no cost to you.

The mortgage balance of $45,000 could be divided by 11, as well as all the other costs to maintain the property, the idea being that since you had the idea—it was you that went out and found the facility and put it together—why not get in for one month as your "profit"?

No one would really object to this arrangement, because they are getting a damn good deal as it is. A lawyer would set it up for you at a reasonable expense (if not, change lawyers), so don't be frightened by the complication of the legal aspects.

Your deal would start by finding the property you want to time-share. It can be a house or any other kind of living facility, including a condo. You need to be sure, however, that there are no restrictions on your multiperson use of the facility. Some apartments and homes (due to homeowners' associations, etc.) may restrict this kind of multiperson use. If that is the case, don't fight it—just don't buy that property. Protect yourself here; suggest that your lawyer or broker insert a provision in the contract that will cover you in this respect. I'd use something like this:

> This agreement is conditioned on there being no restrictions, either by local government, or otherwise, that would prevent the use of this property as a time-share facility whereby ownership would be divided among several owners, each having the right to separate use of the facility at different times of the year.

You might want to make sure you or your broker also covers you on the right to rent out to nonowners as well.

Don't Start Selling Until You Are Set

Never go to a friend or anyone else and ask if he would be interested in buying into a time-share you are thinking about putting together. That will cause you to get discouraged, and you may abandon the idea before you get rolling. The reason for this is simple. Your best buddy will be thinking. "Why should I commit myself to something he is just thinking about? Hell, he'll end up in this thing free. Why don't I do this myself?"

He won't do it, mind you, but he will give you some flak about coming in with you (it always happens this way). Also, you might feel a bit awkward about this kind of situation, and you don't really know what you are going to have to do to make this a reality, so you are apt to give away too much.

"Charlie, hell, I'll even take the last pick of time . . . all I want to do is make sure we all have what is good for everyone." Sounds good, but it softens the deal, and Charlie, if he is smart, will guess that your chance of success in this venture is about 30%.

To make your success factor jump to 100%, tie up the property first. It will be easy in most cases. In fact, if it isn't easy, move on to another property until you do find something you can tie up.

All you have to do is to find what you want, then make an offer to buy. Negotiate the deal just as though you were going to buy tomorrow, but inform the seller, in the offer you first make (never before), that you are putting together a few friends to buy this property and you need sixty to ninety days to make that deal. Your contract to buy should be conditioned on your achieving success. If not, then you would be excused from the contract, with any and all deposits returned.

If you are doing your negotiating in the less-than-peak-market times of the year, you won't find the resistance to this technique strong. The seller doesn't really have a whole lot to lose by going along with you except some time, and in many areas of the world you will find time is less important than other motivations.

Once you have the property tied up, you need to work out the cost factors on the deal. Follow this checklist:

1. **Cash down.** How much cash is needed to close on the purchase?

2. **Closing costs.** Get the lawyer's fee for setting up this time-share deal figured in here, plus all costs to close on the property and the time-share program.

3. **Additions to the property.** New furniture, some kitchen fixtures or appliances, dishes and glassware, all that would be needed to set up the facility as 100% livable. You'll want to buy more glassware and dishes than you think you'll need, to allow for breakage. Store the extras in a safe place.

4. **Advance deposits needed.** What needs to be put down on the utilities and other public services right away?

5. **A cash reserve in the name of the time-share.** You will want to have a cash reserve in the amount of three months' expenses, to be on the safe side.

6. **Add up all the above and divide by the number of units you plan to sell.** Oh, yes—if you want to make some extra profit here, add it in before you divide by the number of units. Remember, the usual time-share deal in a big complex down the road is going to be selling at much more than your piece of a more comfortable home or apartment.

7. **Work up the rules and regulations.** You need to have this set down and clearly shown. Your lawyer will help, but it should be simple and not complicated. All you need to do is spell out some "don'ts" in living—no pets, maximum number of people in the place overnight, that sort of thing. Write it for your own comfort and that of your friends going into this deal.

8. **Have the legal aspects on paper.** You don't need to have

the lawyer work out the final details, but show how future divisions of sale will be covered. Show how the costs of annual expenses will be paid and collected from the buying members. If you are going to take care of all this monetary end yourself, then get paid for it over and above the other benefits to you. It might be a good idea simply to let an accountant take care of that for you and divide the cost.

9. Have a mini sales presentation. If you want to sell anything, be ready to answer some tough questions. Have some photographs, an aerial view, and other things such as maps of the area and a booklet from the local chamber of commerce on the benefits of the locale where the property is located.

10. Offer your friends a chance to join you in this investment. "Charlie, I'm buying a property up in a delightful town in North Carolina. It is only a few minutes from a nice winter ski area, and in the summer it is an ideal spot to go to get away from Florida. I've decided to break up the ownership into twenty-four increments of about two weeks each, but each person who joins me will take two of these time spans, so there will be a maximum of twelve of us in this together. I'll need $3,000 down from you if you're interested."

11. Close on the deal. The moment you have your eleven checks, go to closing. By the way, when you said you were buying a property you were correct. You do have a contract and you can and should show it. Be open, and you will close your time-share deal.

Time-share Anything

There is no reason you can't use this technique to time-share a sailboat, an airplane, a power yacht, or whatever. Your ability to bring in your friends and their friends will always depend on your being able to control the situation. This control comes from having the property tied up, and no other way. Trust me on this one.

16

Recreational Property

NOT EVERYONE wants to own a time-share property to have a stay of a week or two guaranteed over the next twenty years. It gets back to what you can afford, of course, and judging by the statistics on the number of people in this country who own second homes, a lot of people can afford to go in style.

When you own your second home, you can go whenever you want. This ability to have a spur-of-the-moment holiday is a very attractive benefit to a busy person. After all, many people may not be able to plan ahead twenty years for the first two weeks of July, as might be needed in the time-share property. The ability to pick up and go to the cabin in the mountains, or by the sea, is one of the major motivating factors that sells thousands of second homes each year.

7 Critical Factors in Buying a Second Home

When you buy a second home there are some factors that you should pay close attention to. The second home is going to be more expensive than the time-share, and in a sense more limiting. You won't have the advantage of falling back on the exchange programs that are open to the time-share properties.

How you buy will determine which kind of property you have. So look over these seven critical factors governing second homes.

1. Your goal. What do you want to accomplish in buying a second home? Is it a bachelor pad for getting away from the local scene when you want to, or do you really dig the location and think about moving there someday? The investment in a second home should follow a good understanding of what you want to do. The emotional purchase that comes when you are on a holiday and see a home that just knocks you flat is okay, but it's not as good as a cold sober look at what in the hell you are doing buying a home a thousand miles from where you live. There are a million good reasons for doing this, and all you need is to be sure you have picked the one that best represents your goals. Don't rationalize away these good reasons with "I'm sure it will be a good investment" when the fact of the matter is you want to get a place in the country because you like to ride horses.

2. Be aware of all the advantages and disadvantages. These will be specific and oriented to you only. What is an advantage to you might be a disadvantage to me. The goal for buying will give you a clear direction as to what the advantages are, of course. But this is where most people go wrong in the second-home market. They get sold a property, tying in emotion and a beautiful day; the goal isn't clear, and therefore the advantages and disadvantages are all mixed up. The economics must be in your favor right from the start. You don't want to get into a purchase program that you can't handle. Even if the property looks like it can be rented out, you can't always count on that to carry the load. By the time you finish this chapter you will have a good idea what advantages and disadvantages will pertain to you.

3. Location. Start with the geographic location first. Is it where you want to own? I mean, really. It is possible that five miles down the road there is a place you will like better. Have you looked around?

What about the actual physical location of the property? Have you spent much time there? How about the neighbors? All this is very important. You don't want to buy and move in to find there is a railroad track behind the house that is heavily used from midnight on.

Avoid buying from a developer who takes you to his project in the mountains and doesn't let you check out the competition. If he has the best product, he'll want you to see his competition.

4. The real estate itself. Don't ever buy an improved property that hasn't been inspected by qualified people to advise you on the condition of the structural, electrical, mechanical, and plumbing elements. There may be other factors you will want to have inspected, depending on the part of the world in which it is situated. Seawalls, docks, retaining walls, snow roofs, and the like all require special eyes to spot problems that may not be evident.

And what about the land? Are the boundaries clearly marked? Is there a recent survey that indicates there are no encroachments on the boundaries? It's possible a neighbor may have inadvertently constructed a driveway or a wall or a building over on your side of the line. The time to get that straight is before you buy, not after, as legal problems may be more costly than you want.

What about the title? A lawyer may be needed to check that out for you to assure that the seller delivered you a title that is good and marketable, and I'd recommend you also insure that title just in case. Title insurance is not expensive, and if you have a lawyer close the property for you he will include the title insurance at a very nominal cost. Some lawyers will close for you at the cost of the title insurance alone.

By the way, if you decide to rent with option to buy, make sure you have done everything you would do if you were going to buy—all inspections, all title work, surveys, etc. If there is any problem, you want to be sure you have found it before you get in on a lease. There must be a direct connection between your goal and the real estate. If the real estate part of the deal doesn't serve your goal, then you've picked the wrong property.

5. The economics of the deal. This is the point where one deal might look better than another. How much down, what is the payout on the balance—that sort of thing. Everything is relative in this, so if you find one property much more suitable than another, you can afford to pay a bit more (or a lot more). You will never find two identical properties, due to the locations. Two models of the same floor plan will look different on different lots. So it boils down to the dollars and cents in that type of comparison if you are willing to give on other factors. To move away from the best view and take an inside lot instead of a waterfront lot will save you lots of money, but in the long run the trade-off may not be worth the savings.

6. Investment potential. Whatever you buy should have some positive investment potential. Never buy anything that has a negative potential unless you just like throwing your money down the drain. Sometimes it may be hard to tell if there is a positive potential or not, and that's where careful attention to the trends comes in.

The aspects of an ideal investment discussed in the previous chapter apply to resort properties, both time-share as well as full ownership. You need to look for properties that meet as many of these criteria as possible.

Resort properties, however, have some peculiar aspects about them that can make their potential either great or not so great. Such as: A recreational industry that goes down the tube. With the changing times and with gasoline selling for $2 per gallon, you can bet things will change. Major population growth in nearby areas is bound to make the recreational area more popular. That will increase demand and raise prices.

7. The fun factor. Investing in a recreational anything must have a very high fun factor. That is the reason you are buying this thing in the first place, so don't let it get away from you.

The fun factor is the realization that sometimes you should do things for the fun of it rather than for the dollars and cents of it. If you like it and can afford it, and you can have some enjoyment out of it, then I'd say that is a major criterion in defining a good buy.

Don't ever underestimate this fun factor. After all, life is too short not to enjoy it. Right?

Putting it all together, recreational property can be a good alternative. I look back over the years and see the thousands of Canadians and New Yorkers who have been buying recreational properties in Florida. For them the seven factors have panned out nicely. Big profits have been made in the later resale of these properties.

Nearly all kinds of living accommodation have gone up in

value over the last ten years, so it is doubtful that anyone has made a bad investment—if they followed the seven critical factors I've just given you. Bad investments are generally those investments which in hindsight turn out to produce a loss, or not as much profit as you thought you should have made. Often the sale of the recreational property is done with less prudence than the purchase of the property. "Hell, sell the damn thing. I've only used it once in the past eighteen months and it is costing me an arm and leg to keep it." This sort of thinking prevails in the recreational property market and sometimes results in sales at less than best value.

How and When You Should Dispose of Recreational Property to Get Top Dollar

THE first thing to decide is whether you want to sell. The fact that you haven't been using the facility as much as you had intended doesn't mean you should sell. There are other options you should consider.

First, you might decide to do a private time-share. This was described in the previous chapter and can be put into play nicely on a property you already own. After all, you know more about this property than anyone else. That should help you put together an effective sales package. Keeping a piece of the action after you have sold at a nice profit isn't a bad way to go.

Or you might want to exchange it for something else. Keep in mind that there is a big market for second homes and there are many people who feel as you do. After they have bought a place and had the use or lack of use of it for several years and are ripe for another place, a change of pace, why not exchange with them?

The time of the year you sell, assuming you have come to the conclusion that you want to sell, is when people are thinking about going to this place. Summer resort areas sell best in the late spring, when people are thinking about their holiday. Winter resorts do well in late summer and early fall. To take advantage of this, isolate your market and the buying times and concentrate on selling when selling is ripe for your property. If you are listing the property with a broker, govern yourself by this cycle and plan on getting the best price by listing prior to the season, not just after.

Should You Sell It Yourself or Use an Agent?

The best advice I can give you is to list it exclusively with a salesman who gets turned on by the property and has the enthusiasm to sell it. In the first place, it is unlikely you will be able to get the best market by yourself. If you have a recreational property away from your home town, then you don't have the capability to handle the sale long distance (no matter what Ma Bell will tell you). The live-wire salesman on the spot or in the market area will be the best bet. He will earn his commission.

Some of you will want to try to sell your own property. If you are in an area that is so hot that all you have to do is hang a sign on the tree in the front yard, why not give it a try? But follow these tips on selling your own property.

Have the Facts at Your Fingertips

Have the up-to-date facts and figures on the property. Nothing is more frustrating to a seller (or a buyer) than having the wrong answers when the right ones are needed. Follow this list for the basic facts to have.

- Exact size of the property.
- Year the improvements were built or added on.
- Public utilities available or not available.
- Inventory or general list of items that go or don't go with the improvements.
- Price. Quote only one price to everyone. The best trick you can learn is to figure on paying a commission and include it in your price. If a broker calls, quote that one price. Always one price.

• The amount you will take down.

• The existing mortgage—its terms, interest rate, and how many years it has to go. Have a copy of the mortgage handy.

• Purchase-money mortgages you will hold. Spell them out clearly.

• Restrictions, if any. Know what they are and who imposes them.

• Benefits. Make a list of all the benefits to any potential buyer, even if these benefits don't apply to you. You aren't buying, you are selling.

• Know the disadvantages. Try to be realistic about them. See what they are and think of advantages to offset them.

Learn to Qualify the Buyer

You aren't going to make another sale somewhere else, as a professional salesman might if the buyer doesn't like your property, but you don't want to waste your time dealing with a buyer who can't or won't buy your property because of some outside reason. (Such as he can't afford your price.) Also, you don't want to have someone going through your home or property who is looking to case the place for some illicit motive.

There are five qualifying questions you can ask prospective buyers to help you tell if they are wasting your time:

1. "Does this property suit you as it is, or would you need to make any changes?" This will aid you in determining how the prospective buyers like the property as you are showing them through. If the results are positive you will hear "It's fine as it is" or "I think I'd want to add a pool over there." The negative response is "I don't know. Sure is a pretty day, isn't it?"

2. "Would you be using your own furniture?" or "Can you use what's in the house?" You are looking for a mental commitment that they like the property.

3. "Do you need to move in soon?" You want to find out their time element to buy. If they have lots of time, they may not be pressed to make a deal and may just be looking around for a bargain.

4. "Do you want to take over my existing mortgage?" An-

other commitment is being called for here, and at the same time you will get into the financing end of the transaction.

5. "Would you like me to draw up the deal?" Get right to the point if everything is moving along nicely. Ask them to buy.

Be creative. You can change the questions to suit your prospective buyer and yourself.

Negotiating

Recognize that it is tough; negotiating your own deal is a very tough row to hoe. The reason is simple. You are emotionally tied in. The buyer is emotionally tied in. There is no mediator here, and that makes it hard. ("What in the hell do you mean you don't like my blue and yellow carpets! My wife picked them out . . .") You face a buyer who won't trust everything you say because you are too closely connected to this deal. The professional salesman doesn't get so emotionally involved and can be eager to put it together with both of you.

Don't Be Anxious, but Show Reason for Some Urgency

If you are desperate to make a deal, you need to seek a true pro in this area. If you are out to see what you can do, then you need to tell the prospective buyer something like "Mr. Buyer, I'm glad you are showing interest in my property. I've made the decision to sell and I've priced the property with that in mind. I believe I've given you all the facts on this property, but if there are any changes I'll give them to you." (This leaves you open to contact the buyer for any other facts you may have neglected to give.) "I realize dealing with an owner can be difficult sometimes. Please be candid with me, as I want to conclude this transaction and move on to other things. I am a sincere seller, have placed a fair market price based on the facts of this marketplace, and believe I'm reasonable in my terms."

Be ready for something like this: "You've got to be kidding! Mr. Seller, I've looked at fifty properties better than this one this week, and you're the top price yet. If you want to sell, then get your price in line."

Don't Blow Your Cool

Negotiating is not difficult as long as you can put yourself in the middle. "I have a partner who needs to be convinced," you could say. "I really want to sell, but he is firm on the price." In this way you can be the cool one and try to work the deal out for the buyer. If you separate yourself from being the seller, you will have an easier time nailing down the sale at the top price.

If you don't have a partner and are the sole owner, you may have a problem. Remember, many buyers want to get the better of a deal. You can't negotiate and win in those situations if you are dealing one on one. You need a separation of authority. "I guess I'd take the deal after all, Mr. Buyer, but my partner just won't give in and says we need another $5,000 to clinch the deal. I might be able to convince my partner to drop that to $4,000. What do you say?"

Don't Give In to the "Cut of the Commission" Bit

You have been quoting one price, and that's as it should be. Then along comes a guy who tells you, "I'll pay your price, but after all, since there's no agent here, drop the price by the amount of a commission."

If you give in here you have lost the advantage of selling the property yourself and have wasted a lot of time and effort. If you are able to sell your own property, you deserve the commission. It is harder for you than for a professional real estate salesman.

Know Your Options

All good salesmen know more than one closing option. If you expect to get the best deal for yourself, you've got to know all the options you have. The more there are, the better the chance of clinching a favorable deal. This book is your source for these options; you can always turn to it for guidance and advice.

Options are your way of making a deal come together when it looks like it is about to fall apart.

5 Major Things That Turn a Buyer Off

1. Price. If the price isn't within the buyer's budget, then there isn't a whole lot you can do. However, it is possible the buyer doesn't really know if he can afford the property. I'm constantly surprised to learn that many people don't know what they can afford. Some overspend their budget; others are too conservative.

2. Terms. Much the same as the price, but not quite. Terms can be more flexible if you are also. The fact that you need a lot of cash at closing doesn't mean the buyer has to pay all cash. There go the options again. Know them and you can overcome a lot of these turnoffs.

3. Sloppy entryway. Remember, the first impression is the most important, and you get only one shot at that. A messy walkway or a front door in need of paint will create an attitude that will carry through in a lower offer or no offer at all. This is very easy to rectify, so attend to it before you put the property on the market.

4. Housekeeping that is strictly the Three Stooges. I don't care what kind of property it is, the neat, clean, and well-cared-for property will command more attention and interest and a higher price than the same exact property that is a mess. Smudged walls, cigarette butts and ashes in every ashtray, a kitchen that is full of dirty dishes, a bedroom with dirty clothes piled high in a stinking heap, and the like won't make things go easy for you. The remedy is a little elbow grease.

5. Animal and other smells. When you have dogs or cats or hamsters, anything that flies, runs, walks, or crawls, you will have smells. Some can turn off the most ardent buyer.

"My god, what in hell is that stench coming from this room?"

"What stench? I don't smell anything."

"Good lord, you must smell that! It's like an old wet raccoon fur coat."

"Oh, *that*."

Most owners of animals live with the old-wet-raccoon-fur smell so long they even don't realize it is there. But if these sweet little creatures live on your property, you better believe they make an odor. (Snake lovers, don't send me any letters about how snakes don't smell; the waste from the nicest of all cobras stinks.)

The remedy isn't easy. Opening up the property before showing will help, as will air sprays and the like. The only true solution is to remove the source and all its contaminants. This may be something you will have to do in stages or only partially.

Ah, "animals" includes you, too. I'm referring to the smoker of tobacco and more exotic stuff. Sometimes these odors never seem to leave a room.

I visited a nice home one day and the owner, a woman in her late fifties, met me at the door. The smell of coconut incense wafted out the front door and nearly knocked me off the step. Later, when I got to know her better, she showed me her collection of pipes. It would have made any head shop envious.

Remedy: Remove the source, or find buyers who like coconut incense.

Recreational properties are out there for everyone to own. They can be a fun way to invest in real estate and enjoy yourself at the same time. When you own your own home by the sea, or apartment in Vail, you can use it and rent it out the rest of the time. (That is, if the condo association or home association permits.)

If you followed the advice in this chapter, you will find that well-selected recreational properties will go up in value faster than the average year-round property. After all, we are living in a society of leisure time, and we are all seeking more and better ways to use that time. Why not take advantage of this trend and invest in your own getaway?

17

The Ins and Outs of Vacant Land

INVESTING in income-producing property can be a solid way to make big profits. However, the only fast and proven way I know to make it really big is through investing in vacant land.

No real estate investment is more forgiving of your mistakes than vacant land. It doesn't call you up in the middle of the night and make you go over to fix a broken window; it doesn't have the monumental people problems that exist with most other real estate. Vacant land just sits there, going up in value (you hope), making money for you all the while.

There are thousands of stories of how investors have made money investing in vacant land. So many, in fact, you may get the idea that all you have to do to make money is get in your car and drive around until you see a lot and buy it. Another method that may seem equally effective is the DTAM system (Dart Thrown At Map)—you buy whatever the dart hits. These methods will work only some of the time.

Modern society has invented ways to keep speculation in land risky, and the purpose of this chapter is to show you the benefits you can reap as well as the hazards in wait for you in buying vacant land. Investing in vacant land has obvious advantages, and if you are ready and capable, you will find the profits out there waiting.

SUCCESS STORIES TO WHET YOUR APPETITE

WHEN I just started in real estate I didn't know much about investing. I was an eager salesman who tried my best to sell what I had listed. In that process I decided that if I was going to be successful in selling real estate, I would have to become an owner myself. (The old story of using your own product works in real estate as in any other profession.)

One of the first investments I made required $5,000 down on a half interest in a four-acre tract of land. Within two years after purchase, I had paid off the balance of the mortgage. I now had about $20,000 invested and I owned one-half of the deal. The land was sold for $385,000 in the third year, with $100,000 down. The buyer made two interest-only payments on the mortgage, throwing in another $45,000 to my pot. At this point my $20,000 investment had returned me $72,000 in cash and the buyer owed me another $142,500 as my half of the deal. The owner went bankrupt due to outside business problems, and my partner and I made a deal to get ownership of the land back. Part of the land is now leased on a short-term basis at $10,000 per year, and the rest is in negotiation for lease at $40,000 per year. The present value of the land is well in excess of $600,000 and should go to over a million in a couple of years.

Why? Because in the five years since all this took place, new roads have come in, new cities have sprung up all around the area, and what was on the outskirts is now right in the middle of it all.

My original investment of $20,000 has been returned many times now and I still have my half interest in the land. Once the property is fully leased I will get more income each year than I paid for the property. When the full value of the land is reached in a few years, I will reexamine the leases and put the land to more productive use by building on it or leasing for other uses.

You might think I stole this land from the sellers, right? Wrong. Over the years I've developed a method of doing business from which I never vary. I never buy into any real estate that I don't offer to someone else first, often offering the deal to dozens of clients before acting on my promise that "if you don't want to buy, I plan to."

I do this for two reasons. First, I've known real estate salesmen and brokers who used their own profession to scout out good deals for themselves. I had decided I wanted to be unique in that area and deal for my clients first. Second, I discovered (what I thought would happen) that by offering a truly good deal to my clients, I was selling a lot of real estate. I discovered I learned more about the land because I was looking at something I wanted to buy.

In offering these truly good deals around, taking advantage of the occasional deal that wasn't picked up by my clients, I could go back to those clients later on after I'd made a big profit on the deal and say: "Remember that site I showed you last year? I bought it as I said I was going to. I've just made a 2,000% profit on a deal I first offered to you. Now come with me this afternoon and let me show you something else I'm looking at. I'll give you a shot at it before I buy." What do you think the reaction was?

In the case of the land I was telling you about, I showed it to at least twenty clients over a two-month period. I ran ads and did everything I could do to convince people that it was a winner. The agent who had it listed had a large sign on the site and was also running ads. The opportunity was there for anyone to take. It wasn't something I had ferreted out that no one knew anything about. The knock of opportunity was at the door, unanswered until I bought the land.

Another deal was a single-family lot I was interested in. I showed it to many clients over several weeks before taking an option on the land for one year. (I'll give you the option technique later on; it's great.) I knew the value was going up fast, but I didn't have the cash to buy right then. I gave the owner $5,000 for one year against the purchase price of $30,000. If I bought within the year, the option money counted as part of the $30,000, and all I had to do was give her another $25,000. If I didn't buy, I lost the $5,000.

I scraped up the other $25,000 by year end, and one week

after I had closed I was offered $60,000 for the lot. Five years after that, the lot would cost over $180,000.

This lot was the second-to-last vacant lot in one of Fort Lauderdale's oldest waterfront subdivisions. The lot was plainly visible. It had been owned by the same woman for over twenty years (she paid $5,000 for it). Every real estate broker and salesman in town had the same information that I had. The point? Most pots of gold are right out in the open for you to see. Your gold is in your back yard. All you have to do is open your eyes.

5 Rules for Investing in Vacant Land

1. Not everything goes up in value fast enough. Realize that not all land is going to go up in value at all, and even if it does, the cost of holding the land might eat up your profit.

While this might sound like a really big disadvantage, it is the major reason you will be successful. This is because many people don't know this rule and will buy land without following the prudent rules of investing or the trends of the area. A steady market in all vacant land, therefore, creates a special market for the wisely chosen land.

Land investment is risky, as I have said, and you must recognize that you can lose. Nothing is sure in real estate. The best you can do is eliminate as much risk as possible.

2. Everything that will happen already has happened. Some land goes up not at all, other land lags behind cost, and some takes off. Learn to see why these events occur. What caused them to happen in your area once before will cause them to happen again.

If there is anything we can learn from history, it's that we don't learn from history. I've heard hundreds of clients say, "Jack, I wish I'd have known of those investments you told me about where everyone made a killing. Too bad you can't make those kinds of investments now," or "I could have bought that corner back when it was only $10,000—now it's a million dollars."

Learn from history. Nothing happens in real estate that can't be predicted at a close range. Follow the trends, because they are the guide to profits.

3. Don't buy for the long haul unless you can carry the haul a long way. Many speculators have gone down the tube buying land that was a long way off (more than ten years) from reaching its value potential. They do this hoping beyond hope that luck will come their way and the long haul will arrive sooner.

The way things work is this: If you buy something that you feel will mature in a few years, it probably will take longer on the average—but it might jump right into your lap and be hot overnight. Generally the long-haul stuff is clearly a long haul. No roads are planned which would make a difference; no new airports or factories to open up the area. These are the kinds of elements that make speculation in vacant land that is cheap and on the verge of opening up a good buy, but long hauls are just that, so avoid them unless you've got good carrying power.

4. Stick close to home. One of the real joys of vacant land is driving over to it every now and then, walking out on it, and saying to a friend, "I own this."

Staying close to home will give you the advantage over the out-of-towner. Take Florida, for example. The investor who makes the most money isn't the home-towner, but the outsider who comes into town every now and then. With the perspective given by contrast, the out-of-towner sees opportunity while the majority of home-towners complain about growth.

Your advantage is that you can see what is going on in detail, but you must know what to look for and how to see it.

The details you have to look for are the little things, such as the political scene that is shifting in favor of a new road bond issue that will open up one area and bypass another. Or a new mayor who is strongly in favor of the new industrial park or the stadium or whatever that is going to have great impact on one or more areas in town. There are things that the out-of-towner has to rely on his broker to inform him about, and that process can be slow. You can act right away. Buy now, profit later.

As a home-towner you have the best chance to finance through the local bank if you need to, and can deal year-round, making offers on a greater variety of properties in searching for the right deal at the terms you want.

5. The profit potential is greatest in vacant land. No other form of real estate investment offers the tremendous potential of vacant land. All other investments—homes, apartments, office buildings, industrial buildings, whatever—are tied to one or both of two economic criteria that determine the maximum value at any given time. These criteria are the economic approach and the replacement approach.

In the economic approach, you simply take the income and expenses and arrive at the bottom line. Value is then based on that bottom line to the extent of how much you are willing to invest to get that return. There is a limit to the extent to which you can increase the bottom line, as you must increase rent to do this. Some properties, such as hotels and older apartment buildings and some commercial buildings, are good buys because the income is in for a large increase in the near future. However, for the most part the amount of increase available is limited to what the rental market will bear.

The replacement approach will give you a more dramatic view of values, as the cost of replacement has continued to skyrocket. If you can buy a property for half the price of what it would cost to build, you have found a good buy. But how much profit potential is there, 100% or 200%? Perhaps, but there is a limit to that potential, and it is rarely so great that the age and the inconvenience of having to redo the existing building don't take away somewhat from the potential.

A Dollar Today, a Million Tomorrow

If you look at the biographies of millionaires, you will note that most of them got that way because of the vacant land they bought and later sold or developed. The money made in getting the wagon rolling then enabled them to branch out into tax shelter kinds of real estate to keep the money made in vacant land.

Those five rules will get you thinking in the right direction when it comes to vacant land. Land is the easiest for you to buy, as frequently it can be bought with little or nothing down. You will find sellers who are highly motivated and will hold paper, thus enabling you to have good financing without having to go to the banks and pay high interest rates.

I bought twenty acres in the North Carolina mountains in an area I used to visit quite often. It was a cheap land buy, as I paid only $120 per acre, for a total of $2,400. I kept the land for two years and sold it for $18,000. No income deal would have been so productive.

Another land deal was a group investment I got into. Twenty of us bought a tract of three hundred acres. We got fantastic terms and paid $2,000 per acre, with about $100,000 down. I put $5,000 into the deal, and before the first year was out we had begun to sell land off at $5,000 per acre. We later sold land at $6,000 per acre to the same person we had bought the three hundred acres from. Income from the sales brought in more than was needed to carry the mortgage, and the ultimate profit was tremendous.

The value of land can jump overnight, climbing to heights you would never imagine. It does so on a basis that is simple to understand and not impossible to predict. The variables are few and predictable.

But land is still speculative. For one thing, your profit can disappear with a vote of the city council or other people who have control over the use of the land. These include zoning officials, county commissions, and land planners, who will often arbitrarily rezone you out of existence, or make the use of your land so expensive that a buyer has to have his head examined to consider paying your price.

Let's look at the things that affect the value of vacant property.

5 Five Things That Can Make the Value Go Up or Down

1. Growth. This generally has a positive effect on the value of the land. When the growth is moving in the direction of the land or encompassing it, the need for more vacant land increases within the area. This increase in demand increases the value. One detrimental aspect of this growth is the viewpoint that too much of any good thing isn't so good anymore. Look at the inner cities where the growth has come and gone. If the value potential isn't taken advantage of early in this cycle, you can be left with a vacant lot next to a run-down building, the value lessened because of excessive and matured growth.

2. Traffic routes. I always pay a lot of attention to what the traffic engineers tell me when I make my periodic visits to the city and county agencies in my area. They are looking at the needs of the counties and cities on a long-range basis and will know before the general public what roads are in line to be widened, cut through, or developed. They know where bridges and overpasses are to be built. All these things will have an impact on the value of the land that these roads now serve or will serve in the future.

Interestingly, most people don't pay much attention to the announcement of new roads and the like. Land values don't jump up just because the land is on a road right-of-way that was announced in the evening paper. The value eases up slowly as the professional investor who knows and understands this magic starts buying in. When the roadwork starts, much of the land is already in the hands of the new investor and asking prices skyrocket. But even then there is generally tremendous room for improvement in the values.

The terrible slowdown occurs during road construction. The value and the market don't seem to go anywhere. Interest in the area frequently wanes rather than increases at this moment, but this is the lull before the storm, as the value will go up again once the road is open for traffic. The increase of traffic in an area benefits commercial properties more than most other kinds, and your ultimate use of the site will depend on the need for different commercial services.

Sometimes increased traffic can decrease the value of a property, as would be the case if a superhighway were cut through a private and secluded residential neighborhood of expensive homes. Or a major roadway is so busy that the contractors close off median cuts, and while there is a lot of traffic, access to the businesses is so restricted that patrons can't make their way to the location. Should this occur, the use of the site would be limited, and so would the profit. Fortunately for the investor, the traffic ways are easy to follow and take so long to develop that long-range planning gives you a place to start when it comes to land.

3. Zoning and use. This covers the broad topic of the use of the land. Whatever it is zoned for will establish how you can use the land. When it comes to ultimate value, the final user of the land will establish the maximum price by purchasing the site. Thus, the ultimate use will be greatly determined by the zoning at that time.

Zoning ordinances are devised by counties and cities. Depending on where the land is situated, it is possible to come under the control of both governing bodies. The current trend is a standardization of land use within counties, and a rash of land plans are being developed around the country. These comprehensive and total-picture plans are an attempt to regulate the future growth of cities and counties. It is the opportunity for the governing bodies to say, "Hey, we've made lots of mistakes with the developed part of this county and we don't want to make any more." The problem is, land plans are rarely mistakeless. For example, in some of the recent South Florida land plans I saw business-zoned land next to industrial land (a factory already there) get rezoned down to low-density apartment use. This down-zoning from a more logical business use reduced the value of the land, and there was little the property owner could do.

I know, because it was my land, and I fought and squirmed through a half dozen town council hearings. I lost simply because every time I'd say something several hundred community members would shout me down. One of the hazards with vacant land is that when everything builds up around you, those who move in around your vacant land want it kept vacant.

A property owner doesn't even have to be notified of these zoning changes, in most cases. All that happens in most cases is that the county or city runs a few ads in the newspaper. You've seen the kind—a million words so small you can't read them, and if you did it would say something like this:

> . . . is holding a public hearing to discuss the pros and cons of the new countywide Land Use Plan, and in particular, how the proposed changes in land use will affect those areas which are located in Township 30 South Range 72 West all Sections except 7, 12, and 33 . . .

Ah, so now you know exactly if your land is in trouble, right?

I'm spending a lot of time on this one topic because it is important if you plan to invest in vacant land. Your right to the free use of your land doesn't exist. You must adhere to setbacks, provide this or that, build in accordance with building codes, get permits, pay taxes, give easements, tear down if they tell you to, give up if they demand it. These are the restrictions on your property rights, and those rights are being snipped and chipped away by nearly every city council and county commission in existence. If you own vacant land, you may be aware of this and want to do something about it. There is something you can do: Don't vote into power those people who are the snippers and the chippers of your property rights.

The land plan and the ability to snatch away your zoning is just the latest of government efforts to reduce your influence over what is yours (your land). Therefore, this must be watched carefully. Before you buy you should get a feeling for how the trends are moving in that community. Of course, things might be really smooth and positive when you buy and then go sour quickly. There is nothing you can do in those cases except make a decision to hold and wait it out or sell before it gets worse.

Don't believe in logic being on your side. I've seen some of the most illogical things come out of city council meetings. Land planners select uses for sites they haven't seen; zoning ordinances are voted in that can't be enforced or are ridiculous.

". . . In all new construction the owner is required to put in at his expense a five-foot sidewalk along the property line that borders a public street . . ." No matter if you discover that there are only a handful of vacant lots in the city and that none of the other homes have sidewalks. It was a good ordinance, only a little late.

Zoning and use can be changed in your favor as well, of course, and I've been successful at that task many times. However, it is growing more difficult all the time, and everything must be very carefully examined and weighed before you attempt it.

Keep in mind that knowing the zoning pitfalls gives you the edge. It is possible for one city in a county to be more lenient toward property owners' rights than others, and investing in the lenient area instead of the restrictive area can be more profitable as well as less frustrating.

4. Location. "Get me a site near . . ."; "I want to be on Commercial Boulevard between U.S. 1 and Bayview Drive." These are users talking, the guys who will pay you a fortune for that land you bought. Location is the major factor in real estate. It is mitigated only by use. "I need five acres, but I don't need to be on Commercial Boulevard." This user is willing to trade off a prime site for a less expensive location because this site doesn't fit his needs. This doesn't reduce the value of the Commercial Boulevard location unless all buyers make a similar choice.

How to Choose a Good Location

If you had a crystal ball and could look into the future, ascertaining all the prime and desirable locations (based on their future use or proximity to other uses), you would become rich, right?

Well, you can do exactly that, with only a little less accuracy. Trends are the first key. What is planned is the second. The long-range thinking of the governing bodies of any area will point to areas of town that are going to grow and prosper more than others. Become a student of areas in the country that have grown and prospered. It is possible to find towns that in the '20s grew and prospered, just like towns in the '30s, and then like others in the '40s, and so on. History repeats itself time and time again. Specific things to look for are listed at the end of this chapter.

Location is so important that one tract of land can be valued many times over another which may be just around the corner.

Your ability to recognize what will be a good location will give you the edge over the average investor. Pay careful attention to your home town's growth and watch the patterns. These are some of the things that will create prime locations out of swamps.

5. Your ability to become a user. If you are simply a speculator in land, you must be careful to sell it before it reaches the top of its value. The reason for selling early is to avoid getting caught at the top. This occurs because land reaches a point in its vacant history when the most likely buyer is someone ready to use it—build something on it, dig it up, whatever.

I advise speculators, who are not in a position to consider the ultimate use of the land they have bought, to sell when there is plenty of time left for the buyer to get some profit of his own.

When you are selling an investment that will do well for the buyer (but not as well as for you), you will get the best and most favorable terms to you in the sale. Wait a bit too long and you can sit holding the land longer than you anticipated, with greater cost than you had hoped, with mortgages requiring your capital input, rather than having made a clean sale a few months before.

You risk having time work against you by passing up a good profit when you aren't sure there is a better one around the corner. This doesn't mean you should sit back and wait. I've done that many times and been glad of it. But it was for a solid reason, not a whim. When you see the trends in your favor and you can afford to hold on and wait for the greater profit, then do exactly that.

On the other hand, if you can become the user yourself, then the hold isn't painful at all. You can ride the land right up to the market, then decide if you want to sell or take advantage of the ultimate and maximum profits. I've bought lots that I was fully prepared to build on, if I needed to, only to sell them to builders when the value topped out. I've seen many investors buy with the intention of selling for a future profit, only to go ahead and build when the trends of the area indicated that construction was going to be much more profitable than any future sale.

Frequently you will have such great appreciation in the land that you can come out ahead of the deal by building instead of selling. For example, Richard purchased fifty acres for $1,500 per acre. He held the land for five years, at which point he could sell it for $7,500 per acre. He felt the trends were in his favor to develop rather than sell, so he went to a lender and told them he had land worth nearly $400,000 and asked would they lend him $200,000 to develop the site into 100 lots? He showed them the sales potential on the lots in the current market was over $8,500 per lot, so that the loan would be amply secured.

The development went nicely, and Richard took another look at the project and decided not to sell just the lots, but to sell homes on the lots. He went into partnership with one of the area's best home builders, and ended up selling the lots to their joint venture at $10,000 per lot, giving him an average of $2,500 more on each newly built home as his share of the venture. He had invested $75,000 in fifty acres, and in about five years he had $1,250,000 to show for it. Not bad, Richard, not bad.

Don't fret if you aren't a user and can't see yourself ever doing what Richard did. He could have made a nice profit anytime along the way in that deal and no one would ever have questioned his motives for selling.

Okay, so now you have a good understanding of what can make the land more valuable to you, and at the same time see some of the pitfalls. What about finding those good locations that are going to go up in value?

13 Insider Tips

1. Always know the future road plans.

2. Converse from time to time with the long-range planners of all governing bodies that can have any effect on the land or its use in the area you are anticipating buying.

3. Attend one or more city council meetings to get the feel of the local sentiment (county, town, whatever).

4. Know everything you can about the zoning ordinances of the area.

5. Know the status of the land plan for the area. Is there one? What is it? Is there one planned?

6. **Check the land records** (or have your broker do it for you) **to see who is buying and who is selling.** This information can be most interesting and can lead to your getting in on something only the "big boys" knew about ahead of you.

7. **Select sites that are in sizes that are more valuable to a user.** Not enough road frontage and too deep isn't good even if the square-foot price is less than that of the tract next door. Road frontage at the right depth for a shopping center is more valuable.

8. **Choose sites with public utilities either already in or coming in over sites without them, if everything else is nearly equal.**

9. **In small commercial sites, the far corner is best.** (The far corner is the corner opposite the cross street on your right as you drive on the more important of the two streets.) There will be two such corners and their value will be more than that of the other two. This is because these corners are easier to turn in to by cars and are more visible.

10. **Buy any land that can pay for itself.** Farmland can be leased to pay the mortgage, for example, or a vacant commercial lot used as a parking lot or open storage for truckers.

11. **Buy with option contracts to give yourself time to see what is happening without risking much or anything.** (See Chapter 21.)

12. **Have a user already lined up and build to his specifications.** (Easy to do if you work at it a little.)

13. **Don't ever assume that because it's openly on the market, it isn't a good buy.** I've made my best and most profitable deals with land that had been on the market for a long time, passed over by all the investors who didn't see the potential I did.

Take these tips to heart and you will not only reduce your risk, you will increase your profit potential. Land is the greatest of all investments. It is the classic of all trade-offs in that its appreciation can carry you on to the top of the heap in a very short time. The best part is that the bottom side of the deal isn't that tough to swallow, and your land is clearly in sight all the time.

18

Fixing Up and Renting Commercial Buildings

EVERYTHING DEPENDS on the market in your own area, of course, but the trends across the country indicate a need for more commercial rental space. Office buildings are at a premium in most cities, and that means the rental vacancy factor is very low. With high occupancy factors, the rents will start to ease up to higher levels, increasing the value at the same time.

All rents are matched against the current market for the type and category and location of the property. One tenant will pay $10 per square foot for one location and not half as much for another. At similar locations the age and condition of the building itself will determine to some degree the rent which can be collected.

This is where you can make trends work for you.

The move back to the inner city will mean a greater demand for office space. It is simply a matter of economics. The cost of new construction is growing out of sight, and when you have to charge $15 or more per square foot for office space in order to cover the cost factor and get a reasonable return, refinishing older commercial buildings makes sense.

In addition, old buildings often command ideal locations. Some of the best locations in any commercial area are taken by the oldest buildings. In fact, they helped make the area what it is.

WHERE DO YOU START?

FIRST you need to know what to look for. The idea is to find a building that can be purchased on the basis of its present income, yet can easily be converted into a building producing much more income. As you increase the income you increase value by ten times that amount.

Therefore, you must know a great deal about the rental market in the various areas of your town. You will find this information by talking to property managers of different office buildings or management companies you find in the phone book. Tell them you are doing a study of the rental market because you are interested in buying a building in the area. Most of the professional management companies will be glad to spend some time with you on this topic, because you might be a client of theirs in the near future.

Drive around and take down for-rent-sign numbers and ask to speak to the rental agent for any building you might want to check out.

Be sure you compare apples with apples when it comes to rent. This means the tenant is apt to get everything for his rent payment, such as janitorial service, electricity, water, and the like. Some buildings will even paint and replace carpet for a large tenant, as well as partition off offices if needed. Other concepts of turnkey aren't so liberal, so when the rental agent tells you, "Oh, this is a turnkey rental," be sure to question him on what is *not* included as well as what items are specifically included.

Other leases are net leases (or net, net; or net, net, net, depending on the area); this generally refers to the fact that the tenant will be responsible for everything from maintenance of the building's exterior to real estate taxes. When referring to any lease that has the term *net* in it, always make sure you distinguish what items the landlord will pay.

To aid you in arriving at equal comparisons of rental build-

SERVICES AND BENEFITS IN COMMERCIAL LEASES

	MOST COMMON IN TURNKEY LEASES	USUALLY OPTIONAL	TYPICAL NET, NET
Answering service		X	Tenant pays
Janitorial service	Included		Tenant pays
Electricity	Included		Tenant pays
Water	Included		Tenant pays
Private bathroom	Varies		Tenant pays
Air-conditioning apparatus	Included		Varies
Carpets	Included		Tenant pays
Private parking		X	Tenant pays
Covered parking		X	Tenant pays
Guaranteed parking	Included		Tenant pays
Telephone service		X	Tenant pays
Exterior maintenance	Included		Tenant pays
Real estate taxes	Landlord pays		Tenant pays
Sewage charge	Landlord pays		Tenant pays
Rubbish charge	Landlord pays		Tenant pays
Common-area maintenance	Included		Tenant pays
Snow removal	Included		Tenant pays
Common tenant advertising		X	Tenant pays
Insurance	Tenant		Tenant pays
Partitioning/office space	Varies		Tenant pays
Interior painting	Varies		Tenant pays
Renewal options on lease	Varies		Landlord's option
Pro rata share of tax increase	Usual		Landlord's option
Cost-of-living increases		Landlord's option	Landlord's option
Rental commissions	Landlord pays		Varies
Interior repairs	Landlord pays		Tenant pays
Exterior repairs	Landlord pays		Tenant pays
Office or shop space	Included		Included
Free rent for a while	Varies		Varies

ings, I've given you a list of different things which may or may not be included in the lease. Leases may call for the tenant to pay these items separately, or provide them as options either free or for a charge.

7 Key Steps to Buying and Improving Commercial Buildings

1. Know the rental market for your area. This has already been covered, but can't be overemphasized. Learn the amount in rents the competition is about to get and what they have to give up or do to get their rents. If you find a building that seems to be averaging $10 per square foot in an area that commands only $7.50 on the average, look for the hidden "free rent" trick. Builders or new owners will frequently resort to a proven incentive to fill their empty building by offering "free rent" for the first several months. In exchange, the tenant pays a lease based on a higher per square foot. Over the course of the first twelve months the rent per square foot might average only $8, but the space got rented and an empty building was filled up. When the year is over, it is likely that the tenant will stay on, paying the same monthly rent ($10 per square foot). If you are not aware that this tactic is being used to get tenants, your statistics will be thrown off. So watch for this and know your rental market.

2. Have an idea of what it costs to fix up and repair buildings. If you aren't in this field now as a carpenter or other building tradesman, you may find experience the best teacher. I wouldn't let the fact that you don't have all the answers now stop you from making a move in this direction. You can make your offer to buy subject to your having a general contractor give you the quotes on fixing up the building. You might need time to have an architect make some drawings (keep it simple) to aid the contractor and you. Never buy a building that needs a lot of work without either knowing yourself how much it is going to cost or having a firm bid from a qualified general contractor.

3. Look for buildings that have low-paying tenants. If the leases are well below the rental market for the area, you have a potential winner. The condition of the building may account for the low rent, or it might be poor management. Both will have a devastating effect on the income picture.

Don't worry about poor management unless the leases are long and the tenants paying the low rent can't be removed or the leases converted to more reasonable (for the market) terms.

4. Don't get locked into long low-rent leases. The advantage of finding a building that has low rent and few, or better yet no, leases works for you. The reasons are clear. When you are going to upgrade rents you need to be able to get rid of tenants, if necessary. Also, low rents with unsavory tenants generally lessen the building's value. Thus, you have the best of everything going for you. The price will be more in line with a "bargain," and you will have a free hand in clearing out the old and low-paying tenants.

5. Look for buildings where the numbers work for you. This is the pure and simple economics of the deal. If you find a building of 7,000 square feet with a current rent roll of $28,000 and the market for the area is $8 per square foot, you can see an increase of the rent to $56,000. Assuming the value of the building (and its corresponding price) is based on the current economics, you should be about to buy the building for under $300,000. The value of the building with more current market rents would be around $575,000. This increase in value of $275,000 is one of the positive numbers to look for.

The deal becomes even more interesting when you realize that you probably can buy the building for only 25% or so down. This means you might invest $75,000 or less in this building, plus whatever you need to spend to revitalize it. Assume it takes $50,000 for this purpose.

New value		$575,000[a]
Cash down	$ 75,000	
Cash to remodel and rent up	50,000	
Mortgage owed to seller	225,000	
		350,000
Profit		$225,000

[a] Based on increased rent.

With a total cash investment of $125,000, your return on investment of $180%.

Once you have completed the building rent-up (or, prior to that, once you have a track record and the lenders love you), you can refinance. In this event you might look to a conventional loan at 80% of the new value. This would give you $460,000 in cash (less loan costs of about $10,000 or so). You could pay off the existing financing, keep the building, and have some cash left over.

Loan proceeds (mortgage amount)	$460,000[a]
Less loan cost	10,000
Net loan proceeds	450,000
Less existing financing	225,000
Cash in your pocket for the next deal	$225,000

[a] Based on new value.

This is about double what you started with, and you have a building you didn't have when you began.

6. Look for deals you can make on your terms. If you have little cash to put into the building, or need to conserve your cash, look for deals where the seller needs out, but not much cash. You will find the best of such deals in situations where the management problems are more than the current owner can handle. What is a problem for one person might be a piece of cake for another. It is possible that you won't be any better a manager than the last guy. Don't let that worry you. If you *know* that, you can make sure you have professional management. The worst mangement is generally the owner who gets caught in the trap of poor management. It goes like this: The owner thinks he'll save money by managing the property himself. When things go sour, he can't afford new management because there isn't enough income to pay for it.

You can find a deal for you if you aren't picky about the deal. Remember what I've said about money—all it does is enable you to have more selection in your purchases. When you are dealing with run-down properties you are with the most motivated sellers of them all. You don't find sellers with beautiful shopping centers who must sell tomorrow and will take nothing down.

7. **Be creative.** A good friend of mine recently took over one of those multi-cinema buildings. You know, the kind that has more than one theater under one roof. He discovered that the ceilings were high enough to accommodate a second floor under the roof, which just about doubled the space available for use. The cost to do this was much less than that of adding on a new floor or constructing a new building of the same size. Almost as though this were contagious, another friend of mine bought a dinner theater, a large building designed for live performances. It too had high ceilings, and is now an office building with a very high return.

You will find that some of the older run-down buildings have a lot of charm, and in fact may be built better than what is being put up today. Once you update them (paint and carpet will often be enough) you can make a quick turn and be on your way to another building.

My father and I bought a small frame building that was on a local commercial street. It hadn't always been a commercial zone, and the building was in fact a small home. It had been rented to two women who were moving out of town, leaving the owner with an unrented building. The house looked terrible, the yard had grown up all around it, and the inside and outside both were in pitiful shape.

The first thing we did was have everything taken out of the building. We gave some of the furniture to the Salvation Army (what they would take) and threw away the rest. The yard was cut and the few trees pruned. The whole house was painted inside and out, and back on the market she went.

This house was now a pretty little place, ideal for someone who wanted a freestanding office. It was partitioned with a nice entryway and several rooms (living room, kitchen, two bedrooms, etc). We sold it at a profit within a couple of weeks.

The deal was a small one. I put in $3,000 for my half of the down payment and about another $1,500 for the paint and the fix-up. I got back $9,500 for less than a month's work.

Warehouses make interesting restaurants, churches make ideal doctors' offices, and on and on. A fire station near my office was converted to a church. A church was converted to a school.

San Francisco, Atlanta, and Savannah are three places where there are countless examples of warehouses and factories which have been converted to shopping centers and office buildings. All it takes is some creative mindpower.

MULTIPLY YOUR INVESTMENTS BY TEN IN FOUR YEARS

Now that you have the keys and see what you have to do, get cracking. But do this only if you feel you are meant to do this sort of thing. It requires some dedication to numbers and a lot of hard work. You won't be lucky in this; you have to earn your profits. You can make mistakes easily by trying to shortcut the hard part, like doing your homework. Who needs to know about the rental market? You do.

So off you go. You've got the rental market down pat, and you scout some buildings. You make an offer or two, trying to feel out some owners. Never hesitate to do that, but keep an out for your own protection. Use the "inspection" escape or the "general contractor remodeling bid" clause to allow you time to inspect the property or to have your general contractor give you a firm bid on the cost of construction needed to make the building what you want it to be. If you don't approve the inspection or get a bid that makes the numbers work for you, back off. This will give you some negotiating experience, and the second time around you can do a better job of it.

Buying right is one of the most important parts of any transaction. That doesn't mean buying with the least cash, but simply making the best deal for your situation. Often that means paying cash (but you refinance and pull out of the deal, having little or no cash in it).

Remember how leverage works. If you put 20% down and the price goes up 20%, you have made a 100% profit on your investment. If you put 20% down and the price doubles, then you have multiplied your investment by six.

Multiplying your investment by ten or more within four years is hard work, but can be done if you apply yourself.

If you start with $10,000 in cash, you will have to look to properties you can get into with little or nothing down so that you can use your cash in the fix-up period. If you begin small you can quickly pyramid up into other properties.

The greater the loan-to-value ratio in your income property deals, the greater your yields are apt to be when you sell. You are leveraging up on borrowed money which stays fixed in the deal. If you buy a $100,000 property with $5,000 down (possible with run-down properties), for every $5,000 of increase in value, you double your money.

If you are able to make a quick turn on the property (sell it soon after making the improvement), you can take the cash and move on to another property and do it over again. Don't take the fast profit unless you are looking to move on to another deal. Taking the cash and spending it is counterproductive unless it will maintain the momentum of the deal. When you find the real gem you want to keep for the long haul, then keep it, as the profit will climb even higher.

The fast deal is available, however, and is most dramatic in run-down properties in moderately good or better areas. In fact, the greatest sudden increase in value usually comes right after you have finished with the fixing up. Mind you, often it is just paint that is needed.

Other times you will have to plow heavy money into a deal to see the true benefits. Stay away from these deals until you have lots of experience in fixing up properties.

If you can (and you can), get in on a property each year and double your invested capital each time. In four years you will have taken $5,000 and turned it into $50,000. Add to that the income earned from rents and the fact that you are preparing yourself for even better profits, and you can see how to become your own boss in a hurry.

19

Pyramid Yourself into a Fortune

OF ALL the buying and selling techniques that you can learn, the most spectacular is the pyramid. With this technique you can buy property that was otherwise not available to you because you didn't have cash to put down. The pyramid will provide a source of extra financing at terms you want and can pay back. It is a truly fantastic tool in the hands of the determined real estate investor.

Pyramids in Action

BRENT takes stock of his total assets. He owns a small home in a nice and improving neighborhood. This house is worth an easy $90,000, and Brent owes only $50,000 on it. In addition, Brent has $20,000 in cash and is caught up on all his other liabilities. The only payment he makes each month is on the mortgage on his home.

So Brent looks for and finds a small apartment building to buy. He doesn't need the cash flow, so he has the advantage of being able to highly mortgage the property. All that is important to him is that the property pay for itself, as Brent knows all about the trade-off of cash flow for equity buildup, and the increase in equity and the improvement of his estate is worth more to him than anything.

The apartment complex is a ten-unit building and the owner wants $150,000. The complex has a $110,000 first mortgage already on the property. Brent needs $50,000 to meet the down payment. But he doesn't have it. Enter the pyramid plan.

Brent sits down with the owner and presents his offer. He will give the owner the $50,000 he is asking for, but on these terms: $20,000 in cash and $30,000 in the form of a mortgage on the home. Brent shows the owner some photos of the beautiful home and outlines how he will pay off the $30,000 mortgage.

The seller takes the deal because he got his price, he got some cash, and he didn't have to take back a mortgage on his own property. The fact the seller took back a second mortgage on Brent's home doesn't count. There is at play here a phenomenon called "the security looks greener under the other guy's property."

You can see that in essence the pyramid is nothing more than taking equity you have in property you already own and using it as all or part of your down payment on the next deal.

Nadia is the owner of ten acres of beautiful pastureland about five miles out of town. It was given to her by her father, and she dreams of building a home on it one day. It is worth at least $40,000 and it is free and clear. She could use some extra cash to put down on a duplex she is interested in buying. Of course, she could go to a bank and borrow on the land, but she'd have to pay the bank's terms on that loan, and that's not for her.

Nadia goes to the owner of the duplex and offers to buy the property. Instead of the $60,000 the owner is asking, she feels that $55,000 would be fair, so that is the amount of her offer. As the property already has a good $35,000 mortgage, all she needs is $20,000. But she doesn't want to spend what cash she has, and she doesn't have that much anyway.

Nadia offers the duplex owner $55,000, with no cash down. Instead, she offers him a first mortgage of $20,000 on the ten acres. The terms on the mortgage are reasonable for Nadia to pay. She is now paying rent on an apartment, and she'll be living in one side of the duplex and renting out the other, so she can handle the mortgage payments.

The owner of the duplex checks out the land and realizes

that if Nadia fails to make the payments, he'd get the ten acres, worth twice what he'd get otherwise. It's a deal.

So Nadia got the duplex, no cash down, and made the payments with ease. The mortgage she paid on was at a lower interest rate than she'd have gotten at the bank, and she didn't have to pay any closing costs.

PYRAMID POWER

THE real advantage of the pyramid comes when you make the second deal. Brent and Nadia were just beginning to use the pyramid. Take Brent, for example. Now he has the ten-unit apartment complex. He paid a total of $150,000 for it and it has a $100,000 first mortgage. At this moment, Brent has $50,000 equity in the apartment complex, as he paid $20,000 down and secured the balance of $30,000 on his own home.

Six months later, with some tender loving care and by plowing back some of the rent money into the complex, Brent looks back on the project and sees that he has increased the rents and is now making more money. This naturally means his property has gone up in value.

Calculating the increase and relating it to value, Brent assumes the apartments to be worth $185,000. As he has a first mortgage of $100,000 against the property, he has a new equity of $85,000.

Using the pyramid properly, Brent looks for and finds another property to buy, an eight-unit apartment complex. The owner is asking $90,000 for the property, which is free and clear. Brent likes this property and knows that if he spends about $25,000 on the building he can more than double the rents and the value of the property.

This time Brent offers the seller $50,000 in cash and a second mortgage in the amount of $40,000 against his ten-unit building. Brent goes to a local savings and loan with the contract showing the purchase of the building and tells them of his plans to remodel the apartments. He shows them his ideas and how much the rents will increase. He believes the value of the property will increase to at least $150,000, on the conservative side. All he wants to do is to borrow $80,000. He agrees to the hold-back of $25,000 to be spent in remodeling costs.

He takes the loan and gives $50,000 to the seller, along with the second mortgage on his ten units. That leaves $30,000, of which $5,000 will go for closing costs and plans for the remodeling. The remaining $25,000 will go for the remodeling job itself.

This pyramid didn't take any cash, and Brent now has a new apartment building that is 100% fixed up. After a short time—a year or so—he might be ready to take this property and pyramid from a new value of $180,000 or more.

What makes the pyramid investment program work is that other-side-of-the-fence aspect about people. When you buy a property that has been owned by the same person for several years, you can assume the seller is making a profit. In some cases the profit is considerable, in others not, but a profit nonetheless. When you go to that seller and use the normal second-mortgage approach, you must anticipate putting down some cash. It is unlikely that the seller will take nothing down and hold his entire equity in a second mortgage against the property he just sold. Also, presumably he paid less for it than he is selling it for, and this weighs heavily on his mind. "You mean you want me to hold $40,000 in second mortgage behind a $100,000 first mortgage? Hell, I paid less than $100,000 for the property when I bought it. Let the buyer pay cash."

Ah, but the pyramid is a new animal. It takes the seller out of his property and gets him into another investment—in this case, a second mortgage against a property on the other side of the fence. "Look at the ten-unit building over there, dear, we hold a mortgage on that."

6 Steps to Pyramids That Work

1. Know your goal. The pyramid is a means to an end. It is only a method of financing a purchase, and not a goal in itself. It is a highly creative form of finance and can be used in many different ways. You will find numerous combinations of these new tools, but you must understand your own goals and work in that direction. Only by clearly understanding where you want to go will you get there in a hurry.

The purchase you are about to make should be in a positive direction toward your goal. If it is inconsistent with your goal and has no other positive benefit to you, then the investment and the use of the pyramid are probably going to be incorrect. A successful investor is constantly looking to improve his position, and he knows that the final goal is rarely reached in one step. A constant move forward is the best and most successful way to go.

2. Know your ability to risk your cash, equity, and time. Pyramiding is very risky because it is the maximum extension of mortgage-to-price ratio possible. You are buying and creating new value by improving the property. You generate the new mortgage by simply causing it to be in existence. This puts a heavy load on the property in the form of debt service. You can see that the progressing pyramid, where you add new mortgages on top of new equities, works best in a rising economy. A stagnant or declining economy can cause the pyramid to collapse. What happens is a domino effect: One property gets in trouble, and then they all can go.

3. Substantiate your new equity by making sure the new expense can be covered by the income from the property being mortgaged. If you are putting a $40,000 second mortgage on top of the existing $100,000 mortgage, the income from the property (Brent's ten units, for example) should cover the mortgages. If you have to look to any other income source to pay that second mortgage, you have overburdened the property and have an out-of-balance pyramid. Make sure you stay in balance.

4. Look for income property that has not reached its peak income potential. You must have room to improve the income in order to improve the value. This is only logical. You will profit when you sell to the armchair investor who wants only the peak and no hard work getting there. You will build your fortune by improving properties and profiting.

5. Be aggressive. In real estate this means *make offers*. Don't ever ask someone what he would do; make an offer, telling him what *you* will do if he accepts. The advantage is tremendous if you make offers. It makes people make decisions. When you ask a question you can get an answer that may or may not be reality. When you make an offer, that *is* reality.

Sometimes sellers may not fully understand your intentions. You might get a reaction that is negative out of ignorance more than anything else. Don't shy away from the deal because the seller doesn't instantly fall in line. Continue to press the deal without being overly anxious, and at the same time continue to search for an opening in the deal. You will be using agents in many of your dealings, and even your broker or salesman might not be aware of this technique. Let him read this chapter. He will be your best ally in making such deals.

6. Do not move to a new pyramid until you are sure the new property can support a new value. That means, of course, that you have reached the stage where you can carry more debt and you are ready to add to your holdings. If you can generate some cash reserve, you will be ahead of the game.

Following these six key steps should be easy, but watch for some of the hazards in dealing with pyramids. There are reasons why sellers will avoid the technique you may want to use.

Objections You Will Run Into

One is the charge of "artificial equity." It is easy to simply say, "This apartment building is worth $200,000, and as I have a $90,000 first mortgage, my equity is $110,000." However, saying it doesn't make it so. Of course, you could have just bought the property two weeks ago for $110,000 and that extra $90,000 in equity just came in the window, poof, just like that! If a seller of another property were to take a second mortgage back in the amount of $70,000 against this "$200,000" property, I'd say it is likely it is insufficient equity (unless there was genuine reason for the value having risen from $110,000 to $200,000). Because of this reality, many sellers (and their lawyers) will look at the pyramid as a potentially dangerous deal.

Overcome this by justifying your value. Show them the income and expense. You must be able to justify your ability to pay the existing financing out of the income as well as the new mortgage you are about to create, or you are kidding yourself.

Many sellers won't see the pyramid achieving their goals. Many sellers enter the market with the idea they will get all cash for their property. This is their goal, and when you come along you may find resistance to this element the hardest to overcome.

Sometimes you can't overcome it. It is possible that the needs of the seller can be met only by a cash sale. On the other hand, if you or your agent can find out why the seller is selling, you have a much better opportunity to use the correct tool to make the deal.

For example, a seller wishing to buy another property may believe that he must have cash for that purpose. Show him that he can take the mortgage you are going to give him and use it to buy what he wants (i.e., he can pyramid with your mortgage).

A seller in the market to invest his cash can be shown how this investment in a sound second mortgage that meets his primary goal (to sell the property) also achieves a secondary goal (to invest the proceeds of the sale wisely).

The pyramid may not be the best direction for the seller. It is a tool you chose to use, not the seller. He has selling options, too, and perhaps would rather use one of them to better the deal. It doesn't have anything to do with his goal, just the deal.

You need to find out clearly what it is this seller wants to do *in the deal*. There are ways you can deviate from the pyramid to make the deal more secure.

Security is generally the name of this game, and if you look at any of the techniques of finance (pyramids, wraparounds, blankets, purchase-money mortgages, partial mortgages, balloon mortgages, and the like) you will find that sellers can be motivated to take something they would have avoided when you can show them that what they wanted to do isn't as beneficial to them as what you are willing to do for them.

For example, it is possible for you to double the pyramid as additional security. In this situation, you would offer a mortgage in the amount of $40,000, secured by a second mortgage on the ten units and a third mortgage on the house (see Brent's deal). In this way you are combining two techniques, the pyramid and the blanket. You can offer any amount of equity and anything as security. All of these extra items will increase the security (and ease the peace of mind) of the seller.

But if the deal falters, the domino effect can happen. When one deal of the pyramid falters, the danger of *all* the transactions falling down increases. This occurs not because of the connection between each deal—there is no direct connection, and each transaction should stand on its own two feet—but from the potential overmortgaging of all properties in the pyramid. Heavy financing produces heavy debt service, and if the economy slows down and vacancies increase, the whole situation can reach the point where one or more properties will start to slip. The natural tendency is for owners to try to shore up the falling property, and that usually means economic help from the still-successful properties. This violates the principle of pyramiding, of course, in that you should not pyramid unless the property can carry its own debt service. Yet trends aren't so clearly defined that investors can be sure the downward move is permanent and not just a temporary slump in the economy. Thus, instead of bailing out quickly on a losing property, most of us will chip in from the winners for a while. A sudden worsening in the economy, a full-fledged recession, and all can be lost.

So pyramiding can be risky, but the risk can be kept to a minimum if you follow the investment rules and techniques in this book. Because the pyramiding investor has little capital tied up in the deal in relation to the total price, the capital which can be lost is generally well worth the risk involved.

How You Can Use the Pyramid If You Are a Seller

While the pyramid is more often a tool used by buyers, you can find a way to make your property more salable and convert this buyer's tool to a seller's tool. For example, Eric wanted to sell his home in Chicago and move to Florida. He was asking $80,000 and had a first mortgage of $30,000. He found the market not as firm as he had thought, and his asking price of $50,000 cash to his mortgage didn't move the property. On the advice of his broker, he went to Florida and found a nice apartment to buy. In that deal he offered some cash and a $30,000 second mortgage secured by his home in Chicago. The Florida market being no firmer than Chicago's at that time, the seller of the Florida property was glad to get the cash Eric paid along with the second mortgage. The mortgage Eric offered was, in fact, a pyramid mortgage, which changed the picture on the Chicago home. Instead of having $50,000 equity in the property in Illinois, Eric now had a total of $60,000 existing financing and his equity was only $20,000. If he needed to, Eric could hold a small third mortgage to close a sale on the home in Chicago, as he had already met his Florida goals.

What Eric did was simply find what he was going to buy and use a pyramid to help achieve that end. At the same time, he improved the chance of selling the property in Chicago by having a second mortgage at terms and interest rate beneficial to the deal. If he hadn't been careful, of course, he could have placed a second mortgage that would have made the marketing of the Chicago house more difficult instead of easier. The terms placed on a property in pyramid must be beneficial to the deal, whatever that deal is, or you are not using the tool properly. ("Beneficial" depends on the current market and the overall existing financing.) Helping any marketing program become more acceptable to buyers is always something a seller should be concerned with. You will get the best price (*always*) when you offer the best terms. If you can pyramid out part of your equity and then sell the property subject to the existing financing plus the pyramid mortgage, the amount of equity taken in the pyramid will be the same as cash.

PYRAMID YOUR FORTUNE

IF you wait until you can buy using cash as your down payment, you might have to wait longer and miss out on some of the best deals. By using the pyramid as a method of making your equity work for you, you can keep your good properties while letting them give you new credit you didn't think you had. The pyramid is a strong and very viable method of buying with little or no cash down. It works on the "grass is greener on the other side of the fence" principle and will make a reluctant seller take paper when he has rejected every other buyer's offer.

It won't solve every problem you come up against. Whether it is a good tool for you will depend on your ability to put it into play in situations where it benefits the deal and improves your journey to a position of wealth.

20

Three Creative Mortgage Buying Techniques

HERE ARE three very interesting and effective buying and selling techniques which involve moıtgages. Each has drawbacks as well as benefits, so it isn't a matter of simply choosing any of the three, but of knowing which is the best for your specific situation.

The three methods are: balloon mortgage, wraparound mortgage, and blanket mortgage.

BALLOON MORTGAGE

THE name *balloon* comes from the fact that at a certain moment the mortgage swells, as all or at least a large part of the unpaid balance becomes due and payable. The mortgage provides for a pay-out to be based as though it were to continue for a longer time than it actually is.

For example, you borrow $40,000 and agree to pay it back at the rate of $6,000 per year until the whole amount is paid. This payment of $6,000 includes both interest and amortization, and the repayment of the $40,000 could take ten years or more, depending on the interest rate. At 11%, it would take around twelve years. If you or the seller wanted to have the payment come due earlier, it would be possible to balloon the payment in, say, the fifth year. In this plan the first four annual payments would still be $6,000; the fifth payment would include the total unpaid balance of the mortgage. Here is the payment schedule:

End of Year	Payment	Owed	Balloon
1	$ 6,000	$38,400	$ 0
2	6,000	36,626	0
3	6,000	34,655	0
4	6,000	32,068	0
5	35,595	0	32,068[a]

[a] Plus $3,527 interest.

With the normally amortized mortgage the payment schedule continues until the balance owed is paid off. In the balloon mortgage the amortization schedule is interrupted at a set time in the future, when all or part of the balance then becomes due.

How to Use the Balloon Mortgage as a Buying Tool

Cheryl wanted to buy a duplex that she had checked out. It was only a few blocks from where she worked, she knew she could get a good rent from the side she wouldn't be living in, and she was tired of paying rent. The duplex had all the earmarks of a property she could fix up in her spare time, so she felt she could improve the value of the property and the income.

The duplex had a low-interest mortgage on the property, as it was an older mortgage. However, because the mortgage-to-price ratio was low, she would not have enough cash to add to the mortgage, so she needed to work out some alternative form of financing.

The money market was very tight at the moment and she knew it was not a good time to go to any institutional lenders to refinance the property. Not only would she pay heavy points to get the mortgage, but the interest rate on the new mortgage would kill the income picture. She also hated to give up the low interest rate on the existing financing.

Through her broker, Cheryl offered a low-down-payment deal, not using all her available cash. She asked the seller to hold back a second mortgage payable over fifteen years at a reasonable interest rate.

The seller told her that he didn't mind holding the paper, but fifteen years was out of the question. He countered with a seven-year mortgage at the same interest rate Cheryl had offered.

Let's look at the numbers of the deal thus far.

The price of the duplex negotiated was $42,000. The property had a first mortgage of $18,000, and Cheryl was able to put $5,000 cash into the deal. That left $19,000, which the seller was willing to hold for seven years at 10% interest. That made her payments on the second mortgage $315.40 per month.

The total annual debt service picture looked like this:

Existing mortgage	$1,807.20[a]
Second mortgage	3,784.80[b]
Total annual debt service	$5,592.00
Monthly payment	466.00

[a] 20 years at 8%.
[b] 7 years at 10%.

Cheryl took one look at the annual debt service and knew that she wouldn't be able to make a go of this investment with that kind of payment. She countered with a balloon mortgage having the following terms: same cash down, same first mortgage to be assumed, same amount of a second mortgage, same due date seven years from now. The only difference Cheryl made was that the second mortgage was to be paid out on an interest-only basis for seven years, at which time the entire principal would be due. At 10%, that made her mortgage payment on the second mortgage $1,900 per year. That, coupled with the existing first mortgage, gave her a total debt service of $2,707.20 per year, or $225.60 per month, a savings of $240.40 per month over the seller's counter. The monthly payment Cheryl had worked out was less than what she was paying in rent, and the duplex would provide some extra income to carry the other ownership costs.

The seller went along with the deal because he saw that he was getting a nice interest on his investment, more than he could get in a regular passbook at a savings and loan, and it was secure enough for his purpose. He also won his point in having the mortgage come due within seven years.

From Cheryl's point of view, she did nicely too, as she knew that within that seven years she was going to improve the value of the duplex considerably. She could refinance the property in a few years when the value increased, pulling out her investment and moving up into more real estate. Cheryl used the interest-only mortgage primarily as her counter, although she was prepared to go to a long amortization pay-out if she had to, paying principal along with interest. The seller's acceptance of the interest-only part of the deal was a feather in Cheryl's cap she hadn't expected to win.

The result in this example was a buy for Cheryl that might have eluded her otherwise. The balloon enabled her to buy a property that she liked and to have a debt service that the facility could support. The circumstances of this deal were such that the older mortgage was worth keeping for a few more years anyway, and five years down the road Cheryl anticipated she would have improved value to the point of $80,000 or so; with that kind of value she could put a new mortgage on the property in the low $60,000 range, pulling out profit (not taxed) and her total original investment as well.

The balloon is generally used by buyers as a way to gain time, keeping the total debt service down at a manageable level until new financing can be obtained, or until the values are sufficient to finance the deal institutionally. Because sellers are usually in a hurry for their cash and don't like long-pay-out mortgages, the balloon helps keep them happy while getting time on the side of the buyer.

This aspect works for any mortgage, balloon or not. The idea is that you write the terms and conditions of the mortgage to make the deal, not because the deal makes the terms. If you are buying a seasonal income type of property it is not uncommon to have terms that call for interim balloon payments. These would occur during the term of the loan and only partial payoff of the total balance owed would happen.

The interim balloon could be tied to income performance of the property just bought, in such a way that if the seasonal income was excellent (or at least equal to what the seller said it would be), an interim balloon of a set amount or an amount based on the income would occur.

These interim balloon payments are usually tied to something the seller has told you, and will sometimes bring out "new truth" in the negotiations. When you have just asked the seller to take such a mortgage based on a large balloon in two years if the income reaches the amount the seller just told you he got last year and the seller balks, that's a good time to examine the income statements more carefully.

The Balloon as a Selling Tool

When you sell your real estate you should know what the buyer is looking for. He is just like you in that he wants to get as good a deal as possible. As a smart seller, you should know you will get your best price when you offer the best terms.

Assuming that you don't need to sell for all cash and can pyramid any paper you would have to take back, you can use the balloon to make the sale. For example, Harley wanted to sell his lot down in Key West. He had bought it as an investment and it had gone up in value from $5,000 to $45,000. He was now ready to convert the value to something else. He sold it to a builder for $10,000 down, the remaining $35,000 to be paid over twenty-five years at 10½% interest. This kept the carrying costs for the builder relatively low, and the builder didn't mind the balloon payment that Harley had created—the total amount would come due in three years. As the builder planned to start construction within that time, he would pay off the loan then.

The balloon idea worked for Harley because the builder liked the almost interest-only cost for the first few years, and Harley created a mortgage that was easy to swap for something else.

Drawbacks of the Balloon Mortgage

The best plans sometimes blow up because of unforeseen events. A too-short balloon can catch you in an economic condition worse than the one you are trying to wait out. This has happened to many builders and will no doubt happen again. You want to avoid a balloon of less than three years. Any balloon shorter than that is too dangerous, too short, unless you are absolutely sure it can be handled.

Don't forget about the balloon, either. I've seen many sellers in a tough situation simply because they forgot about the balloon payment coming up. It can sneak up on you as the years go along. In the first place, the amortization is set on a long payout, and you get in the habit of making monthly payments in the same amount month after month. Then all of a sudden the seventh year's balloon is on you and where will you get the hunk of cash needed to pay off the mortgage?

In moving from the balloon mortgage to the wraparound mortgage you will see that ballooning can occur in almost any mortgage. Therefore, it is more a technique used in mortgages rather than a form of mortgage itself.

The wraparound is a form of mortgage, mostly misunderstood and frequently misused. Yet it is a very effective form of financing that benefits both buyer and seller *at the same time in the same deal.*

Wraparound Mortgage

A wraparound mortgage is a mortgage that includes in its amount some existing financing already on the property.

Brad wants to sell a $100,000 house. The house has a good low-interest first mortgage in the amount of $60,000. Brad is willing to take some paper in the deal but wants to get a minimum of $20,000 cash down. He chooses the wraparound mortgage as his selling tool.

Brad offers the home with an $80,000 mortgage on terms less than the current market. This wraparound of $80,000 includes the existing mortgage of $60,000, so Brad's interest in the wraparound is only $20,000. The buyer in this deal would buy the home with $20,000 cash down and pay on the amortization terms of the wraparound. Brad will take the payments from the buyer and make the first-mortgage payments, as that remains his obligation.

Because the function of the wraparound is to give Brad the advantage of leveraging up on the low interest rate of the existing mortgage, he is able to offer the buyer a nominal interest rate less than the current market to entice the buyer into the deal. On the other hand, because of the upward leverage in the transaction (say the interest rate on the existing mortgage is 8% and Brad charges only 11% on the wrap), for every $100 of existing mortgage outstanding, Brad gets $3 in interest each year.

In simple terms, the buyer of this property is paying 11% interest on the $80,000 mortgage. This is a good deal for the buyer because he didn't have to pay points to a lender and he buys the property with only 20% down.

Brad is doing okay too. He is holding paper on the deal in a wraparound form with a contract rate of 11%. However, $60,000 of the deal at the outset is borrowed at only 8% interest. Interest paid in by the buyer for the first year on the wraparound mortgage would be about $8,800 (11% of $80,000). Brad would pay out interest on the existing first mortgage at 8% of $60,000, or only $4,800.

Brad took in interest on the wraparound	$8,800
He paid out interest on the first mortgage	4,800
He has left the net interest on $20,000 equity	$4,000

The effective return to Brad this year was 20%. The buyer got a good deal and the seller got a fantastic deal.

7 Most Common Uses of the Wraparound Mortgage

1. To leverage the seller's return upward. You just saw a good example of the movement of a yield from a contract rate of

11% to an actual cash-in-the-pocket return of 20%. Such returns are common in wraps, depending on the circumstances. It should be clear that the greater the spread of interest between the existing financing and the wrap, and the greater the dollar amount of the existing financing, the greater the leverage advantage to the seller. In the example above, if the first mortgage had been $70,000, the seller's equity in the $80,000 wraparound would have been $10,000. Using the same interest rates of 8% and 11% as indicated, look at the result:

Interest on wrap	$8,800
Paid-out interest on first mortgage	5,600
Net interest to Brad on $10,000 equity	$3,200

The yield to Brad is now 32% on the $10,000. Good gets better quicker. Remember, in each case the buyer was getting a mortgage rate better than what he could have gotten in the market.

The point you should see quickly here is that the wraparound is highly effective when you are dealing with any set of numbers where the bulk of the wraparound is in the existing financing. That means that even in small mortgage situations where the seller might balk at a $10,000 paper, you could show him that he might be in an ideal position to get 32% on his money. You would never be able to sell a buyer on paying 32%, by the way, but that's exactly what he will do in a wraparound, and he won't bat an eyelash.

2. To induce a seller to hold secondary paper. There are times when you as a buyer need to get the seller to hold financing. Normally it is because the financial marketplace is closed or so tight that you can't anticipate reasonable financing from that sector. If you are buying a property where you need to obtain the maximum mortgage-to-price ratio, the wraparound may permit you to do that through the seller. Remember, if you allow the seller to leverage up over the existing loan interest rate, he will be inclined to take the paper himself instead of insisting that you seek financing in the market.

The one factor you must remember in seller-held financing is the inducement to the seller to hold the paper. Sometimes the motivation for selling is sufficient in this event, but more often not. If something stronger is needed, the wrap will give you that edge.

3. When the existing financing has provisions that make the sale difficult or costly. There will be times when the existing financing has provisions that call for large prepayment penalties. These penalties might cause the buyer to shy away from the deal, as the seller will want to pass this cost on. If you are the buyer, or perhaps the seller stuck with this situation, the wraparound mortgage may be the answer. As the existing mortgage isn't assumed but merely encompassed within the wrap, the original lender (on the existing financing) doesn't have the opportunity to "call" the penalty.

There are some situations, however, where the mortgage might have a "due on sale" clause. This is quite common in federal savings and loan association mortgages made after 1972, and while courts have yet to decide on the validity of this, the wraparound will not circumvent this issue by lack of assumption. The fact of the matter is, there will be a sale, and unless you are ready and willing to fight the lender in court, you will have to wait until others do that for you. A word of caution: Lenders have a habit of putting restrictive clauses in their loans and then telling you that it is regulation for those items to be there. Don't believe it. This is a free economy, and lenders tend to do their own price fixing in this respect. The point isn't is it regulation or not, but will the public put up with that kind of business tactic? My suggestion is not to borrow money from a lender who uses conditions that do not improve his security and will most certainly hamper your rights to sell the property later on.

The due-on-sale provision that the savings and loan associations have been passing on to their borrowers was at first an attempt (so they say) to make sure a good-risk client didn't sell the property to a bad-risk buyer. It doesn't matter in their eyes that the property securing the loan is still the same. Further, a new buyer is apt to create *more* security, as he probably paid more for the property. The simple fact (which judges and the public don't seem to know or understand) is that the average savings and loan association loan is written for over twenty-five years, but the average payoff term is well under ten years, due to advance payoff consequent on a sale of the property. In many areas of the country the average term of loan lasts only seven years. This means the savings and loans are getting a natural turnover within seven years—but that doesn't seem to be enough, so the due-on-sale provision is used. Why? Well, while the current turnover of savings and loans is ten years or less, the turnover (resale) of homes in many cases is less than half that time. If a twenty-seven-year loan can be called each time the property is sold, the added interest, points, etc., will be out of sight.

4. **To keep the existing financing intact despite nonassumption provisions in the mortgage document.** Frequently private as well as institutional loans have clauses that restrict the assumption of the mortgage by a new owner. These restrictions range from approvals needed by the lender to more informal registration of the new owner. In each case, the lender is restricting the actions of the buyer, and some buyers will balk at that. When the restriction gives the lender the right to "require the new owner assume the loan at current interest rates," the new, more current, interest rates might blow the deal altogether.

The wraparound should work in these situations, as there is no actual assumption of the existing financing. The previous owner (the seller) holds the existing mortgage and makes the payments. In the event of a default, the lender looks to the property and the original borrower, not to the buyer.

5. **Maintain an installment sale in a mortgage-over-basis situation.** One of the most effective methods of lessening the tax bite on a sale where there is a substantial capital gain in the year of the sale is the installment sale. One of the several items that will disallow the installment sale is receipt of more than 30% of the sale price in the year of the sale. While it seems simple to calculate 30% of this sale price, the danger comes in several areas, the most overlooked being the mortgage-over-basis. This occurs when the basis on a property is less than the amount of the exist-

ing financing at the time of sale. The basis on a parcel of real estate is the book value of that property: the price paid for the property plus any capital improvements over the tenure of ownership less any depreciation taken during that time. The basis is the figure from which all gain is calculated. If you sell for $100,000 and your basis is $40,000, you have a $60,000 gain. Even if you paid $100,000 for the property many years before, and depreciated it down to a $40,000 basis, your gain would still be $60,000. IRS is getting back at you for the shelter you took.

Madge bought a tract of land for $10,000 over twenty years ago. It was out in the sticks then, but now it is on the edge of town. The site was worth around $200,000 several years ago, and Madge borrowed $80,000 on a one-year mortgage of interest only. This mortgage was renewed each year, and as the property increased in value was finally converted to a ten-year pay-out loan.

Madge has a $10,000 basis, and as the property was vacant land and there were no improvements, there was nothing to depreciate. When Madge put the $80,000 loan against the property, she created a $70,000 mortgage-over-basis situation. The $70,000 over her investment went to her and was not taxed by IRS.

When the property reached $300,000 in value, Madge decided to sell. Her gain was going to be $290,000, and her taxes on that gain were out of sight. So she knew an installment sale to spread the tax over several years was important. However, she had a problem in that the IRS would say that any amount of mortgage which was in excess of her basis came back to her in the year of the sale. Thus, she was going to get $70,000 over her basis even though she wasn't going to get that money now. (She got it several years ago, when she put the mortgage on the property.) Under any circumstance, the maximum she could take in an installment sale would be 30% of the sales price. That would amount to $90,000 (30% of $300,000 = $90,000). As $70,000 of that comes to her in the form of the mortgage-over-basis, to have a proper installment sale she could get only $20,000 in cash at the closing. To sell the property for only $20,000 cash didn't seem realistic to her, so she needed another way to go.

The wraparound solved her problem. She set up a wraparound mortgage encompassing the existing $80,000, on which she would continue to make the payments. The sale was handled under the contract-for-deed form of sale to provide further protection in the non-passing of title in the year of sale.

While this method worked for Madge and may work for you in a similar mortgage-over-basis situation, you must, as in all legal situations, seek the advice of a lawyer to bring yourself current with the law. IRS and case law are ever changing, and you just might be the example when IRS wins.

6. As a marketing tool, the wraparound works magic. There are many things the wrap does in helping a deal come together. For the most part the wraparound is a seller's tool and can be used when you sell to maximize the advantage of the rate spread between the existing financing and the wrap. When you are selling a property that has several existing mortgages, you might find the wraparound to be a benefit in simplifying the terms for the buyer. The overall best package makes the deal work for you in achieving a higher price when you can offer an easy way to buy. Offering the property at terms that are at or below the current interest rate is to your benefit.

You can narrow down the negotiations when you take a property and offer it with reasonable terms and a moderate down payment. A $100,000 property that is free and clear has a lot of room for negotiation. The same property with an existing $50,000 mortgage has only $50,000 of flexibility between the price and the mortgage. Quote the same property with a new mortgage of $80,000 (a wraparound) and you have cut the negotiating room down to only $20,000. When you can narrow the negotiations you can hold your price and terms far more easily.

7. To give the seller control over the existing mortgages. When you sell a property that has several mortgages and you are being asked to or decide you want to hold additional paper, the wraparound will give you some added protection in comparison to holding a second or third mortgage that is not in the wraparound form. The most important protection comes in the default area. If you sell a property and take back a second or third mortgage as part of the transaction, you may not know when the first mortgage goes into default until it is too late for you to protect your stake in the deal. If you know of a potential default prior to the actual default, you can protect yourself to the point where the existing financing does not go into a foreclosure proceeding.

The wraparound mortgage is wonderful in this respect. You (the seller) are making the payments on the existing financing out of the payments on the wraparound that the buyer is giving you or your collection agent. When the buyer is late or defaults on the wraparound you will know this instantly. You still have to meet the existing mortgage payments, but it is far better to have this kind of problem when the mortgage is only one month late and you can take legal action to protect yourself in foreclosure. What happens otherwise is that the mortgage will go several months late before the first mortgage gets foreclosed, and by then the cost just to bring a mortgage current can be economically difficult. Knowing early of default is worth a great deal when there are several mortgages ahead of your position.

Escrowing for taxes and insurance is another matter that you can control as a seller holding a wraparound. If the existing first mortgages don't have such provisions, you can install them in the terms of the wrap and account for that annual payment yourself. Just another item that can let you get another good night's sleep.

3 Problem Areas

1. Legal advisers unaware of the benefits of the wraparound. This technique isn't in every textbook and there are many lawyers and CPA's who have not run up against the wrap yet. It would be natural for these fellows to want to avoid the use of something that is foreign to them. Whenever you feel there is a good reason to use the wrap, don't let a lawyer deter you on the ground that he is not familiar with the form. And all you lawyers and CPA's reading this book should spend a little time looking up some of the case history of wraparounds in your state. See some of the ways the wraps have been used, and you will begin to get a feel for this truly magnificent tool for increasing wealth. (Become proficient as a real estate lawyer or CPA who knows all about wraparounds and you will get much more of that kind of business.)

As investors, you must assume that there will be things you will learn and put into practice that the general advisers haven't seen or become proficient in. The wrap is just one of many buying and selling tools in this book that simply aren't common knowledge even in the real estate profession. Seek out advisers who are familiar with the terms and practices of real estate and the unique and creative forms of buying and selling.

2. Paying on a wrap to a seller who skips town to Buenos Aires. As the buyer makes the payment on the wrap to the seller and the seller is supposed to make the payments on the existing financing, there is always the danger that the seller will keep the total payment and not make the existing mortgage payments. The solution to this problem is to have the wraparound payments made to a third party who acts as a collection agent, disbursing the payments on the prior mortgages and then to the seller. This escrow or collection agency should be set up very carefully to insure that it is in fact the seller who is making the separate payments and not the buyer.

3. Fear of the unfamiliar. One of the problems that frequently comes up with the wraparound is that its infrequent use makes for caution when it is used. There is no reason to be afraid of the wraparound; it is a mortgage much like any secondary mortgage. The unique aspect is that it contains one or more of the existing mortgages. Note the flexibility of this fine form of financing:

• The wraparound can wrap any or all of the existing financing. There is no reason you can't wrap just a second mortgage if it makes more sense to leave the existing first alone. If the first mortgage is due and payable in a year or two, putting it in the wrap might only complicate the situation, especially if there is a big balloon on the first. It is possible to wrap a third and fourth mortgage in this same way, leaving the first and second alone.

• Title can transfer just as it would in any other kind of deal. The wraparound doesn't affect the way you pass title.

• The wraparound takes a position in rank of mortgages below the most recent recorded mortgage. If, prior to the deal, there are in existence a first and a second mortgage, the wraparound will automatically become a third mortgage. This position or rank doesn't have anything to do with the wraparound effect, but with the position you will fall into in a recovery of foreclosure. A third-position mortgage is behind the first and second mortgages in the event of a foreclosure. The first mortgage always gets paid out first from the proceeds after IRS gets theirs.

Blanket Mortgage

A blanket mortgage is any form of mortgage that has as its security more than one property. If you give someone a mortgage and secure it with two vacant lots, or your home and a lot, or any two or more properties, this mortgage becomes a blanket mortgage.

The blanket mortgage works much like the wraparound in that it covers two or more of something, but the something isn't another mortgage but property. Of course, you can have a wraparound mortgage that has blanket provisions incorporated into it so that the wrap itself covers two or more properties, but where blanket provisions excel is in opening up a pyramid situation where the seller isn't convinced that the security on the one property is sufficient to entice him to take that paper in the deal. It is another low-cash-down form of finance that works for your equity buildup.

Remember how the pyramid works—you go to a seller and offer him as part of the purchase terms a second mortgage on an existing property you own. This pyramid deal is highly effective, but isn't possible in every situation. As a seller, you would be advised to go beyond the pyramid when a buyer comes along and offers you such a deal. If you can increase your security in the transaction, you have improved the deal from your point of view. One such way is by using the blanket mortgage.

You are the seller and along comes Simon, who, being no simpleton, offers you cash and a second mortgage on his fine home on the greener side of the street. You, however, recognize a pyramid when you see one. It isn't a bad deal, but to improve your situation you ask for one small favor: Would Simon also include the property you are selling as additional security on the second mortgage? Now you have a deal that is secured not only by the other property but by the property you are selling as well. This additional security improves your situation and makes the second mortgage much stronger. If you wanted to sell or exchange this mortgage, you could do so with better credentials, and because the mortgage has more security you will widen your chances of making the trade or selling at par instead of taking a discount.

Builders and developers use the blanket mortgage all the time. When a builder buys a large tract of land from a developer, he frequently has a blanket mortgage from that developer. If he buys twenty lots in a subdivision, he might have one mortgage covering the entire twenty. As he reduces the mortgage, some of the lots become free and clear and he builds on them.

In addition, he may have subordination granted to him as he goes along.

Subordination is a word used to describe a series of events. The lender, or mortgagee, agrees to let his mortgage rank secondary to another mortgage. (This concession is made by the lender in order to make the deal.) The same thing happens in a land lease when the owner of the land agrees to permit the lessee of the land to mortgage the property (and a building) over and above the rights of the landowner.

Subordination can come in any mortgage as a technique to permit the mortgage to lapse into a lesser position. This frequently is used with the blanket mortgage. In the case of the builder with his twenty lots, instead of the mortgagee releasing a lot from the mortgage, he simply subordinates on a repeated basis to an institutional lender's construction loan so the builder can go out and obtain additional funds for the development of a home or whatever on that lot. Through subordination the lender keeps an interest in the lot without allowing a full release. The mortgagee's paper drops from a first mortgage to a second mortgage, of course, but that is more protection than if there were no position at all.

When used less cautiously, subordination is a very easy way

to risk all for little gain. It is something you must be very careful of and avoid unless there is some benefit to you. In the case of the land sale where the builder obtains subordination on a per-lot basis, the deal would be good for the developer only if there was sufficient additional security or the risk was warranted on the gains in the transaction. A developer building houses in a new subdivision might make all the remaining lots go up considerably in value. Early sales to promote such development might call for such subordination as a prudent business decision.

In the situation described, the subordination was an additional security to the developer, who might have simply released the lots with a minimum down payment. For the most part, however, subordination is something to watch with caution.

As a buyer planning on building on vacant property, you will ask for subordination whenever you can get it. It will enable you to buy a $40,000 lot, for example, for a reasonable down payment (say, $10,000) and then go to a bank and borrow on the lot and building. The lender doesn't look to the fact that you owe $30,000 on the lot, as their loan is in a first position if you received subordination when you bought the lot. You might find the lender giving you all the cash you need to build the building. If you were a builder who could sell the home (or other building) and make a nice profit, you might be able to pay off the loan on the lot and still have a sizable profit from the deal.

The blanket mortgage will aid you in these subordinated deals as a buyer because you can offer the seller a mortgage on something else, as additional security to the deal, in addition to a subordinated mortgage on the property you are buying.

Gardner had a nice home with about $30,000 equity. He wanted to buy a lot to build a duplex on. He offered the seller $25,000 for the lot on the condition that the seller take $5,000 down and a $20,000 mortgage secured by a second mortgage on Gardner's house and a first position on the lot itself. However, Gardner wanted the owner to subordinate that first mortgage on the lot to a development loan not to exceed 80% of the value of the project (lot included).

The savings and loan that was willing to make the development loan of $75,000 knew that Gardner was buying the lot, and they were willing to make the deal knowing that Gardner was going to spend about $65,000 on the building itself. That meant Gardner would actually take $10,000 out of the loan for his own pocket, so thus far he was $5,000 ahead on the deal. Of course, he still owed $20,000 to the seller of the lot. Gardner could have sold the duplex at a profit, but instead he rented both sides of the duplex and plowed all the rent income back into paying off the lot. Over the next few years, once the loan to the seller was paid off, he had the duplex with no capital tied up in the lot. In fact, he pulled out his original down payment on the lot right off the bat.

Use a Blanket When You Can't Pyramid

For the most part the blanket mortgage is a step back from the pyramid. You don't have to think of it as a drawback, however, because if you are only making a few deals here and there you won't have to pyramid on top of your deals anyway. The idea is to make the best deal you can, and if that means using a blanket to add to the security of the mortgage (and that by itself allows you to make a deal with little or no cash down), you have succeeded.

Do not, however, jump up with good equity on a bad deal. You can put your other property in jeopardy by allowing too broad a blanket. If you own several tracts of land and some buildings, don't let them all be covered in a blanket if the income from the new property isn't sufficient to cover the debt. You can reach into your pocket for a while on a vacant land deal if you are going to build, or hope for a quick profit, but remember that this is where speculation comes in and you are risking more than perhaps you should.

21

Two Professional Techniques That Build Wealth

One of the primary rules of smart investing is: reduce your risk. I have referred to this concept several times. You reduce your risk in a variety of ways, and risk is relative to your knowledge and ability. One man's risk is another man's fun.

"I'll pay your price if you accept my terms." This works for any savvy buyer as long as the buyer knows the alternatives available to make the terms fit the price he is willing to pay. What happens is this: I find a property I want to buy and then approach the seller with the news that I'm interested in buying and will pay a reasonable price. The seller views reasonable price in different terms than I do, but let's not argue at this stage of the game. "Tell me your price, Mr. Seller. As long as I can work it out, I'm interested in buying."

The proper avenue to take when dealing through a broker is to tell the broker of your intent and begin there. As long as you're not buying for all cash, you know that whatever the price offered, there will be some terms that you can work out to bring the price in line with what you can afford. This chapter will give you two good and creative techniques that can be used by themselves or in combination, and there are many different and highly creative formats of offers you can devise using these two techniques. You can even interject the three mortgage techniques covered in the last chapter to broaden your scope of options and alternatives.

The two techniques to be covered in this chapter are the preferred purchase deal and the option.

Preferred Purchase

One of my early clients taught me about this deal. It is a magnificent way to get down to the nitty-gritty in a deal where the seller is telling you, "I'd love to keep this property but I need some cash." Mind you, this kind of transaction is based on a sizable amount of cash coming into the deal and is usually not an option available to the low-cash-down buyer. Of course, frequently the "cash" can be obtained from other sources, but from the seller's point of view cash is what is going to talk.

Let me set the stage for a preferred purchase deal.

Charles owns a beautiful office building in downtown San Francisco. It is fully rented, or nearly so, and Charles has a nice suite of offices in the building. He has a pro forma showing the income and expenses, and projects that within a year or so, when he can increase the rents in the building, the investment will provide a very good return to a prospective buyer.

"I need some cash," Charles says, and your broker has conveyed this to you.

Now, buying an office building is one thing, but assume that you aren't in the business of managing office buildings. You like the idea of the rent and the income and the tax shelter, but the idea of management isn't to your liking. Besides, you live in Chicago.

In this deal Charles reports the following:

Price	$1,500,000
Mortgages	750,000
Cash to buy	$750,000

The debt service on the existing $750,000 mortgage is $94,000 per year. On top of that Charles reports that the operating expenses and taxes and the like total another $50,000 per year. Gross revenue at the moment is $220,000.

If these figures were correct and you paid $750,000 cash for this deal, you would be making the cash flow shown below:

Gross revenue	$220,000
Operating expenses	50,000
Net operating income	$170,000
Debt service	94,000
Cash flow	$ 76,000

This is slightly more than 10% on your invested capital. This is not bad, because you have lots of other benefits going along with this deal. There is ample tax shelter and lots of future equity buildup. If the rents can be increased and costs held down, there is even appreciation. Not a bad deal at all.

Except that Charles has overestimated on the pro forma a little. The expenses are probably low by $10,000 or more, and there is no vacancy factor accounted for. There is about $25,000 in income at risk here, although that's being conservative from the buyer's point of view. But the property is a very nice building and you would like to own it.

Offer a preferred purchase deal.

You offer to buy 50% of the building and will pay $400,000 cash for that opportunity. All you want is the following:

• To be preferred (to receive from the top of the cash flow), 10% on your cash invested. The seller takes the next equal amount, and everything else is split 50/50.

• All or most of the depreciation. This is a negotiating point; depending on the deal and the motivation of the seller, you might end up with the building and the seller with the land (land is not depreciable).

• When the property is sold or refinanced, you will share in the proceeds on a 50/50 basis.

There are other points you could have asked for, such as the right to buy out the seller's interest at a time in the future at a formula to be offered in this deal, or just a first right of refusal down the road. You might find that as the loan is paid off and the value increases you would be able to buy out the partner through the funds obtained in refinancing the property.

You could also have asked for the deficit (if any) of your preferred interest to build up and add to your investment. For example, say there is a bad year and the total cash flow is only $30,000. As you would get the first 10% of your invested capital, which was $400,000, you would get the entire $30,000. Yet you are $10,000 short. If you have a buildup on deficit, then your invested capital for next year's calculations is now $410,000. This would go on until some defined point where the partner would see his share eaten up and would drop out of the picture.

Why would a seller accept a deal like this? Well, look at it from his point of view. He is getting $400,000 in cash and still has 50% of the deal. He will be given a management contract as a part of the deal, so he will be allowed to take a management fee off the top. If he has confidence in the deal, he will quickly see that within a few years he is going to profit far more than if he had sold the property and taken the $750,000 cash to the mortgage. But note one very important aspect here: Charles isn't being given the choice of $750,000 or the preferred deal. He must choose between this preferred deal or his best offer (if any).

The buyer's advantage is easy to see. You as the investor in this deal have bought sound management with motivation to stay in and do a good job. You would offer a preferred deal, by the way, on the condition that the seller to do exactly that—manage the property. If you were concerned about that ability, then you had best stay away from the deal unless it was so good that outside management could be found easily and quickly.

In making this kind of deal you might well find the seller suddenly changing his tune about how good the project is. "Well, I don't think the income will be *that* good" is the aftermath of some preferred presentations.

Big smart money uses the preferred deal to nail down solid projects with good management and a motivated seller who needs some cash. In the development business there are often good managers and developers who get cash-short on a new project and have to spin off one of their existing developments to make up for construction overages or whatever. These deals make for the mainstay of the preferred deals, but they aren't necessarily limited to that kind of project.

You can buy a business or any small venture on this preferred plan. Whatever you buy that is income-producing has the potential of being financed in this way. If you are looking at a business, don't buy 100% of the deal, but instead keep the current owner in at a percentage of the deal. That way you can move into many varied deals without losing your flexibility.

The Option

Buying with an option is an ideal way to put time on *your* side for a change. The option contract gives you the opportunity to put up some money that can build into a sizable equity in a hurry if you are right about the trends. If you are wrong, then you have kept your risk at a minimum.

There are several kinds of option agreements, but for the most part they fall into two categories, the straight option and the conditioned option.

The straight option is, as the name would suggest, a standard type of agreement that simply provides for the would-be buyer to pay to the seller a sum of money for the right to buy the property at a set date in the future at a price agreed to in the present.

Nearly all aspects of the contract are flexible and open to negotiation up until the contract is signed. For example, you can have a price that is tied to some third element, such as the price of gold, or income. You can have a date for the ultimate purchase that is flexible. Whatever those items are, they should be spelled out in detail at the time the option is given and the money is paid. A contract to buy and sell is part of the option agreement.

In the straight option there is no guarantee of sale, of course, and the seller is being compensated by the option price for the time the property is taken off the market. Also, the seller is fixed to the terms of the sale agreed on in the option, and if the value goes up well above the set price, it is the buyer who has profited.

At the signing of the straight option the money goes to the property owner, and there is no possibility of a return of that money to the buyer unless the seller cannot deliver the kind of title called for. The inability of a seller to deliver a clear title doesn't occur often, but it is a possibility. Because of this, it is advisable for the option buyer to check the title early in the period. If the idea is to hold the option and sell the contract, the whole plan can be ruined if the seller can't deliver good title.

The Conditioned Option

Here the optionee has included in the contract some conditions that can cancel or change the contract. These conditions might be such that the price will change, or the time to buy will be increased or decreased; most important, the conditions may call for a full return of the option money if something doesn't occur (or does occur, as the case may be).

From the buyer's point of view the conditioned option is the least risky of deals. If you have an option agreement and can tie up a tract of land for a period of time, and because of some condition in the agreement (which you may control) you can get your option money back, you haven't risked anything.

Conditions frequently used in conditional options include:

1. Soil test. Your right to test and approve the subsoil conditions.
2. Survey certification. Your approval of the exact dimensions, etc.
3. Bering test. A more detailed subsoil examination.
4. Site plan approval. Government approval of your planned development.
5. Issuance of building permit. Actual and final stage before building.
6. Partner's approval. A clear out if your partner nixes the deal.
7. Corporate ratification. Similar to the above.
8. Obtaining satisfactory financing. Necessary in many deals.

9. Government approval. This covers a wide range of sins.
10. Prior sale of a third property. When you need to sell something else.
11. Prior development of a section 1031 exchange. You have to develop an exchange before you can close.
12. Preleasing of to-be-developed space. Many lenders will demand this.

Of these twelve items, you can see that some can be simply accomplished and would not normally take a long time, while others can take months or in some cases, such as government approval, years. In all cases you (the buyer) have control over these items and can make sure the condition fails to be met.

The seller in the conditioned option contract will naturally object to tying up his land with the buyer having a full right to a refund of option money in situations where the buyer can back out of the deal. In essence, what has been created is a free option, with the money being not much more than good-faith deposit. Yet despite the fact that many sellers will object to such contractual agreements, many conditional agreements are made each day. Sellers try to limit the time for these conditions, realizing that the option is "free," and to provide for other safeguards to counterbalance the lack of security in the refundable deposit. Such counterbalances are in strict timetables, elements of past performance being a main criterion in the decision to go along with the condition if it is time-consuming. In essence, if the optionee is genuine and can give the impression he is going to buy, his chances are improved in using a conditioned option agreement.

All twelve items used in the option contract can be conditions in the actual sales agreement as well, and when they are used in that form of purchase they convert the buy-and-sell agreement into a conditional option agreement.

USING OPTION AGREEMENTS

THE scenario is as follows: A tight money market, high interest rates, and unrest in the real estate market. It is a growing buyer's market, and while the trends indicate that there is a turnaround somewhere down the road, you aren't sure when that is going to be. You have found a property that you want to buy. You know that the more you reduce your risk, the more profit potential you have in the future.

The price you feel you can get the property for is $100,000. The seller has been asking more, but that's what you want to pay. You find that current interest rates are around 15% in the prime market, around 12% in land sales.

Your first offer is a conditioned option agreement. You offer $10,000 option money for the right to buy the property for $100,000. You agree to give the seller $10,000 right away. As a condition to the deal you call for your unqualified approval of a subsoil test. You want to make sure that there are no subterranean conditions which will make building on this site very expensive. You allow for ninety days for this to be made. If you disapprove of the results, you get your money back and the deal is off.

If you approve the test, you have nine months in which to exercise the option to buy. All you have to do to exercise the deal is to sign the buy-and-sell agreement attached to the option and return it to the seller. You have sixty days to close on the deal after that. (By the way, when you close on the property the option money you paid is to be applied to the sales price.)

The soil test condition gives you three months to examine the property and decide if you want to go through with the deal. If you go ahead, you have another nine months to exercise the option to buy, and then another sixty days to close on the purchase. In all, you have one year and two months to make the deal. You paid $10,000 at the beginning, which is counted as a part of the purchase price. Even if the seller had insisted that the $10,000 not be counted at closing, you would have tied up the property for under 10% interest for those fourteen months.

When You Know You Are Going to Buy, Use the Option

You can see that when you aren't sure about buying, the option gives you some time to make the final decision. It locks up the price and terms so that you know exactly what to base the decision on. But when you *know* you are going to buy, the option gives you added appreciation and reduces your carrying cost for the first year or so.

In the deal described above, you would have tied up a $100,000 property for fourteen months at no real cost in the long run. You would have gotten fourteen months during which time you didn't have to pay the real estate taxes on that property and you got all the appreciation. As long as you don't need immediate title to the property, the option-to-buy deal is a great way to get a head start on appreciation.

Using the Option to Sell

The seller likes the option because he is a gambler. If you were a seller and you didn't have a buyer for your property and someone came along and said, "I'll give you money just to let me decide if I'll buy the property," you might be inclined to take the deal. After all, if the option fails to be exercised, you still have the property. In the meantime, the investor has paid you for the time which passed, during which you might not have sold the property anyway.

Options work because people like to gamble and options are a safe way to risk little from the seller's point of view.

As a seller you can use the option to help entice a buyer into your hard-to-sell property. If a buyer will pay your price if you accept his terms, then you should be able to get a better price by offering better terms. In the case of a tough-to-sell property, you may have to resort to some very creative selling techniques. There is nothing wrong with being creative, and moving a dog in a tough market may call for all the creativity you can generate.

One of the problems of the real estate market is that there are times when value has little to do with the ability to sell something. The inability to finance a deal might cause a builder to shy away from your kind of land, or a potential user to decide not to buy your vacant building. Use the option to get their interest, then sink the hook.

It's like anything else. If you can get someone's attention, then you can often create an environment that didn't exist before.

In dealing with builders and developers, getting them involved is often the first step in making the deal.

A tough deal may need lots of good ideas and some hard work running around getting tenants, getting sites rezoned, etc. The builder won't do that if he has to lay out heavy bucks to tie up the land. So offer him an option.

When the potential buyer has an option, he will start thinking how he can make a profit. Once the would-be buyer starts thinking about making a profit, then his creative mind is working in your favor as well as his. He will have to buy your land or building to make his profit.

The idea is to find a probable buyer for your property and establish some rapport with him. You can't walk into his office and say, "How do you do; by the way, I'll give you an option on my land." Sure this sounds fresh and creative. but also a little nuts.

A better approach is to have your broker make a presentation to the buyer. ("How would you like to buy Jack's land?") You will get feedback when you do that and you will see if there is any interest. One of the first signs of interest comes with the statement, "The price is too high." There is no reason to knock your price unless there is some interest (or he is just one of those guys who likes to knock everything).

Your broker can take this approach:

"Mr. Prospective Buyer, I understand your reasons for saying the price might be too high. But I feel that someone with your experience could put this site to its best use. The owner is so conscious of your ability that he'll give you a sixty-day option to buy this land. I know that if you truly become interested in this land you will profit by it."

22

The Four Stages of Every Purchase

THERE ARE FOUR STAGES that transpire from the start of your quest to invest in real estate to the moment you sign a contract to buy. They are:

1. Laying the foundation to buy.
2. Selecting a property to buy.
3. Negotiating to win.
4. Offering/contracting to buy.

These stages have moments when all seems to be going according to plan. Everything is smooth and no hitches appear. Then the storm can come crashing in and in a second the whole thing seems to fall apart. It is in those moments you see your dream purchase disappear.

Each of these stages has people involved: you, of course, your real estate broker and salesman, the other party to the contract, your lawyer, the other party's lawyer, the CPA, the closing agent, the escrow agent. Each one takes time and adds to the complexity of the transaction.

Buying and selling real estate for a profit is not a one-man job. There is no highly successful investor who has ever done it all on his own. There simply isn't enough time, and once the money begins to build up, the time it would take for some of the simpler tasks will best be left to others you can hire. It becomes a matter of priority as your wealth grows, not a matter of your not being able to do the job yourself. Wealth does have its rewards.

Laying the Foundation to Buy

Without the proper foundation you will have a hit-or-miss chance at success. Granted, there are people who do have success at things they do and they have no foundation at all. You can read about them or you've known people like that. And what did you say when you learned about the guy down the street who sold his house for twice its value because he was the key piece to a redevelopment of that block? "That lucky son of a gun."

That's right, he was lucky, and there are many other investors who will be just as lucky due to no act of their own. They just happened to make a buy that turned into a small pot of gold.

Unfortunately, for every one of these lucked-out investments, there are dozens of not so lucky ones. Buying real estate just is not an absolute guaranteed deal. Not everything you buy is going to go up in value fast enough (if at all) to cover the cost of holding on to it. Not every property will produce a profit; not every apartment building will be fully occupied and become a money machine. It is possible for you to lose your shirt investing in real estate no mater how much you know.

In fact, some of the smart boys lose their shirts. Not every investment I've made has turned out the way I wanted it to. I've taken a few high flyers that could have turned out like a diamond mine, but instead developed into a latrine. The risk in these investments was higher than you might be able to absorb; I thought I'd be able to overcome it. But the best-laid plans of men can be thwarted by men—or time.

So the occasional high flyer (risky deal) should be left to the big boys who can anticipate and afford the potential loss. Building your wealth in real estate won't always be an uphill ride. There will be times in even the most conservative investment when you may have to pull in the belt a notch or two to counteract temporary setbacks, such as high unemployment in your area (which does nasty things to rental projects), or city projects such as new roads that will have a future benefit, but in the meantime can cause you to lose tenants in your strip store because of the torn-up pavement for twelve months.

Being able to bend with these elements of the game is all part of the road to success. If it were easy, it wouldn't be so rewarding when you got there. Success is simply attained. Not easily, just simply. It requires only your dedication and persistence.

The development of your foundation is, of course, up to you. Some of you will get it in the school of hard knocks. That is, you will experience a bit more failure early in your learning, and if you hang in the success will come later. Hard knocks, by the way, is really a misnomer. If you succeed, you will look back on all your failures as important stages in your success. You simply cannot have success without failure. This is the most important part of your total foundation for success.

People who are failures in life find a reason why each failure was not their fault. People who succeed found out what they did to cause each failure, and did not do it again. The successful embrace failure, as it is essential to advancement and success. Into every real estate investor's life a little rain must fall.

I've given you all the basics you need to know to get ready. Applying them is up to you. The six elements of success—knowledge, enthusiasm, motivation, perseverance, clear goals, and no fear of failure—are within you if you pull it together and make them work for you. You can be a little success or a big success depending on your balance of elements. You will find the balance, or you simply will find that real estate isn't your thing.

There's nothing wrong with that. I have many tenants who feel exactly that way.

Finding a Salesman

There are two categories of real estate brokers and salesmen. There are realtors, and brokers who are not realtors. Let me explain it this way. The National Association of Realtors is a nationwide professional organization, the largest of its kind. The members of the realtors' association, in order to join, must agree to be bound by a series of rules which govern their activities in many ways. They have their own internal professional standard code, and a strict self-policing of that code as well as its enforcement. The realtors make up the majority of the brokers dealing in real estate. But not all brokers are in fact realtors. No state law requires the holder of a real estate license to be a realtor.

As a realtor I feel the major benefit to an investor in dealing with a fellow realtor would be simply that the realtor has a wider access to the product than the nonrealtor. There may be other reasons to choose realtors, and the National Association of Realtors would be quick to point out that realtors adhere to a more strict code of ethics, but while that may be true, I've known many fine and qualified brokers and salesmen who didn't want to bother to become realtors.

Yet, because your interest is in finding the best selection of property for your invested capital, look first among the realtors in your neighborhood to see if you can find the person with whom you can develop rapport; someone who will put his (or her) total knowledge at your disposal so that you will profit. It is your interest that you want this person to have at the top of his list.

The best way to find this ideal salesman is to look for him. Ask around in your own circle of friends to see if a name will be recommended. The good salesman usually has a wide range of satisfied clients who are that salesman's best source of new clients. Let your friends know you are looking for a good real estate salesman and pretty soon you will have several names to choose from.

Of course, that may not produce a person you feel you can work with. The importance of your having rapport with this person cannot be overestimated. He might be the best salesman in town, but if you can't get along with him, then seek out someone else.

Visit some real estate offices and ask to speak with a broker. Tell the broker that you are planning to invest in real estate and you feel you need to meet several salesman so you can find one you can work with over the years. If the broker is smart, he will discuss your needs with you and introduce you to one or two of his salesmen he feels would be right for you. If he was wrong, then try another office.

It is a good idea for you to explain to the salesman that you want to find a salesman you can work with and you don't want him or her to spend any time on your behalf until you are ready. The salesman will appreciate the fact that you want to find one salesman to deal with and will respect that. There is nothing worse for a real estate salesman than to be working with a client who hasn't told him about the other salesman from a competitor's office that he is currently working with. A lot of time and effort are wasted in the real estate business because of this.

Ask questions and expect answers that demonstrate to you that the salesman is knowledgeable about the area and can be of help to you. If you don't get a good feel for the setup, then don't waste your time or the salesman's—move on. The time you spend in searching out a salesman to work with will pay off benefits later on, and you will be glad you were cautious.

The Kind of Real Estate Salesman You Don't Want

• The salesman who doesn't ask you questions. This shows this salesman doesn't know enough to find out what your goals, your needs, and your time requirements are. If the salesman does ask questions but they are disjointed and unrelated to your goals, the time you have spent was for nothing. Move on.

• The salesman who talks and doesn't listen. (The worst thing any salesman can do!) Some do it because they feel they must impress you. It is okay for the salesman to give you a brief history of himself and/or his office, but you are there to have your problems solved, your goals met. He has got to listen to do it effectively.

• A salesman who is in a rush to make a sale. The first sign of this is when he wants to take you out to see a property before he has found out sufficient data about your needs. This is a common trait with real estate salesmen and may be a sign of lack of confidence. Understanding your needs is important, so he will save time by showing you property that is closer to your needs.

• The salesman you are uncomfortable with. It doesn't matter why—he smokes and you can't stand smoke, or the accent of his voice, or his hairstyle, or the funny mole on the side of his nose. If you are uncomfortable and can't get rapport, move on.

8 Traits of Top Real Estate Salesmen

1. **They listen.**
2. **They are prompt.**
3. **They ask pointed and direct questions aimed to help you shape your goals so that they will understand what they are.**
4. **They are constantly learning.** Real estate is a profession that demands constant update and learning.
5. **They are enthusiastic about their ability to solve your problem.**
6. **They demonstrate self-confidence.**
7. **They look successful.**
8. **They know the techniques of the trade which will enable you to make more deals.**

Once you have a real estate salesman on your side and you have been candid with him about your financial position, you are ready to move on to the second stage of the transaction—

Selecting a Property to Buy

Much has been said already about this stage. You know that the selection of real estate is very important because it sets the theme of the kind of real estate investing you are going to do.

If this is to be your first buy, then you will seek a living investment, that is, one you can live in yourself. That might be a single-family property or an apartment complex. Whatever it is, you will make the proper selection by following the many suggestions I've given you in this book.

10 Key Factors in Finding the Property
You Will Ultimately Buy

1. **Stick close to your back yard.**

2. **Don't get beyond the scope of your ability, but know what that ability is.**

3. **Be willing to stretch yourself to the maximum limit of your economic capability.**

4. **Remember that risk is relative, and you can ease, reduce, or even remove risk by knowing as much as possible about the area, the market, and the property.**

5. **In building wealth you must look for property you can improve.** The top of the heap has no place to go but down.

6. **Have property inspected for problems by qualified people.** The cost is nothing in comparison to the benefit of knowing the real condition of the property.

7. **Recognize that if you like it and can afford it, this is one of the most important parts of buying real estate.**

8. **Don't overanalyze a deal.** If it is really good, by the time you have made up your mind to buy it someone else will have bought it. Besides, the likelihood is your long-range projections won't be accurate anyway.

9. **Trends are generally clearly visible if you know where to look for them.**

10. **History repeats itself in real estate, so to know what is going on, look back to the past.**

In reality you don't select the property you are going to buy, but instead you select property you would like to own. The time between wanting to own it and actually owning it has yet to come. It is highly possible that once you begin negotiating to buy, you will change your mind about the property in the first place. Price and terms the seller is willing to take can be the deciding factors. Or, as you continue to progress in the selection process you might start negotiating on one parcel of land or one building only to find another which suits your goals better than the first. In that event, simply break off negotiations and go on to the second property.

Sellers should recognize that a savvy buyer will not be bound to a deal until the deposit is placed and the contract fully executed on all sides. The highly motivated seller, then, should keep in mind that a bird in the hand is worth a whole flock in the bush (in real estate that's the way it goes).

Naturally, it depends on the status of the real estate marketplace. If it is a sellers' market, that is, if the demand to buy is greater than the supply to meet that demand, then the sellers sit in a good position. They usually will have several potential buyers out there, so the prices are firm and terms not as easy as in other markets. There is a danger here, however. If you are a seller and it seems to be a sellers' market, it could well be that your property isn't in that market at all. Real estate isn't one marketplace; it is many. There is the single-family-homes market, but even that is divided into different strata, then vacant lots, acreage, office buildings, hotels, and so on. Not all markets are up at the same time, and fortunately not all are down at the same time either.

When you enter the market to buy, the condition of that market will affect the method in which you negotiate. Obviously, if it is a sellers' market for the kind of property you want to buy and you can't be detoured to buy another kind of property, then you can't be too standoffish in your attempts to bring the price down or to get better terms in the negotiations. If you do, you are apt to lose the deal to a less finicky buyer.

In a buyers' market, the conditions are such that there are more sellers than there are ready and willing buyers. This is more often the case in vacant land and acreage, as there is a lot of that kind of property. However, even this can become a hot item in a local area and then switch overnight from a buyers' market to a sellers' market.

A buyers' market might seem to be the ideal time to buy a property, but this is not always the case. You have to look to your own reason for buying and decide based on your own goal. If you wa ıt to utilize the property right away, or you anticipate the need for immediate income, a sellers' market could be your best market The buyers' market might have been created because of a recession or a slowdown in the growth of the area. These conditions might work against your goals, and buying at this time might not suit your needs. Price is a function of the use of a property, so as the need for the use (in the marketplace) goes down, so will the price.

Hotel sites in an overbuilt area will be a buyers' market. However, unless the buyer can find another use for the site or wait out the overbuilt condition, the purchase of that site at this time may not be prudent. To wait until the time is right to build and pay more might be wiser. Builders and developers have long since recognized the fact that in a development program the cost of the land is only a fraction of the total picture anyway. It makes no economic sense to buy cheap and have the risk of holding for a long time when only a slightly increased price (when compared to the total picture) will produce a ready and set property. You should remember this as well.

Now it's time to move into the third stage of the deal.

NEGOTIATING TO WIN

THERE are six key factors in negotiating and winning. These are:

1. Avoid personal confrontation during the actual offer. This is absolutely essential to successful negotiating. The buyer will do far better if he has a mediator, a broker or salesman, in between him and the seller, at least at that crucial moment when the offer is presented. Every professional arbitrator, negotiator, politician, salesman, broker, lawyer, and judge knows that placing the two parties (buyer and seller) face to face is not in the best interest of the best deal.

Here's why. A buyer attempting to make the best deal for himself is going to press the transaction. If that pressure is direct and face-to-face the seller can and generally will react in a defensive way.

Buyer: "Mr. Seller, I realize you want $150,000 for this property, but the most I am prepared to offer is $95,000, and that's a good price."

Seller: "Well, you can take that $95,000 offer and stick it."

As you can see, negotiations have broken down. Another example of the same kind of thing happening:

Buyer: "Mr. Seller, if it weren't for the blue and pink drapes in this house, which I'll have to replace, I'd be offering more, but whoever picked those colors out had to be nuts."

Seller: "My wife picked them out, and if you don't like those colors then you don't have to buy this house. In fact, I don't think I want to sell to you."

And so on. I could continue giving you examples of what can happen. Now, granted, there are those rare people who can sit down and make a deal face-to-face with the seller. However, it is too risky in my opinion. It is far too easy to say the wrong thing in such an encounter and end up with a seller who doesn't like you, and who will not be reasonable from that moment on.

Good salesmen who know the art of negotiation can deal with a difficult seller (or when things are turned around with a difficult buyer) without compromising your interest in the deal. The salesman can absorb (as he should) the heat of the negotiations so the other side of the deal can vent his frustrations to his broker and not at you.

2. Review your goals prior to making the offer to be sure the property fits in the scheme of things. There is no sense in starting out on a negotiation that will end up with a property not suited for your goals. A simple review of those goals will put you back on the right track. You will find on occasion that what has happened is that emotion has become an insider to the deal and has, at least temporarily, replaced your goals or at best clouded those goals from a clear sight. Watch for that, because once you get away from the goals and let emotion run wild with the deal, you will find yourself rationalizing away the best part of your plan.

3. Try to learn something about the other party's goals. If you know what the seller (or buyer) is really attempting to accomplish, then you might have a better way to help him reach his goal and at the same time benefit yourself. One example that comes to mind involved a client of mine interested in selling a lot he owned in a subdivision west of Fort Lauderdale. A prospective buyer made an offer through another office. My client rejected the offer and countered $5,000 higher. The would-be buyer balked and said he'd think about it. As he and the other broker were about to leave my office, he asked me what the seller was going to do with the money. "He wants to get a summer home in North Carolina," I said.

"Hell," the buyer said. "I'm a builder in Asheville. I have several homes I'll trade."

The story didn't end there. The owner of the lot never ended up with a home this client had, but an exchange was made in which the builder from North Carolina did participate, and he did get the lot he wanted. The seller of the lot got what he wanted because of the North Carolina builder.

Learning the true reasons for a sale or the real use to which the money is going to be put can be next to impossible sometimes. Your broker or salesman will have to dig a little to find out what he can, and sometimes you are well into the negotiations before you find even anything that resembles the truth.

Yet it is simple and should be clear to you that the more you know about the other party to the deal the better you will be able to come out on top of the negotiation.

In fact, it is more important for the seller to know more about the buyer than the other way around. And best of all, the seller is in a better position to find out information about the buyer once the negotiations start. Sellers being asked to hold secondary financing, for example, can rationally and logically ask for and usually receive financial information on the buyer. References and the like are a good source of data on the buyer, and most buyers attempting to buy hard will be forced to give up some of this information. You should be careful about relying on such references, however, as a buyer wouldn't give you the name of someone who would badmouth him. But you can get leads from a reference on where else to go to get more information about a person, so they are highly useful in that sense.

4. Be flexible in the negotiations, but firm at the same time. Does this sound like a contradiction? It's not. The idea is to decide where you want to be flexible and where you want to be firm. If the deal is all cash, then you are closing the options you are giving the other party and the only place where there is any flex left is in the price. This is, in my opinion, a bad stand for a seller, as it places him in the tightest of all boxes to make a deal. Naturally, this stand must be taken at times when cash *is* the only way out, and there is no way to generate that cash from some outside source. But the fact of the matter is there are so many options open to buyers to give a seller cash and yet keep their own out-of-pocket cash investment at a minimum that it is folly to assume that all cash to one party means all cash paid by the other.

Financing from a third party can usually be found in one form or other to help the deal along.

Remember "I'll pay your price if you accept my terms." Or, said another way, "I can't budge on the cash down, but I can work out the terms," or "I know I can get the best terms to suit my deal if I'm flexible in the price."

You will see a clearer path in the decision on where you want or need to be firm by having a good understanding of your goals, of course, but it is more than just that. The property and its ability to sustain a profit while it produces income is very important. You don't want to overburden the transaction with heavy debt that can't be sustained unless a miracle happens, just because you are getting the price you were willing to pay.

5. Remember there are other fish in the sea. I've seen buyers go into deep depression because they lost out on a property they wanted to buy. Losing deals will happen to you if you plan to buy and sell real estate. There will be other investors who have snookered you out of a great deal, and other times it will be turned around. Yet, crying over spilled milk won't get you anything. Move on to the next deal. Be careful, however—you might act a little quicker the next time out of fear of losing the next deal, so watch out for this overreaction.

6. Sellers should be careful about holding out too long. There is a time and place for holding out for a better offer. In typical hindsight I'll tell you that the time and place is only when you get a higher offer. Unfortunately, many sellers turn down offers that are never bettered. It might be possible that the seller will get a higher price sometime in the future by holding out longer, but you must consider the time element. If you are a tough seller and yet you really want to sell, keep in mind that as you hold on to a property you are losing the potential from the reinvestment of that capital. Not selling at $100,000 because you are sure you will get $110,000 is okay if you get the $110,000 within a reasonable time. If you had to hold on to the property for twelve months or more, the chances are you have lost ground rather than come out ahead. This depends somewhat on your motivation, of course, and what you might have done with the money from a sale. Remember, time is the key factor to profit.

These six factors will help give you some edge in the negotiation of the contract. You win, however, in every transaction that takes you closer to your goal. Naturally, the real win is viewed from the nineteenth hole. The fifth-quarter viewpoint of the game is always the easiest, and most investors look back at every transaction to decide if they have won or lost.

While this might give the investor a more satisfactory view of his analysis of winning or losing, it does provide the investor with the rationalization of that win or loss. This is natural, however, even though it will distort the true win or loss. The seller says, "You should have negotiated a little harder, because I would have taken much less than you paid."

In retort the buyer says, "That's okay, because if you would have held out for more I was ready to give you double what I actually paid."

Your viewpoint on winning should be tied to what it is you want to accomplish. Your flexibility in the negotiations will be very important to keep alive all possibilities to achieve what you wanted in the first instance. Try to keep personalities out of the picture by avoiding direct confrontation with the other party. If you have a broker or salesman, let him become the buffer, as he should, in nailing down the best deal for you. Remember, of course, that this salesman or broker will have to see the transaction from three vantage points—yours, the other party's, and his own. As long as you keep track of your own best interest and help point the salesman in that same direction, you won't have to press the deal; the enthusiastic and knowledgeable salesman will do that for you.

You have progressed well along in the buying or selling

process if you have a contract. As a buyer you haven't made up your mind sufficiently unless you are at that stage, and as a seller nothing happens until there is an offer which can generate a contract. Thus, on to the next stage.

Offering/Contracting to Buy

How you present your offers is an essential part of the negotiation process. There are four basic forms of offers—verbal; letter of intent; standard-form agreement; lawyer-drafted agreement. Not all are effective for each situation. Some may not be useful at all.

Verbal

It should be noted that in the transfer of real estate the contract must be executed in writing to be legally enforceable. This doesn't negate the use of the verbal offer, however, as with some people their word is as good as their bond. I've seen many deals hammered out in verbal terms with nothing written down until everything had been agreed to. This is not unusual or uncommon. However, for each deal worked out in such methods I've seen a hundred fall into one hassle or other as one of the parties lapses into forgetfulness as to what was exactly said, and the closing never occurs.

Frequently a buyer will instruct his salesman, "See what the seller will take." This is generally followed by the salesman asking the seller what is the lowest price the seller will take. These tactics generally don't produce any beneficial results and the salesman won't find out the real facts in this maneuver. Most sellers don't know what they will take until a plan is presented to them that suits their goals (at that moment).

For the buyer to tell the seller (directly or through the salesman) that he would like to buy the property and would the seller take, say, $100,000 is equally unproductive. If the seller was foolish enough to answer the question "Yes," the likelihood is that the offer will be $90,000 or less.

Thus, while there is a time and place for verbal offers, most sellers won't respond as effectively to a verbal offer as they would to a cash deposit and written contract. "Here's my offer, Mr. Seller, and here's a big check to show I'm real."

The Letter of Intent: A Written Verbal Offer

What happens in the letter of intent is that the broker or the buyer himself will write a letter to the seller. This letter states that the client (buyer) is interested in buying the seller's property on the basis of terms outlined in detail or in some loose form in the letter. The basics only are discussed, and the buyer leaves out much of the detail that would constitute a contract. One such letter of intent is shown below:

LETTER OF INTENT

Mr. Bradford J. Williams
President
Westmoreland National Insurance Companies
New York, New York

Dear Mr. Williams:

This letter is to indicate to you the intent of our prospective purchaser THE WORLD DEVELOPMENT COMPANIES N.V. from Aruba, Netherland Antilles, to enter into an agreement for the purchase of the apartment complex your company owns known as OCEAN SIDE APARTMENTS which is located in Hollywood, Florida. We have been informed by THE WORLD DEVELOPMENT COMPANIES N.V. that their legal representatives in Miami will draft the purchase offer and have it in your offices within five days from the date of your acceptance of this Letter of Intent. They are prepared to place $200,000 deposit with the offer.

The terms which would be acceptable to THE WORLD DEVELOPMENT COMPANIES N.V. are as follows:

1. A purchase price of: $5,750,000.
2. A cash down payment (of which the deposit is a part) of $2,000,000.
3. The balance of the purchase price would be held by the sellers

as a first mortgage over 27 years term at a variable interest rate to be 2 points below prime as of the first of each month.

4. Closing to occur within 45 days of approval of the various inpections to be made. These inspections will include:

(a) Structural of the buildings.
(b) Electrical of the buildings.
(c) Mechanical of the buildings.
(d) Plumbing of the buildings.
(e) Examination of the leases.
(f) Examination of payment records.
(g) Inspection of the maintenance records of the buildings.

5. In the event there is no approval given of these items within 15 days from the date the agreement of sale is completed, the sales agreement will be null and void and each party released from further obligations to the other.

6. Each party understands and agrees that there will be other terms and conditions in the final purchase agreement, but the first five terms outlined herein are the basic terms being agreed herein.

It is understood that the prospective purchasers will proceed immediately with the legal document if you agree to the basic terms in this Letter of Intent. It is understood also that this Letter is not to be construed as a contract and only in the approval and execution of the final document of sale will there be a bona fide contract.

Your approval of this Letter in the proper place indicated below will demonstrate your interest to proceed on this matter and your approval in principle of the price and sale terms indicated herein. Furthermore, your approval will acknowledge that as seller your firm would be obliged to pay our fee at closing of title; said fee is Three Hundred and Fifty Thousand Dollars.

I have enclosed a packet of information on THE WORLD DEVELOPMENT COMPANIES N.V. which I'm sure you will find highly informative. You will find ample references to check on, and I'm confident you will be impressed with the credentials of these prospective buyers.

Very truly yours,

Jack Cummings, President
Cummings Realty Inc.

I HAVE READ THE LETTER OF INTENT AND DO HEREBY ACCEPT THE TERMS OF THE SALE AS OUTLINED. THIS ACCEPTANCE SHALL NOT CONSTITUTE A CONTRACT, BUT MERELY AN AGREEMENT TO ACCEPT THE PRICE AND TERMS BASED ON THE SATISFACTORY APPROVAL OF A FULL AND BONA FIDE CONTRACT CONTAINING THOSE TERMS. OTHERWISE, THIS APPROVAL SHALL AUTOMATICALLY BE WITHDRAWN WITHIN _____ DAYS FROM THE DATE BELOW.

Date: ______________________________

____

Bradford J. Williams

There are many items in this letter of intent which could be altered or made less specific, of course, and each letter of intent will be different. The idea is to simply indicate what you want to do and to proceed from there. These letters of intent aren't much more than verbal offers, but they do start things rolling. A more impressive way to present a letter of intent and at the same time make sure you have the attention of the seller is to put a deposit with the broker and have him mention that deposit in the letter: ". . . and the prospective buyer has placed a deposit of $10,000 in an escrow account as a statement of good faith. This deposit will become a part of the total cash down at closing."

Many large transactions use the letter of intent format to get moving, as it enables the buyer and seller to negotiate without having the considerable cost of having their lawyers draw full contracts. However, this shortcut works only in some instances, usually in cases where the broker has a good standing with the seller.

As a realtor I never hesitate to use the letter of intent if I know the buyer is sincere. In fact, I recommend using the letter of intent in many situations. But in cases where I know the seller will react more positively to the more formalized and customary form of offer, I shy away from the letter of intent.

The Standard Form of Agreement

There are many forms of "standard" deposit receipt contracts or buy and sell agreements used by the real estate profession. These agreements are easy to spot, as they will have a notice of who the printer is and in many cases a statement showing the forms are approved by the local lawyers' association and/or were formulated by local realtors' associations. These forms will differ slightly around the country and may vary with the kind of real estate being bought and sold. Condominiums, for example, generally require some different terminology to take care of the special items of interest in that kind of real estate. There will be the usual attention to the condo association, the recreation lease (if any), and the percentages of ownership of the common areas. Vacant land also differs in the contractual needs as compared to improved real estate. A contract dealing with vacant land often can be far simpler than one dealing with the sale of a residence.

To see how the standard form works to your advantage, you need to understand some of the selling philosophy which surrounds its use. The form is simple and covers nearly every aspect of the transaction in common, easy-to-understand verbiage. If you are dealing with a board-of-realtors-approved standard form, you will have a form which is up-to-date on the needs of the area. It should have conditions which protect both the buyer and the seller and spell out in detail the important aspects of the deposits and defaults and the like. The magic that works for you as buyer or seller is the simplicity of the form. Nothing will frighten a buyer or seller faster than a twenty-page lawyer-prepared contract, even though the lawyer's agreement might be exactly the same, only spread out over more pages and in a different kind of type.

As a buyer you want the salesman presenting your offer to be able to concentrate on the deal and not on the form of the agreement. As a seller you want your salesman to be able to get the buyer in the heat of the moment to make the offer that might solve your problem and generate a sale.

To give you an idea of what one of these standard forms

looks like, I've provided a copy of the Fort Lauderdale Board of Realtors' Deposit Receipt Contract. This form is used for any sale, although it does have some provisions which are superfluous to transactions involving vacant land. There is ample room for the buyer or seller to add additional terms or provisions, and you can, of course, alter any of the standard provisions.

The form shown on the next pages has been filled out as though I were buying a $100,000 waterfront home. The property has existing financing of $50,000, and I am asking the seller to hold some additional paper. See what other "buyer" techniques you can spot.

Deposit Receipt and Contract for Sale and Purchase

Jack Cummings et al his wife, of *Fort Lauderdale, Florida* (PH *771-6300*) hereinafter called the Buyer, and *Hank Bigdeal* of *Boca Raton, Florida* (PH *n/p*) hereinafter called the Seller, hereby agree that the Seller shall sell and the Buyer shall buy the following described property UPON THE TERMS AND CONDITIONS HEREINAFTER SET FORTH AND CONTINUED ON REVERSE SIDE OF THIS CONTRACT.

1. LEGAL DESCRIPTION of real estate located in *Broward* County, Florida. Tax Folio No. *14-869-2770*
   Lot 11 plus East ½ Lot 12, Block H, Rio Mar Sub. Plat Book 1, page 105, Broward County.
   STREET ADDRESS: *1235 South East 15 Street*
   PERSONAL PROPERTY INCLUDED: *Carpets, drapes, kitchen appliances. The built-in bar. The pool table in den. Master bedroom furniture.*
   Seller represents that the property can be used for the following purposes: *Single-family residence*
2. PURCHASE PRICE IS: .... $ *$100,000.00*
   METHOD OF PAYMENT:
   Deposit herewith .... $ *5,000.00*
   Additional deposit to be paid upon acceptance of Contract by both parties on or before ______ 19 ___ $ *5,000.00*
   All deposits to be held in trust by *Cummings Realty Inc.*
   Time is of the essence as to additional deposit.
   Principal balance of first mortgage which Buyer shall *take subject to* $ *50,000.00*

Interest 9½ %; Method of payment *monthly*

Other: *Seller to hold a Second Mortgage in the amount of* $ *25,000.00*

for a term of 10 years. Payments to be interest only for the first 3 years, annual payments. Beginning the 4th year, monthly amortization. Interest to be 10%.

U.S. Currency, certified or cashier's check on closing and delivery of deed (or such greater or lesser amount as may be necessary to complete payment of purchase price after credits, adjustments and prorations). Said funds to be held in escrow pursuant to provisions of Paragraph R on reverse side of this Contract .... $ *15,000.00*

TOTAL.. $ *100,000.00*

3. SPECIAL CLAUSES: (See page 4 or addendum attached, if any) *This offer is subject to the Buyer's unqualified approval of a Subsoil Test to be completed at his expense. Said test to be made within 10 days of acceptance of this offer and approval made (or not) within 10 days after that. If not approved for any reason this contract shall be null and void.*

4. This offer shall be null and void unless accepted, in writing, on or before *March 1* , 19____.

5. CLOSING DATE: This Contract shall be closed and the deed and possession shall be delivered on or before the *1st* day of *June* ,19___, unless extended by other provisions of this Contract or separate agreement.

WITNESS: Executed by Buyer on ______ 19___ Time: ______

X ____________ */S/ Jack Cummings* (SEAL)

X ____________ ____________ (SEAL)

Buyer

ACCEPTANCE OF CONTRACT & PROFESSIONAL SERVICE FEE: The Seller hereby approves and accepts the offer contained herein and recognizes *Cummings Realty Inc.* as Broker(s) in this transaction, and agrees to pay, as a fee 7 % of the purchase price, or the sum of Seven thousand Dollars ($7,000) or one half of the deposit in case same is forfeited by the Buyer through failure to perform, as a compensation for service rendered, provided the same does not exceed the full amount of the agreed fee.

WITNESS: Executed by Seller on ______ 19___ Time: ______

____________ ____________ (SEAL)

____________ ____________ (SEAL)

Seller

Deposit received on ______ 19___ to be held subject to this Contract; if check, subject to clearance.

By: *Cummings Realty Inc.* By: ____________

Broker or Attorney

BE ADVISED: When this agreement has been completely executed, it becomes a legally binding instrument. The form of this "Deposit Receipt and Contract for Sale and Purchase" has been approved by the Broward County Bar Association and the Fort Lauderdale Area Board of Realtors, Inc.

Standards for Real Estate Transactions

A. EVIDENCE OF TITLE: The Seller shall, within ______ days (17 banking days if this blank is not filled in), order for Buyer a complete abstract of title prepared by a reputable abstract firm purporting to be an accurate synopsis of the instruments affecting the title to the real property recorded in the Public Records of that county to the date of this Contract, showing in the Seller a marketable title in accordance with title standards adopted from time to time by the Florida Bar subject only to liens, encumbrances, exceptions or qualifications set forth in this contract and those which shall be discharged by Seller at or before closing. The abstract shall be delivered at least 15 days prior to closing. Buyer shall have fifteen (15) days from the date of receiving said abstract of title to examine same. If title is found to be defective, Buyer shall, within said period, notify the Seller in writing, specifying the defects. If the said defects render the title unmarketable, the Seller shall have ninety (90) days from receipt of such notice to cure the defects, and if after said period Seller shall not have cured the defects, Buyer shall have the option of (1) accepting title as it then is, or (2) demanding a refund of all monies paid hereunder which shall forthwith be returned to the Buyer, and thereupon the Buyer and Seller shall be released of all further obligations to each other under this Contract.

B. CONVEYANCE: Seller shall convey title to the subject property to Buyer by Statutory Warranty Deed subject to: (1) zoning and/or restrictions and prohibitions imposed by governmental authority; (2) restrictions, easements and other matters appearing on the plat and/or common to the subdivision; (3) taxes for the year of closing; (4) other matter specified in this Contract, if any.

C. EXISTING MORTGAGES: The Seller shall obtain and furnish a statement from the mortgagee setting forth the principal balance, method of payment, interest rate, and whether the mortgage is in good standing. If there is a charge for the change of ownership records by the mortgagee, it shall be borne equally by the parties to the transaction. In the event mortgagee does not permit the Buyer to assume the existing mortgage without a change in the interest rate, terms of payment or other material change, the Buyer at his option may cancel the Contract and all monies paid on the purchase price shall be refunded to him and the parties shall be released from all further obligations. Any variance in the amount of a mortgage to be assumed from the amount stated in the Contract shall be added to or deducted from the cash payment or the purchase money mortgage, as the Buyer may elect. In the event such mortgage balance is more than three percent (3%) less than the amount indicated in the Contract, the Seller shall be deemed to be in default under the Contract. Buyer shall execute all documents required by mortgagee for the assumption of said mortgage.

D. NEW MORTGAGES: Any purchase money note and mortgage shall follow the forms generally accepted and used in the county where the land is located. A purchase money mortgage shall provide for insurance against loss by fire with extended coverage in an amount not less than the full insurable value of the improvements. In a first mortgage, the note and mortgage shall provide for acceleration, at the option of the holder, after thirty (30) days default and in a junior mortgage after ten (10) days default. Junior mortgages shall require the owner of the property encumbered by said mortgage to keep all prior liens and encumbrances in good standing and forbid the owner of the property from accepting modifications, or future advances, under a prior mortgage. Buyer shall have the right to prepay all or any part of the principal at any time or times with interest to date of payment without penalty and said payments shall apply against the principal amounts next maturing. In the event Buyer executes a mortgage to one other than the Seller, all costs and charges incidental thereto shall be paid by the Buyer. If this Contract provides for Buyer to obtain a new mortgage, then Buyer's performance under this Contract shall be contingent upon Buyer's obtaining said mortgage financing upon the terms stated, or if none are stated, then upon the terms generally prevailing at such time in the county where the property is located. Buyer agrees diligently to pursue said mortgage financing, but if a commitment for said financing is not obtained within ______ days (15 banking days if this blank is not filled in) from the date of this Contract, and the Buyer does not waive this contingency, then either Buyer or Seller may terminate this Contract, in which event all deposits made by Buyer pursuant hereto shall be returned to him and all parties relieved of all obligations hereunder.

E. SURVEY: The Buyer, within the time allowed for delivery of evidence of title and examination thereof, may have said property surveyed at his expense. If the survey shows any encroachment on said property or that the improvements located on the subject property in fact encroach on the lands of others, or violate any of the covenants herein, the same shall be treated as a title defect.

F. INSPECTIONS: 1. THE Buyer shall have the right to make the following inspections at Buyer's expense, subject to the provisions of paragraph 4 below:

a) Termite: The Buyer shall have the right to have the property inspected by a licensed exterminating company to determine whether there is any active termite or wood-destroying organism present in any improvements on said property, or any damage from prior termite or wood-destroying organism to said improvements. If there is any such infestation or damage, the Seller shall pay all costs of treatment and repairing and/or replacing all portions of said improvements which are infested or have been damaged.

b) General: The Buyer shall have the right to have a roof, seawall, pool, electric and plumbing inspection made by persons or companies qualified and licensed to perform such services. If such inspection reveals functional defects (as differentiated from aesthetic defects), Seller shall pay all costs of repairing said defects.

c) Personal Property: The Seller represents and warrants that all appliances and machinery included in the sale shall be in working order as of the date of closing. Buyer may, at his sole expense and on reasonable notice, inspect or cause an inspection to be made of the appliances and equipment involved prior to closing. Any necessary repairs shall be made at the cost of the Seller and, unless otherwise agreed by the parties, the Buyer shall by closing be deemed to have accepted the property as is.

2. Escrow for Repairs: If treatment, replacement or repair called for in subparagraphs a, b, and c hereof are not completed prior to closing, sufficient funds shall be escrowed at time of closing to effect same.

3. Reinspection: In the event the Seller disagrees with Buyer's inspection reports, Seller shall have the right to have inspections made at his cost. In the event Buyer's and Seller's inspection reports do not agree, the parties shall agree on a third inspector, whose report shall be binding upon the parties. The cost of the third inspector shall be borne equally between the Buyer and Seller.

4. Limitation and Option Clause: Seller shall be responsible for all costs of the above treatment, replacement or repairs up to 4 % (or 3% if this blank is not filled in) of the purchase price. In the event the total costs of items to be accomplished under subparagraphs a, b, and c exceed this amount, then either party shall have the option of paying any amount in excess and this Contract shall then remain in full force and effect. However, if neither party agrees to pay the additional amount above the applicable percentage of the purchase price, then, at the Seller's or Buyer's option, this Contract may be cancelled by delivery of written notice to the other party or his agent, and the deposit shall be returned to the Buyer.

5. Time for Inspections: All inspections described in Paragraphs 1 (a)and (b) above shall be completed on or before five days prior to closing.

G. INSURANCE: The premium on any hazard insurance policy in force covering improvements on the subject property, shall be prorated between the parties, or the policy may be cancelled as the Buyer may elect. If insurance is to be prorated, the Seller shall, on or before the closing date, furnish to the Buyer all insurance policies or copies thereof.

H. LEASES: The Seller shall, prior to closing, furnish to Buyer copies of all written leases and estoppel letters from each tenant specifying the nature and duration of said tenant's occupancy, rental rate, advance rents or security deposits paid by tenant. In the event Seller is unable to obtain said estoppel letters from tenants, the same information may be furnished by Seller to Buyer in the form of a Seller's Affidavit.

I. MECHANICS LIENS: Seller shall furnish to the Buyer at time of closing an Affidavit attesting to the absence of any claims or liens or potential lienors known to the Seller and further attesting that there have been no improvements to the subject property for 90 days immediately preceding the date of closing. If the property has been improved within said time, the Seller shall deliver releases or waiver of all mechanics liens, executed by general contractors, subcontractors, suppliers or materialmen and in addition a Seller's mechanics lien Affidavit setting forth the names of all such general contractors, sub-contractors, suppliers and materialmen and further reciting that in fact all bills for work to the subject property which could serve as the basis for a mechanic's lien have been paid.

J. PLACE OF CLOSING: Closing shall be held at the office of the Buyer's attorney or closing agent, if located within Broward County; if not, then at the office of Seller's attorney, if located within Broward County.

K. DOCUMENTS FOR CLOSING: Seller's attorney shall prepare deed, mortgage, mortgage note, bill of sale, affidavit regarding liens, and any corrective instruments that may be required in connection with perfecting the title. Buyer's attorney or closing agent will prepare closing statement.

L. EXPENSES: Abstracting prior to closing, State documentary stamps which are required to be affixed to the instrument of conveyance, the cost of recording any corrective instruments, intangible personal property taxes and the cost of recording the purchase money mortgage, if any, shall be paid by the Seller. Documentary stamps to be affixed to the note or notes secured by the purchase money mortgage, if any, or required on any mortgage modification and the cost of recording the deed shall be paid by the Buyer.

M. PRORATION OF TAXES (REAL AND PERSONAL): Taxes shall be prorated based on the current year's tax, if known. If the closing occurs at a date when the current year's taxes are not fixed, and the current year's assessment is available, taxes will be prorated based upon such assessment and the prior year's millage. If the current year's assessment is not available, then taxes will be prorated on the prior year's tax; provided, however, if there are completed improvements on the subject premises by January 1st of the year of closing, which improvements were not in existence on January 1st of the prior year, then the taxes shall be prorated to the date of closing based upon the prior year's millage and at an equitable assessment to be agreed upon between the parties, failing which, requests will be made to the county tax assessor for an informal assessment taking into consideration homestead exemption, if any. However, any tax proration based on an estimate may, at the request of either party to the transaction, be subsequently readjusted upon receipt of tax bill and a statement to that effect is to be set forth in the closing statement. All such prorations whether based on actual tax or estimated tax will make appropriate allowance for the maximum allowable discount and for homestead or other exemptions if allowed for the current year.

N. PRORATIONS AND ESCROW BALANCE: Taxes, hazard insurance, interest, utilities, rents, and other expenses and revenue of said property shall be prorated as of date of closing. Seller shall receive as credit at closing an amount equal to the escrow funds held by the mortgagee, which funds shall thereupon be transferred to the Buyer.

O. SPECIAL ASSESSMENT LIENS: Certified, confirmed and ratified special assessment liens as of the date of closing (and not as of the date of this Contract) are to be paid by the Seller. Pending liens as of the date of closing shall be assumed by the Buyer.

P. RISK OF LOSS: If the improvements are damaged by fire or other casualty before delivery of the deed and can be restored to substantially the same condition as now existing within a period of sixty (60) days thereafter, Seller may restore the improvements and the closing date and date of delivery of possession hereinunder provided shall be extended accordingly. If Seller fails to do so, the Buyer shall have the option of (1) taking the property as is together with insurance proceeds, if any, or (2) cancelling the Contract and all deposits will be forthwith returned to the Buyer and the parties released of any further liability hereunder.

Q. MAINTENANCE: Between the date of the Contract and the date of closing, the property, including lawn, shrubbery and pool, if any, shall be maintained by the Seller in the condition as it existed as of the date of the Contract, ordinary wear and tear excepted.

R. ESCROW OF PROCEEDS OF SALE AND CLOSING PROCEDURE: The deed shall be recorded and evidence of the title continued at Buyer's expense, to show title in Buyer, without any encumbrances or changes which would render Seller's title unmarketable, from the date of the last evidence and the cash proceeds of sale shall be held in escrow by Seller's attorney or by such other escrow agent as may be mutually agreed upon for a period of not longer than ten (10) days. If Seller's title is rendered unmarketable, Buyer's attorney shall, within said ten (10) day period, notify Seller or Seller's attorney in writing of the defect, and Seller shall have thirty (30) days from date of receipt of such notice to cure said defect. In the event Seller fails to timely cure said defect, all monies paid hereunder by Buyer shall, upon written demand therefor, and within five (5) days thereafter, be returned to Buyer and, simultaneously with such repayment, Buyer shall vacate the premises and reconvey the property in question to the Seller by Special Warranty Deed. In the event Buyer fails to make timely demand for refund, he shall take title as is, waiving all rights against Seller as to such intervening defect except such rights as may be available to Buyer by virtue of warranties contained in deed. In the event the transaction is not consummated because of an uncorrected or unwaived defect in title, the Seller will be deemed to have defaulted under this Contract. Possession and occupancy will be delivered to Buyer at time of closing. If Seller provided Escrow Disbursement insurance or if Buyer executes a Disclosure and Consent Statement, then disbursement of closing proceeds shall be made to Seller immediately upon closing. The broker's professional service fee shall be disbursed simultaneously with disbursement of Seller's closing proceeds. Payment shall be made in the form of U.S. currency, cashier's check, certified check, unless in the event a portion of the purchase price is to be derived from institutional financing or refinancing, the requirements of the lending institution as to place, time, and procedures for closing and for disbursement of mortgage proceeds shall control, anything in this Contract to the contrary notwithstanding.

S. Escrow: The party receiving the deposit agrees by the acceptance thereof to hold same in escrow and to disburse it in accordance with the terms and conditions of this Contract. Provided, however, that in the event that a dispute shall arise between any of the parties to this Contract as to the proper disbursement of the deposit, the party holding the deposit may at his option: (1) take no action and hold all funds (and documents, if any) until agreement is reached between the disputing parties, or until a judgment has been entered by a court of competent jurisdiction and the appeal period has expired thereon, or if appealed then until the matter has been finally concluded, and then to act in accordance with such final judgment; or (2) institute an action for declaratory judgment, interpleader or otherwise joining all affected parties and thereafter complying with the ultimate judgment of the court with regard to the disbursement of the deposit and disposition of documents, if any. In the event of any suit between Buyer and Seller wherein the escrow agent is made a party by virtue of acting as such escrow agent hereunder, or in the event of any suit wherein escrow agent interpleads the subject matter of this escrow, the escrow agent shall be entitled to recover a reasonable attorney's fee and costs incurred, including costs and attorney's fees for appellate proceedings, if any, said fees and costs to be charged and assessed as court costs in favor of the prevailing party.

T. Attorney Fees and Costs: In connection with any litigation arising out of this Contract, the prevailing party whether Buyer, Seller or Broker, shall be entitled to recover all costs incurred including reasonable attorney's fees for services rendered in connection with such litigation, including appellate proceedings and postjudgment proceedings.

U. Default: In the event of default of either party, the rights of the non-defaulting party and the Broker shall be as provided herein and such rights shall be deemed to be the sole and exclusive rights in such event; (a) If Buyer fails to perform any of the covenants of this Contract, all money paid or deposited pursuant to this Contract by the Buyer shall be retained by or for the account of the Seller as consideration for the execution of this Contract as agreed and liquidated damages and in full settlement of any claims for damages by the Seller against the Buyer. (b) If Seller fails to perform any of the convenants of this Contract, all money paid or deposited pursuant to this Contract by the Buyer shall be returned to the Buyer upon demand, or the Buyer shall have the right of specific performance. In addition, Seller shall pay forthwith to Broker the full professional service fee provided for on the reverse side of this Contract.

V. Persons Bound: The benefits and obligations of the covenants herein shall inure to and bind the respective heirs, personal representatives, successors, and assigns (where assignment is permitted) of the parties hereto. Whenever used, the singular number shall include the plural, the plural the singular, and the use of any gender shall include all genders.

W. Survival of Covenants and Special Covenants: Seller covenants and warrants that there is ingress and egress to subject property over public or private roads or easements, which covenants shall survive delivery of deed. No other provision, covenant, or warranty of this Contract shall survive the delivery of the deed except as expressly provided herein.

X. FINAL AGREEMENT: This Contract represents the final agreement of the parties and no agreements or representations, unless incorporated into this Contract, shall be binding on any of the parties. Typewritten provisions shall supersede printed provisions and handwritten provisions shall supersede typewritten and/or printed provisions. Such handwritten or typewritten provisions as are appropriate may be inserted on the face of this form or attached hereto as an addendum. The date of this Contract shall be the day upon which it becomes fully executed by all parties.

The form of this "Deposit Receipt and Contract for Sale and Purchase"
has been approved by the Broward County Bar Association and
the Fort Lauderdale Area Board of REALTORS®, Inc.

NOTICE:

Jack Cummings is a Registered Real Estate Broker and is dealing as a principal, and any profit or loss from a subsequent disposition of the Real Estate in this agreement is of no consequence to the Seller herein. This does not waive the rights of Cummings Realty Inc. to collect a commission herein.

This agreement is shown simply as a sample of what is used in my part of the country. Not all brokers here use this agreement, some opting for simpler agreements. Personally, I find the Fort Lauderdale standard form to be adequate for almost all improved-property deals, although I prefer to see sellers use a form which has the real estate being sold in an "as is" condition rather than have repair conditions for damage and the like. However, to a buyer the provision of repairs is attractive.

If you are the seller in the transaction you must take a very special look at any contract that has a condition that you repair items not working or any damage. I've seen many arguments over this lead to the filing of legal actions. The buyer wants anything and everything that might be determined to be in need of repair fixed by the seller, while the seller will have a different point of view. Inspections are important, but often there is a narrow line on many items. Sure the roof isn't new, but just because it is old doesn't mean it needs to be replaced, or even repaired, for that matter.

My suggestion to sellers is to either remove the repair-or-replacement part of the agreement, or count on having to spend up to the total maximum percentage of the price for that repair or replacement and take that into consideration on the counter-offer.

Buyers should realize, too, that sellers will look at the offer this way and should anticipate the removal of these provisions;

see the sample agreement provisions F(1–5). A good way to counteract this is to plan the removal.

When you make an offer to buy a property you should anticipate the seller making a counter to you. It is rare that sellers accept the first offer. This will, of course, depend a great deal on the market and your salesman, but in the majority of instances anticipate a counter.

To focus the attention of the seller on one item that you are flexible on (but he doesn't know that), then, will be wise. You do this by anticipating what factors of the deal are crucial to him or difficult in his situation. The inspections might be one area which you might be willing to bend on. If the total maximum exposure the seller would have in the deal due to the percent of price applicable to repairs was $5,000, then you might reduce your offer by that amount and be ready to drop that entire section as long as you had the right to make the inspections and approve of them. In that way you could firm up a deal and if you found the suspected problem was nonexistent then you won. If the needed repairs were extensive, then you could opt to negate the deal and renegotiate for better terms—or walk away from the deal.

You win by letting the other side win too. A smart buyer will put in some term or other that can be taken out of the offer as a face-saver for the seller. One good way to accomplish this is in the terms. The buyer offers a deal which calls for the seller to hold a second mortgage at 10% for eighteen years. The salesman presents the offer that way and the seller balks at the terms. A counter which the salesman feels would be acceptable is returned to you. The price is the same, the interest rate the same, only now the second mortgage has a ten-year balloon. You win because you anticipate paying off the mortgage within that time anyway, through a refinance of the total mortgage structure.

Sometimes it can be simple things like asking the seller to include some furniture, or to close within three months, when you didn't want the furniture or were ready to close much sooner.

As a seller you don't want to play around with the offers and counteroffers that much. That is the advantage of being a buyer.

However, because you might be the seller, keep in mind that the way in which you offer the property for sale is in essence your first offer. It is here that you can provide your "room to play," and can anticipate the first offer to be less than your offer for sale.

You will keep your negotiations as a seller to a minimum by offering good terms that have some flexibility for that buyer who wants to dicker with you to win a point.

The Lawyer-Drafted Agreement

Important deals might require this agreement, but there's a good argument against its use. I've successfully sold to happy sellers and buyers properties in the millions-of-dollars price range with the simplest of standard forms. On the other hand, I've had twenty-page lawyer-drafted documents on some of the simplest deals that caused nothing but problems. Why?

If you are a seller and along comes a buyer with a high-priced lawyer and he presents you with twenty pages of legal language, what are you going to do? Go to your lawyer, if you see any merit —or throw the thing into the wastebasket.

Let's assume you go to your lawyer. What happens now?

Your lawyer has to spend time reading each and every word, looking for deviations from the standard form he's familiar with. Also, to show that he's looking out for your interests, he will want to change a word or two, or a page or two, or rewrite the agreement.

Now you have a situation that can get out of hand. The two lawyers start to tear apart each other's agreement, and time seems to go on and on, with the heat of the moment cooling down and the deal lost.

Salesmen know and understand well the emotions of the buy-and-sell situation. As a buyer or seller I want my salesman to have everything going for the deal. I know enough about what I want to look out for my interest as long as the legal aspect is taken care of. So in those events when I feel I need a lawyer's advice, or a client of mine wants to have his lawyer draft an agreement, I suggest the use of the standard form with changes or additions to protect where needed.

Most lawyers will go along with that when the contract can accommodate the deal. This will be the majority of the transactions, if the lawyer will acquiesce in allowing the standard form to be used. Some lawyers, however, wouldn't use a standard form under any circumstances.

My advice from the realtor's point of view and as a buyer and seller of real estate is to keep it as simple as you can. If you have the best lawyer in town and you are comfortable with his advice, then you should listen to his advice and act based on that. It is rare, however, to find a lawyer ready and willing to come out in the middle of the night to draft an agreement and then stand by to work on the counter, as your salesman is doing, to nail down the deal.

Every buyer or seller should have the opportunity to seek out legal counsel if the deal warrants it or he feels it is needed. The buyer has more time to do that before the negotiations get to the point of the offer; the seller should know where he is going once the property is offered on the market, before the first offer rolls in.

Make the deal subject to your lawyer's approval. This is a salesman's touch to nail down the deal even though there is an out. It is important to keep the emotions hot. You are the buyer and you make an offer the seller might be inclined to go along with. "I'll go along," he tells the salesman. "But while the price and terms seem okay, I don't know how this part in the offer about my holding a wraparound mortgage will affect me. I want my attorney to review this before I sign."

The salesman, knowing that you, the buyer, might have a change of heart the next day or the seller might have a different point of view after taking the unaccepted offer to his lawyer (as well he might), will opt to get an acceptance subject to the approval of the lawyer the following day.

Two things take place in this kind of situation that are important. First, the seller relaxes in the deal. He does want to sell, and so far everything seems okay. He only wants the lawyer to check it over to see if it is a proper and correct deal. So he accepts the deal subject to the lawyer's review of the contract and approval thereof. The second and most important aspect is the mental release of the property. Sellers frequently hold on to property in their minds, not wanting to let go. If a salesman can get this mental release to take place, then the problems seem to melt away.

As both of these events benefit the buyer and now there is a contract that has been approved by both the buyer and the seller, all that must occur is the approval by the lawyer. Of course, the lawyer can still nix the deal, and sometimes that is exactly what happens. However, it won't occur often, and when it does usually it is for good reasons.

Keep in mind as a buyer or seller that there are times when you will need a lawyer-drafted contract. It is always a good idea for you to have a lawyer you can relate to who understands your goals, to use as a sounding board and adviser for any transaction. Do keep in mind the psychology of the deal and try to keep it simple. Smart lawyers know this and will often use the simplest form possible to get across the most complicated transaction.

Contracts in General

Throughout this book I've mentioned several items about contracts which I want to repeat as a general caution.

1. **Watch out for verbal offers.** Talk is cheap and memories as convenient as the other party wants them to be.

2. **Beware of returned drafts of offers that have been fully retyped except for a slight change that zings you hard**—a neat technique whereby your offer appears to be accepted, but what has happened is the offer was changed.

3. **Shy away from the standard form that isn't standard at all.** Some brokers, lawyers, and investors have developed their own contracts. They look exactly like the standard form I've included in this book except they won't have the name of the authority (Board of Realtors, etc.). Also, they might have some standard-looking phrases that are very one-sided and don't work to your benefit. A protection to you is to deal with a broker or salesman who will give you a copy of his standard form, which you can have

your lawyer check over in advance of a deal. If the form is approved, you don't have to worry about the little things and can concentrate on the importance of the sale.

4. Never be insulted by an offer or a counteroffer. Too many deals are lost by sellers who are insulted at a low offer. As a salesman, I tell my sellers that buyers often want to test the market. Making low offers isn't an insult, it is simply a buyer interested in the property looking to be educated. Don't feel that as a seller you have to counter on an offer that is very low. The best counter to a very low offer is often no counter at all other than a "Thank you, Mr. Buyer, but you had best check around. You'll find the price we are offering *is* a good price as it is."

23

Twenty-six Ways to Get In for Little or No Cash

1. **Paper in.** Make your offer with nothing down, giving the seller a note or mortgage secured by the property you are buying.

2. **Personal services in exchange for down payment.** If you have any specialty or profession you can offer in exchange for the down payment, try that. I know of a surgeon who trades operations for real estate.

3. **Pyramid.** Instead of offering a note or mortgage on the property you are buying, offer to secure it with something else. It doesn't have to be real estate. It can be your car, a boat, whatever. It doesn't even have to be something you own. You could use your parents' home or boat. (They would have to know about this, of course, and sign the proper document.)

4. **Total new paper.** It is possible to simply mortgage out in some deals at the institutional lender's. If the deal is right and you can borrow 100% of the cash needed to buy the property, you're home free.

5. **Third party second.** If the seller wants cash down, then perhaps there is someone else to lend you the down payment. Give him a second mortgage.

6. **Refinance something else to get the cash.** A form of pyramid—except not exactly. You use equity in something else

to raise cash to make the deal. Again, it doesn't have to be real estate.

7. **Sweat deals.** Prove to the seller that your labor will turn the property around and that if he sells to you for nothing down and holds 100% of the paper (or all of his equity over any existing financing), he will benefit.

8. **Sweat option.** In this you take an option on a run-down property and fix it up on speculation that you will be able to refinance it for 100% of your option price.

9. **Sweat contract for deed.** Similar to the above, but you are paying off a 100% mortgage and don't get the deed until it is fully satisfied. The seller holds all paper or paper over the existing financing.

10. **Syndicated equity.** Put a group together and get a piece of the deal because you did all the legwork and made the whole thing come together.

11. **Charitable contribution buy-out.** Each year millions of dollars of real estate is given to schools and other charitable organizations. Most of them sell the property to raise cash or add to their endowment. Frequently these sellers will work deals very easy and attractive to a sincere but no-cash-down buyer.

12. **A piece of the action for the down payment.** Give the seller a piece of the future profit in lieu of the down payment.

13. **Give stock or interest in the whole property to the seller for down payment.** You could incorporate and give the seller some stock as the down payment, with the single asset of the corporation being the property being purchased. Or pyramid this angle by incorporating with an existing property and giving up some action on that parcel. (A land trust or partnership interest might be equally as good.)

14. **Exchange a don't-want.** If you have something you don't need or want, exhange it for the property or at least the down payment.

15. **Exchange a future.** You may have a mortgage which you are collecting on and it balloons in two years. You can keep the mortgage but exchange part of the face amount as down pay-

ment. Or you might have a big commission coming up next year. Exchange a piece or all of that future benefit.

16. Lease with option to buy. If all or most of the lease payments can be applied to the future purchase, you can take over the property and fix it up and refinance or mortgage out with your new equity to pay off 100% of the option price.

17. Long closing on a conditioned contract. In a fast-moving market you might reap large profits from condo investing or other investments with very little capital tied up.

18. Take over payments. Some sellers are just trying to get out from under their mortgage payments. You can step in and save their credit rating.

19. The land lease deal. You buy the improvements (leasehold interest) and lease the land from the seller. No cash down, and you better this deal by having an option to buy the land sometime in the future.

20. Future-event condition. Down payment is to occur when something happens in the future (you sell your other house, your boat, whatever).

21. Look to the broker as a potential source of cash. You might be able to exchange something to the broker or the broker might take paper from you. He can then trade off that for his commission with the seller so it doesn't take a bite out of the seller and the deal.

22. Buy-in and partial sell-off. If you time things right and do some homework you can buy in with little or nothing down and agree to have a hefty payment in a year or so. You manage to sell off some of the property in the meantime, taking care to meet your terms of the mortgage with the seller.

23. Advance rent as the down payment. If you can get a prospective tenant to pay up a year or so in advance, you can use this as your down payment. Other tenants or your other property should be able to carry the debt, however.

24. The blanket mortgage. Use the pyramid scheme, but add security to the deal for the seller by combining several different properties and giving them as security to the mortgage.

25. Use a DPM to reduce the debt service. A Deficit Payment Mortgage is a mortgage which has a payment schedule that is less than interest only. This does two things: It makes the payments easier to handle, giving you a breather to put your act together and improve the property, and it continually increases the amount owed to the seller in the mortgage.

26. Wraparound mortgages entice the seller to hold more paper. A nice way to go, the wraparound. It benefits everyone and gives the buyer a manageable debt service.

Appendix

Appendix

TABLE A.

Constant Annual Percents Expressing the Sum of 12 Equal Monthly Payments Needed to Amortize a Principal Amount for the Term of Years Shown

% Interest	Years .5	1	1.5	2	2.5	3	3.5	4
8	204.694	104.387	70.969	54.273	44.266	37.604	32.853	29.296
8.25	204.836	104.523	71.104	54.409	44.403	37.742	32.992	29.436
8.5	204.991	104.666	71.244	54.548	44.542	37.882	33.133	29.578
8.75	205.139	104.805	71.381	54.685	44.680	38.021	33.273	29.720
9	205.287	104.944	71.518	54.823	44.819	38.160	33.414	29.863
9.25	205.433	105.083	71.656	54.960	44.957	38.300	33.555	30.005
9.5	205.578	105.220	71.793	55.098	45.095	38.440	33.696	30.148
9.75	205.729	105.361	71.931	55.236	45.235	38.580	33.838	30.292
10	205.879	105.502	72.070	55.375	45.375	38.722	33.981	30.436
10.25	206.021	105.639	72.207	55.512	45.513	38.862	34.123	30.579
10.5	206.171	105.779	72.345	55.652	45.653	39.003	34.266	30.724
10.75	206.318	105.918	72.484	55.790	45.793	39.145	34.409	30.869
11	206.464	106.057	72.622	55.929	45.933	39.286	34.552	31.015
11.25	206.615	106.199	72.762	56.069	46.075	39.429	34.697	31.161
11.5	206.766	106.340	72.902	56.210	46.216	39.572	34.842	31.307
11.75	206.911	106.479	73.040	56.348	46.357	39.714	34.986	31.454
12	207.060	106.620	73.179	56.489	46.498	39.858	35.131	31.601
12.25	207.204	106.758	73.317	56.628	46.639	40.000	35.276	31.748
12.5	207.356	106.900	73.458	56.769	46.782	40.145	35.422	31.896
12.75	207.503	107.040	73.597	56.909	46.923	40.288	35.568	32.044
13	207.654	107.182	73.738	57.051	47.066	40.433	35.715	32.193
13.25	207.800	107.322	73.877	57.191	47.209	40.578	35.861	32.342
13.5	207.946	107.461	74.017	57.332	47.351	40.722	36.008	32.491
13.75	208.099	107.605	74.158	57.474	47.495	40.868	36.156	32.642
14	208.248	107.746	74.299	57.616	47.639	41.014	36.304	32.792
14.25	208.396	107.887	74.440	57.758	47.782	41.159	36.452	32.943
14.5	208.544	108.028	74.580	57.900	47.926	41.305	36.601	33.094
14.75	208.691	108.168	74.720	58.041	48.070	41.451	36.749	33.245
15	208.841	108.310	74.862	58.184	48.214	41.599	36.899	33.397
15.25	208.991	108.453	75.004	58.327	48.359	41.746	37.049	33.549
15.5	209.141	108.595	75.145	58.470	48.504	41.893	37.199	33.702
15.75	209.287	108.735	75.286	58.612	48.649	42.040	37.349	33.855
16	209.435	108.876	75.427	58.755	48.794	42.188	37.499	34.008
16.25	209.587	109.020	75.570	58.900	48.940	42.337	37.651	34.162
16.5	209.738	109.163	75.713	59.044	49.087	42.486	37.802	34.317
16.75	209.885	109.304	75.854	59.187	49.233	42.634	37.954	34.471
17	210.035	109.447	75.997	59.331	49.379	42.784	38.106	34.626
17.25	210.182	109.588	76.138	59.475	49.525	42.933	38.258	34.781
17.5	210.331	109.731	76.281	59.619	49.672	43.082	38.411	34.937
17.75	210.483	109.874	76.425	59.765	49.820	43.233	38.564	35.094
18	210.632	110.017	76.567	59.909	49.967	43.383	38.717	35.250
18.25	210.780	110.159	76.710	60.054	50.115	43.534	38.871	35.407
18.5	210.931	110.303	76.854	60.200	50.263	43.685	39.025	35.564
18.75	211.078	110.444	76.996	60.344	50.411	43.836	39.179	35.722

TABLE A (*continued*)

% Interest	Years .5	1	1.5	2	2.5	3	3.5	4
19	211.228	110.588	77.140	60.490	50.559	43.987	39.334	35.880
19.25	211.381	110.732	77.285	60.637	50.709	44.139	39.490	36.039
19.5	211.530	110.875	77.428	60.783	50.857	44.291	39.645	36.198
19.75	211.679	111.018	77.572	60.929	51.006	44.444	39.801	36.357
20	211.827	111.161	77.716	61.075	51.155	44.596	39.957	36.516
20.25	211.976	111.304	77.860	61.221	51.305	44.749	40.113	36.676
20.5	212.129	111.450	78.005	61.369	51.456	44.903	40.270	36.837
20.75	212.279	111.594	78.150	61.516	51.606	45.057	40.428	36.998
21	212.427	111.737	78.294	61.663	51.756	45.210	40.585	37.159
21.25	212.576	111.880	78.439	61.810	51.906	45.364	40.742	37.320
21.5	212.726	112.024	78.583	61.958	52.057	45.518	40.900	37.482
21.75	212.880	112.170	78.730	62.106	52.209	45.674	41.060	37.645
22	213.029	112.314	78.875	62.254	52.360	45.829	41.218	37.807
22.25	213.180	112.459	79.021	62.403	52.512	45.984	41.377	37.971
22.5	213.328	112.602	79.166	62.550	52.663	46.140	41.537	38.134
22.75	213.478	112.747	79.311	62.699	52.815	46.295	41.697	38.298
23	213.628	112.891	79.457	62.848	52.968	46.452	41.857	38.462
23.25	213.780	113.037	79.604	62.997	53.121	46.608	42.017	38.626
23.5	213.930	113.181	79.750	63.146	53.273	46.765	42.178	38.791
23.75	214.081	113.327	79.896	63.296	53.427	46.922	42.339	38.957
24	214.230	113.471	80.042	63.445	53.580	47.079	42.501	39.122
24.25	214.381	113.617	80.189	63.595	53.733	47.237	42.663	39.288
24.5	214.534	113.763	80.337	63.746	53.888	47.395	42.825	39.455
24.75	214.685	113.908	80.484	63.896	54.042	47.554	42.987	39.622
25	214.835	114.053	80.630	64.046	54.196	47.712	43.150	39.789

TABLE A (*continued*)

% Interest	Years 4.5	5	5.5	6	6.5	7	7.5	8
8	26.535	24.332	22.534	21.040	19.780	18.704	17.774	16.964
8.25	26.677	24.475	22.679	21.186	19.928	18.853	17.925	17.117
8.5	26.821	24.620	22.825	21.334	20.077	19.004	18.078	17.271
8.75	26.964	24.765	22.972	21.482	20.227	19.155	18.231	17.425
9	27.108	24.910	23.119	21.631	20.377	19.307	18.384	17.580
9.25	27.252	25.056	23.266	21.780	20.528	19.460	18.538	17.736
9.5	27.396	25.202	23.414	21.930	20.679	19.613	18.693	17.893
9.75	27.542	25.349	23.563	22.080	20.832	19.767	18.849	18.051
10	27.687	25.497	23.712	22.231	20.985	19.922	19.006	18.209
10.25	27.833	25.644	23.861	22.383	21.138	20.077	19.163	18.368
10.5	27.980	25.793	24.012	22.535	21.292	20.233	19.321	18.528
10.75	28.126	25.942	24.162	22.688	21.447	20.390	19.479	18.689
11	28.274	26.091	24.314	22.841	21.602	20.547	19.639	18.850
11.25	28.422	26.241	24.466	22.995	21.758	20.705	19.799	19.012
11.5	28.570	26.392	24.619	23.150	21.915	20.864	19.960	19.176
11.75	28.719	26.542	24.771	23.305	22.072	21.023	20.121	19.339
12	28.868	26.694	24.925	23.460	22.230	21.183	20.284	19.504
12.25	29.017	26.845	25.078	23.616	22.388	21.344	20.447	19.668
12.5	29.168	26.998	25.233	23.774	22.548	21.506	20.610	19.835
12.75	29.318	27.150	25.388	23.931	22.707	21.668	20.775	20.001
13	29.470	27.304	25.544	24.089	22.868	21.831	20.940	20.169
13.25	29.621	27.458	25.700	24.248	23.029	21.994	21.106	20.337
13.5	29.772	27.612	25.857	24.407	23.190	22.158	21.272	20.506
13.75	29.925	27.767	26.015	24.567	23.353	22.323	21.440	20.676
14	30.078	27.922	26.172	24.727	23.516	22.488	21.607	20.846
14.25	30.231	28.078	26.331	24.888	23.679	22.654	21.776	21.017
14.5	30.385	28.234	26.490	25.049	23.843	22.821	21.945	21.189
14.75	30.538	28.391	26.649	25.211	24.008	22.988	22.115	21.361
15	30.693	28.548	26.809	25.374	24.173	23.156	22.286	21.535
15.25	30.848	28.706	26.969	25.537	24.339	23.325	22.457	21.709
15.5	31.004	28.864	27.130	25.701	24.506	23.494	22.629	21.883
15.75	31.159	29.022	27.292	25.865	24.673	23.664	22.802	22.058
16	31.316	29.182	27.454	26.030	24.840	23.834	22.975	22.234
16.25	31.473	29.341	27.616	26.196	25.009	24.006	23.149	22.411
16.5	31.630	29.502	27.780	26.362	25.178	24.178	23.324	22.589
16.75	31.787	29.662	27.943	26.528	25.347	24.350	23.499	22.767
17	31.945	29.823	28.107	26.696	25.518	24.523	23.675	22.946
17.25	32.104	29.985	28.272	26.863	25.688	24.697	23.852	23.125
17.5	32.263	30.147	28.437	27.031	25.859	24.871	24.029	23.305
17.75	32.422	30.309	28.603	27.200	26.031	25.046	24.207	23.486
18	32.582	30.472	28.769	27.369	26.204	25.221	24.385	23.668
18.25	32.742	30.636	28.935	27.539	26.377	25.398	24.565	23.850
18.5	32.903	30.800	29.103	27.710	26.550	25.574	24.744	24.033
18.75	33.063	30.964	29.270	27.881	26.724	25.752	24.925	24.216
19	33.225	31.129	29.438	28.052	26.899	25.930	25.106	24.401
19.25	33.387	31.294	29.607	28.224	27.075	26.108	25.288	24.586
19.5	33.549	31.460	29.776	28.397	27.251	26.287	25.470	24.771
19.75	33.712	31.626	29.946	28.570	27.427	26.467	25.653	24.957
20	33.875	31.793	30.116	28.743	27.604	26.647	25.837	25.144
20.25	34.039	31.960	30.287	28.917	27.781	26.828	26.021	25.331

TABLE A (*continued*)

% Interest	Years							
	4.5	5	5.5	6	6.5	7	7.5	8
20.5	34.203	32.128	30.458	29.092	27.960	27.010	26.206	25.519
20.75	34.367	32.296	30.630	29.268	28.139	27.192	26.391	25.708
21	34.532	32.464	30.802	29.443	28.318	27.375	26.577	25.897
21.25	34.697	32.633	30.974	29.619	28.497	27.558	26.764	26.087
21.5	34.863	32.802	31.147	29.796	28.678	27.742	26.951	26.278
21.75	35.029	32.973	31.321	29.974	28.859	27.926	27.139	26.469
22	35.196	33.143	31.495	30.151	29.040	28.111	27.327	26.661
22.25	35.363	33.314	31.670	30.330	29.222	28.297	27.516	26.853
22.5	35.530	33.485	31.845	30.509	29.405	28.483	27.706	27.046
22.75	35.698	33.656	32.020	30.688	29.588	28.669	27.896	27.239
23	35.866	33.828	32.197	30.868	29.771	28.857	28.087	27.433
23.25	36.035	34.001	32.373	31.048	29.955	29.044	28.278	27.628
23.5	36.203	34.174	32.550	31.229	30.140	29.233	28.470	27.823
23.75	36.373	34.348	32.728	31.410	30.325	29.422	28.662	28.019
24	36.543	34.521	32.905	31.592	30.511	29.611	28.855	28.216
24.25	36.713	34.696	33.084	31.775	30.697	29.801	29.049	28.413
24.5	36.884	34.871	33.263	31.958	30.884	29.992	29.243	28.610
24.75	37.055	35.046	33.442	32.141	31.071	30.182	29.438	28.809
25	37.226	35.222	33.622	32.325	31.259	30.374	29.633	29.007

TABLE A (*continued*)

% Interest	Years 12.5	13	13.5	14	14.5	15	15.5	16
8	12.680	12.397	12.136	11.896	11.674	11.468	11.277	11.099
8.25	12.847	12.565	12.306	12.067	11.846	11.642	11.452	11.276
8.5	13.015	12.734	12.477	12.239	12.020	11.817	11.629	11.454
8.75	13.184	12.905	12.649	12.413	12.195	11.994	11.807	11.633
9	13.354	13.076	12.822	12.587	12.371	12.171	11.986	11.814
9.25	13.525	13.249	12.996	12.763	12.549	12.350	12.167	11.996
9.5	13.697	13.423	13.172	12.940	12.727	12.531	12.349	12.180
9.75	13.870	13.598	13.348	13.119	12.908	12.712	12.532	12.365
10	14.045	13.774	13.526	13.299	13.089	12.895	12.717	12.551
10.25	14.220	13.952	13.705	13.479	13.271	13.079	12.902	12.738
10.5	14.397	14.130	13.886	13.661	13.455	13.265	13.089	12.927
10.75	14.575	14.310	14.067	13.844	13.640	13.451	13.278	13.117
11	14.754	14.490	14.249	14.029	13.826	13.639	13.467	13.308
11.25	14.934	14.672	14.433	14.214	14.013	13.828	13.658	13.500
11.5	15.115	14.855	14.618	14.401	14.202	14.018	13.850	13.694
11.75	15.297	15.039	14.804	14.588	14.391	14.210	14.043	13.889
12	15.480	15.224	14.991	14.777	14.582	14.402	14.237	14.085
12.25	15.664	15.410	15.179	14.967	14.773	14.596	14.432	14.282
12.5	15.849	15.597	15.368	15.158	14.966	14.790	14.629	14.480
12.75	16.035	15.785	15.558	15.350	15.160	14.986	14.826	14.679
13	16.223	15.975	15.749	15.543	15.355	15.183	15.025	14.880
13.25	16.411	16.165	15.941	15.737	15.551	15.381	15.225	15.081
13.5	16.600	16.356	16.134	15.932	15.748	15.580	15.425	15.284
13.75	16.790	16.548	16.329	16.129	15.946	15.780	15.627	15.488
14	16.981	16.741	16.524	16.326	16.146	15.981	15.830	15.692
14.25	17.173	16.935	16.720	16.524	16.346	16.183	16.034	15.898
14.5	17.366	17.130	16.917	16.723	16.547	16.386	16.239	16.105
14.75	17.560	17.326	17.115	16.923	16.749	16.590	16.445	16.313
15	17.755	17.523	17.314	17.124	16.952	16.795	16.652	16.521
15.25	17.950	17.721	17.514	17.327	17.156	17.001	16.860	16.731
15.5	18.147	17.920	17.715	17.530	17.361	17.208	17.069	16.941
15.75	18.344	18.120	17.917	17.733	17.567	17.416	17.278	17.153
16	18.543	18.320	18.120	17.938	17.774	17.624	17.489	17.365
16.25	18.742	18.522	18.323	18.144	17.981	17.834	17.700	17.579
16.5	18.942	18.724	18.528	18.350	18.190	18.045	17.913	17.793
16.75	19.143	18.928	18.733	18.558	18.399	18.256	18.126	18.008
17	19.345	19.132	18.939	18.766	18.610	18.468	18.340	18.224
17.25	19.548	19.336	19.146	18.975	18.821	18.681	18.555	18.440
17.5	19.751	19.542	19.354	19.185	19.033	18.895	18.770	18.658
17.75	19.956	19.749	19.563	19.396	19.245	19.110	18.987	18.876
18	20.161	19.956	19.772	19.607	19.459	19.325	19.204	19.095
18.25	20.367	20.164	19.983	19.820	19.673	19.541	19.422	19.315
18.5	20.573	20.373	20.194	20.033	19.888	19.758	19.641	19.535
18.75	20.781	20.583	20.406	20.247	20.104	19.976	19.861	19.757
19	20.989	20.793	20.618	20.461	20.321	20.195	20.081	19.979
19.25	21.198	21.004	20.831	20.677	20.538	20.414	20.302	20.201
19.5	21.408	21.216	21.046	20.893	20.756	20.634	20.524	20.425
19.75	21.618	21.429	21.260	21.110	20.975	20.854	20.746	20.649
20	21.829	21.642	21.476	21.327	21.194	21.076	20.969	20.874
20.25	22.041	21.856	21.692	21.545	21.414	21.297	21.193	21.099

TABLE A (*continued*)

% Interest	Years							
	12.5	13	13.5	14	14.5	15	15.5	16
20.5	22.254	22.071	21.909	21.764	21.635	21.520	21.417	21.325
20.75	22.467	22.287	22.126	21.984	21.857	21.743	21.642	21.552
21	22.681	22.503	22.345	22.204	22.079	21.967	21.868	21.779
21.25	22.895	22.719	22.563	22.425	22.302	22.192	22.094	22.007
21.5	23.111	22.937	22.783	22.646	22.525	22.417	22.321	22.235
21.75	23.327	23.155	23.003	22.869	22.749	22.643	22.548	22.464
22	23.543	23.374	23.224	23.091	22.974	22.869	22.776	22.693
22.25	23.760	23.593	23.445	23.315	23.199	23.096	23.005	22.924
22.5	23.978	23.813	23.667	23.539	23.424	23.323	23.234	23.154
22.75	24.196	24.034	23.890	23.763	23.651	23.551	23.463	23.385
23	24.415	24.255	24.113	23.988	23.878	23.780	23.693	23.617
23.25	24.635	24.476	24.337	24.214	24.105	24.009	23.924	23.849
23.5	24.855	24.699	24.561	24.440	24.333	24.239	24.155	24.081
23.75	25.076	24.922	24.786	24.667	24.561	24.469	24.387	24.314
24	25.297	25.145	25.011	24.894	24.790	24.699	24.619	24.548
24.25	25.519	25.369	25.237	25.122	25.020	24.930	24.851	24.782
24.5	25.742	25.594	25.464	25.350	25.250	25.162	25.085	25.016
24.75	25.965	25.819	25.691	25.579	25.480	25.394	25.318	25.251
25	26.188	26.044	25.918	25.808	25.711	25.626	25.552	25.486

TABLE A (*continued*)

% Interest	Years 16.5	17	17.5	18	18.5	19	19.5	20
8	10.934	10.779	10.635	10.500	10.373	10.254	10.142	10.037
8.25	11.112	10.958	10.815	10.682	10.556	10.439	10.328	10.225
8.5	11.291	11.140	10.998	10.866	10.742	10.625	10.516	10.414
8.75	11.472	11.322	11.182	11.051	10.928	10.813	10.706	10.605
9	11.655	11.506	11.367	11.237	11.116	11.003	10.897	10.797
9.25	11.838	11.691	11.554	11.426	11.306	11.194	11.089	10.990
9.5	12.023	11.877	11.742	11.615	11.497	11.386	11.283	11.186
9.75	12.210	12.065	11.931	11.806	11.689	11.580	11.478	11.382
10	12.397	12.255	12.122	11.998	11.883	11.775	11.675	11.580
10.25	12.586	12.445	12.314	12.192	12.078	11.972	11.872	11.780
10.5	12.777	12.637	12.507	12.387	12.274	12.170	12.072	11.981
10.75	12.968	12.830	12.702	12.583	12.472	12.369	12.273	12.183
11	13.161	13.025	12.898	12.781	12.671	12.570	12.475	12.386
11.25	13.355	13.220	13.095	12.979	12.872	12.771	12.678	12.591
11.5	13.550	13.417	13.294	13.180	13.073	12.975	12.883	12.797
11.75	13.747	13.615	13.494	13.381	13.276	13.179	13.089	13.005
12	13.944	13.815	13.695	13.583	13.480	13.385	13.296	13.213
12.25	14.143	14.015	13.897	13.787	13.686	13.591	13.504	13.423
12.5	14.343	14.217	14.100	13.992	13.892	13.799	13.713	13.634
12.75	14.544	14.419	14.304	14.198	14.100	14.009	13.924	13.846
13	14.746	14.623	14.510	14.405	14.308	14.219	14.136	14.059
13.25	14.950	14.828	14.717	14.613	14.518	14.430	14.349	14.273
13.5	15.154	15.034	14.924	14.823	14.729	14.643	14.562	14.488
13.75	15.359	15.242	15.133	15.033	14.941	14.856	14.777	14.705
14	15.566	15.450	15.343	15.245	15.154	15.071	14.993	14.922
14.25	15.773	15.659	15.554	15.457	15.368	15.286	15.210	15.141
14.5	15.982	15.869	15.766	15.671	15.583	15.503	15.428	15.360
14.75	16.191	16.080	15.978	15.885	15.799	15.720	15.647	15.580
15	16.402	16.292	16.192	16.100	16.016	15.938	15.867	15.801
15.25	16.613	16.506	16.407	16.317	16.234	16.158	16.088	16.024
15.5	16.826	16.720	16.623	16.534	16.453	16.378	16.309	16.247
15.75	17.039	16.934	16.839	16.752	16.672	16.599	16.532	16.470
16	17.253	17.150	17.057	16.971	16.893	16.821	16.755	16.695
16.25	17.468	17.367	17.275	17.191	17.114	17.044	16.979	16.921
16.5	17.684	17.585	17.494	17.412	17.336	17.267	17.204	17.147
16.75	17.901	17.803	17.714	17.633	17.559	17.492	17.430	17.374
17	18.118	18.022	17.935	17.855	17.783	17.717	17.657	17.602
17.25	18.336	18.242	18.156	18.078	18.007	17.943	17.884	17.830
17.5	18.556	18.463	18.379	18.302	18.233	18.169	18.112	18.059
17.75	18.776	18.685	18.602	18.527	18.459	18.397	18.341	18.289
18	18.996	18.907	18.826	18.752	18.686	18.625	18.570	18.520
18.25	19.218	19.130	19.050	18.978	18.913	18.854	18.800	18.751
18.5	19.440	19.354	19.276	19.205	19.141	19.083	19.031	18.983
18.75	19.663	19.578	19.502	19.433	19.370	19.313	19.262	19.215
19	19.887	19.803	19.728	19.661	19.599	19.544	19.494	19.448
19.25	20.111	20.029	19.956	19.889	19.829	19.775	19.726	19.682
19.5	20.336	20.256	20.184	20.119	20.060	20.007	19.959	19.916
19.75	20.562	20.483	20.412	20.349	20.291	20.240	20.193	20.151
20	20.788	20.711	20.642	20.579	20.523	20.473	20.427	20.386
20.25	21.015	20.939	20.871	20.810	20.755	20.706	20.662	20.622

TABLE A (*continued*)

% INTEREST	YEARS 16.5	17	17.5	18	18.5	19	19.5	20
20.5	21.242	21.168	21.102	21.042	20.988	20.940	20.897	20.858
20.75	21.471	21.398	21.333	21.274	21.222	21.175	21.133	21.095
21	21.699	21.628	21.564	21.507	21.456	21.410	21.369	21.332
21.25	21.929	21.859	21.796	21.740	21.690	21.646	21.605	21.569
21.5	22.158	22.090	22.029	21.974	21.925	21.882	21.842	21.807
21.75	22.389	22.322	22.262	22.209	22.161	22.118	22.080	22.046
22	22.620	22.554	22.496	22.443	22.397	22.355	22.318	22.285
22.25	22.851	22.787	22.730	22.679	22.633	22.593	22.556	22.524
22.5	23.083	23.020	22.964	22.914	22.870	22.830	22.795	22.764
22.75	23.316	23.254	23.199	23.151	23.107	23.069	23.034	23.004
23	23.549	23.488	23.435	23.387	23.345	23.307	23.274	23.244
23.25	23.782	23.723	23.671	23.624	23.583	23.546	23.514	23.485
23.5	24.016	23.958	23.907	23.862	23.821	23.786	23.754	23.726
23.75	24.251	24.194	24.144	24.100	24.060	24.025	23.995	23.967
24	24.485	24.430	24.381	24.338	24.299	24.266	24.235	24.209
24.25	24.721	24.666	24.619	24.576	24.539	24.506	24.477	24.451
24.5	24.956	24.903	24.857	24.815	24.779	24.747	24.718	24.693
24.75	25.192	25.141	25.095	25.055	25.019	24.988	24.960	24.936
25	25.429	25.378	25.334	25.294	25.260	25.229	25.202	25.179

TABLE A (*continued*)

% Interest	Years 20.5	21	21.5	22	22.5	23	23.5	24
8	9.938	9.845	9.757	9.674	9.596	9.521	9.451	9.385
8.25	10.127	10.035	9.948	9.867	9.789	9.716	9.647	9.582
8.5	10.318	10.227	10.142	10.061	9.985	9.913	9.845	9.781
8.75	10.510	10.420	10.336	10.257	10.182	10.111	10.045	9.982
9	10.703	10.615	10.532	10.454	10.381	10.311	10.246	10.184
9.25	10.898	10.811	10.730	10.653	10.581	10.513	10.449	10.388
9.5	11.095	11.009	10.929	10.854	10.783	10.716	10.653	10.593
9.75	11.293	11.209	11.130	11.056	10.986	10.920	10.858	10.800
10	11.492	11.409	11.332	11.259	11.191	11.126	11.066	11.009
10.25	11.693	11.612	11.535	11.464	11.397	11.334	11.274	11.219
10.5	11.895	11.815	11.740	11.670	11.604	11.542	11.484	11.430
10.75	12.099	12.020	11.947	11.878	11.813	11.753	11.696	11.642
11	12.304	12.226	12.154	12.087	12.023	11.964	11.908	11.856
11.25	12.510	12.434	12.363	12.297	12.235	12.177	12.123	12.072
11.5	12.717	12.643	12.573	12.509	12.448	12.391	12.338	12.288
11.75	12.926	12.853	12.785	12.721	12.662	12.606	12.554	12.506
12	13.136	13.064	12.998	12.935	12.877	12.823	12.772	12.725
12.25	13.347	13.277	13.211	13.150	13.093	13.040	12.991	12.945
12.5	13.560	13.491	13.426	13.367	13.311	13.259	13.211	13.166
12.75	13.773	13.705	13.643	13.584	13.530	13.479	13.432	13.388
13	13.988	13.921	13.860	13.803	13.750	13.700	13.654	13.611
13.25	14.203	14.138	14.078	14.022	13.970	13.922	13.877	13.835
13.5	14.420	14.356	14.298	14.243	14.192	14.145	14.101	14.061
13.75	14.638	14.576	14.518	14.465	14.415	14.369	14.327	14.287
14	14.856	14.796	14.739	14.687	14.639	14.594	14.553	14.514
14.25	15.076	15.017	14.962	14.911	14.864	14.820	14.780	14.742
14.5	15.297	15.239	15.185	15.135	15.089	15.047	15.007	14.971
14.75	15.519	15.462	15.409	15.361	15.316	15.274	15.236	15.201
15	15.741	15.685	15.634	15.587	15.543	15.503	15.466	15.431
15.25	15.965	15.910	15.860	15.814	15.771	15.732	15.696	15.662
15.5	16.189	16.136	16.087	16.042	16.000	15.962	15.927	15.894
15.75	16.414	16.362	16.314	16.270	16.230	16.193	16.159	16.127
16	16.640	16.589	16.543	16.500	16.461	16.424	16.391	16.361
16.25	16.867	16.817	16.772	16.730	16.692	16.657	16.624	16.595
16.5	17.094	17.046	17.002	16.961	16.924	16.890	16.858	16.830
16.75	17.322	17.275	17.232	17.193	17.156	17.123	17.093	17.065
17	17.551	17.505	17.463	17.425	17.390	17.358	17.328	17.301
17.25	17.781	17.736	17.695	17.658	17.624	17.592	17.564	17.538
17.5	18.011	17.968	17.928	17.891	17.858	17.828	17.800	17.775
17.75	18.242	18.200	18.161	18.126	18.093	18.064	18.037	18.012
18	18.474	18.433	18.395	18.360	18.329	18.300	18.274	18.251
18.25	18.706	18.666	18.629	18.596	18.565	18.538	18.512	18.489
18.5	18.939	18.900	18.864	18.832	18.802	18.775	18.751	18.729
18.75	19.173	19.135	19.100	19.068	19.039	19.013	18.990	18.968
19	19.407	19.370	19.336	19.305	19.277	19.252	19.229	19.208
19.25	19.642	19.605	19.572	19.543	19.516	19.491	19.469	19.449
19.5	19.877	19.842	19.810	19.781	19.754	19.731	19.709	19.690
19.75	20.113	20.078	20.047	20.019	19.994	19.971	19.950	19.931
20	20.349	20.315	20.285	20.258	20.233	20.211	20.191	20.173
20.25	20.586	20.553	20.524	20.497	20.473	20.452	20.432	20.415

TABLE A (*continued*)

% Interest	Years 20.5	21	21.5	22	22.5	23	23.5	24
20.5	20.823	20.791	20.763	20.737	20.714	20.693	20.674	20.657
20.75	21.060	21.030	21.002	20.977	20.955	20.934	20.916	20.900
21	21.298	21.269	21.242	21.218	21.196	21.176	21.159	21.143
21.25	21.537	21.508	21.482	21.458	21.437	21.419	21.402	21.386
21.5	21.776	21.748	21.722	21.700	21.679	21.661	21.645	21.630
21.75	22.015	21.988	21.963	21.941	21.922	21.904	21.888	21.874
22	22.255	22.228	22.205	22.183	22.164	22.147	22.132	22.118
22.25	22.495	22.469	22.446	22.426	22.407	22.391	22.376	22.363
22.5	22.736	22.710	22.688	22.668	22.650	22.634	22.620	22.607
22.75	22.976	22.952	22.930	22.911	22.894	22.878	22.865	22.852
23	23.217	23.194	23.173	23.154	23.137	23.123	23.109	23.097
23.25	23.459	23.436	23.416	23.398	23.381	23.367	23.354	23.343
23.5	23.701	23.679	23.659	23.641	23.626	23.612	23.599	23.588
23.75	23.943	23.921	23.902	23.885	23.870	23.857	23.845	23.834
24	24.185	24.164	24.146	24.129	24.115	24.102	24.090	24.080
24.25	24.428	24.408	24.390	24.374	24.360	24.347	24.336	24.326
24.5	24.671	24.651	24.634	24.619	24.605	24.593	24.582	24.573
24.75	24.914	24.895	24.878	24.863	24.850	24.839	24.828	24.819
25	25.158	25.139	25.123	25.109	25.096	25.085	25.075	25.066

TABLE A (*continued*)

% Interest	Years 24.5	25	25.5	26	26.5	27	27.5	28
8	9.322	9.262	9.205	9.151	9.100	9.051	9.005	8.961
8.25	9.520	9.461	9.406	9.353	9.303	9.255	9.210	9.167
8.5	9.720	9.663	9.608	9.557	9.508	9.461	9.417	9.375
8.75	9.922	9.866	9.812	9.762	9.714	9.669	9.625	9.585
9	10.126	10.070	10.018	9.969	9.922	9.878	9.836	9.796
9.25	10.331	10.277	10.226	10.177	10.131	10.088	10.047	10.008
9.5	10.537	10.484	10.434	10.387	10.343	10.300	10.260	10.223
9.75	10.745	10.694	10.645	10.599	10.555	10.514	10.475	10.438
10	10.955	10.904	10.857	10.812	10.769	10.729	10.691	10.656
10.25	11.166	11.117	11.070	11.026	10.985	10.946	10.909	10.874
10.5	11.378	11.330	11.285	11.242	11.202	11.164	11.128	11.094
10.75	11.592	11.545	11.501	11.459	11.420	11.383	11.348	11.315
11	11.807	11.761	11.718	11.678	11.639	11.603	11.570	11.538
11.25	12.024	11.979	11.937	11.897	11.860	11.825	11.792	11.761
11.5	12.241	12.198	12.157	12.118	12.082	12.048	12.016	11.986
11.75	12.460	12.418	12.378	12.340	12.305	12.272	12.241	12.212
12	12.680	12.639	12.600	12.563	12.529	12.497	12.467	12.439
12.25	12.901	12.861	12.823	12.788	12.755	12.724	12.695	12.667
12.5	13.124	13.084	13.047	13.013	12.981	12.951	12.923	12.897
12.75	13.347	13.309	13.273	13.240	13.208	13.179	13.152	13.127
13	13.571	13.534	13.499	13.467	13.437	13.409	13.382	13.358
13.25	13.797	13.760	13.727	13.695	13.666	13.639	13.613	13.589
13.5	14.023	13.988	13.955	13.925	13.896	13.870	13.845	13.822
13.75	14.250	14.216	14.184	14.155	14.127	14.102	14.078	14.056
14	14.478	14.445	14.414	14.386	14.359	14.334	14.311	14.290
14.25	14.707	14.675	14.645	14.618	14.592	14.568	14.546	14.525
14.5	14.937	14.906	14.877	14.850	14.825	14.802	14.781	14.761
14.75	15.168	15.138	15.110	15.084	15.059	15.037	15.016	14.997
15	15.399	15.370	15.343	15.318	15.294	15.273	15.253	15.234
15.25	15.632	15.603	15.577	15.552	15.530	15.509	15.490	15.472
15.5	15.865	15.837	15.811	15.788	15.766	15.746	15.728	15.711
15.75	16.098	16.071	16.047	16.024	16.003	15.984	15.966	15.950
16	16.333	16.307	16.283	16.261	16.241	16.222	16.205	16.189
16.25	16.568	16.542	16.519	16.498	16.479	16.461	16.444	16.429
16.5	16.803	16.779	16.757	16.736	16.717	16.700	16.684	16.669
16.75	17.039	17.016	16.994	16.975	16.957	16.940	16.925	16.910
17	17.276	17.254	17.233	17.214	17.196	17.180	17.165	17.152
17.25	17.514	17.492	17.472	17.453	17.436	17.421	17.407	17.394
17.5	17.752	17.730	17.711	17.693	17.677	17.662	17.649	17.636
17.75	17.990	17.970	17.951	17.934	17.918	17.904	17.891	17.879
18	18.229	18.209	18.191	18.175	18.160	18.146	18.133	18.122
18.25	18.468	18.449	18.432	18.416	18.401	18.388	18.376	18.365
18.5	18.708	18.690	18.673	18.658	18.644	18.631	18.619	18.609
18.75	18.949	18.931	18.915	18.900	18.886	18.874	18.863	18.853
19	19.189	19.172	19.157	19.142	19.129	19.118	19.107	19.097
19.25	19.431	19.414	19.399	19.385	19.373	19.362	19.351	19.342
19.5	19.672	19.656	19.642	19.628	19.617	19.606	19.596	19.587
19.75	19.914	19.899	19.885	19.872	19.861	19.850	19.841	19.832
20	20.156	20.141	20.128	20.116	20.105	20.095	20.086	20.078
20.25	20.399	20.385	20.372	20.360	20.349	20.340	20.331	20.323

TABLE A (*continued*)

% Interest	Years 24.5	25	25.5	26	26.5	27	27.5	28
20.5	20.642	20.628	20.616	20.604	20.594	20.585	20.577	20.569
20.75	20.885	20.872	20.860	20.849	20.839	20.831	20.823	20.816
21	21.129	21.116	21.104	21.094	21.085	21.076	21.069	21.062
21.25	21.373	21.360	21.349	21.339	21.330	21.322	21.315	21.308
21.5	21.617	21.605	21.594	21.585	21.576	21.568	21.561	21.555
21.75	21.861	21.850	21.840	21.830	21.822	21.815	21.808	21.802
22	22.106	22.095	22.085	22.076	22.068	22.061	22.055	22.049
22.25	22.351	22.340	22.331	22.322	22.315	22.308	22.302	22.296
22.5	22.596	22.586	22.577	22.569	22.561	22.555	22.549	22.544
22.75	22.841	22.832	22.823	22.815	22.808	22.802	22.796	22.791
23	23.087	23.078	23.069	23.062	23.055	23.049	23.044	23.039
23.25	23.333	23.324	23.316	23.309	23.302	23.296	23.291	23.287
23.5	23.579	23.570	23.562	23.555	23.549	23.544	23.539	23.535
23.75	23.825	23.817	23.809	23.803	23.797	23.792	23.787	23.783
24	24.071	24.063	24.056	24.050	24.044	24.039	24.035	24.031
24.25	24.318	24.310	24.303	24.297	24.292	24.287	24.283	24.279
24.5	24.565	24.557	24.551	24.545	24.540	24.535	24.531	24.528
24.75	24.811	24.804	24.798	24.792	24.788	24.783	24.779	24.776
25	25.058	25.052	25.046	25.040	25.036	25.031	25.028	25.025

TABLE A (*continued*)

% Interest	Years 28.5	29	29.5	30	30.5	31	31.5	32
8	8.919	8.879	8.841	8.805	8.771	8.738	8.706	8.676
8.25	9.126	9.087	9.050	9.015	8.982	8.950	8.919	8.890
8.5	9.335	9.297	9.261	9.227	9.194	9.163	9.134	9.106
8.75	9.546	9.509	9.474	9.440	9.409	9.379	9.350	9.323
9	9.758	9.722	9.688	9.656	9.625	9.596	9.568	9.541
9.25	9.972	9.937	9.904	9.872	9.842	9.814	9.787	9.762
9.5	10.187	10.153	10.121	10.090	10.061	10.034	10.008	9.983
9.75	10.404	10.371	10.339	10.310	10.282	10.255	10.230	10.206
10	10.622	10.590	10.560	10.531	10.504	10.478	10.454	10.431
10.25	10.841	10.810	10.781	10.753	10.727	10.702	10.679	10.657
10.5	11.062	11.032	11.004	10.977	10.952	10.928	10.905	10.884
10.75	11.284	11.255	11.228	11.202	11.177	11.154	11.132	11.112
11	11.508	11.480	11.453	11.428	11.404	11.382	11.361	11.341
11.25	11.732	11.705	11.679	11.655	11.632	11.611	11.591	11.572
11.5	11.958	11.932	11.907	11.884	11.862	11.841	11.821	11.803
11.75	12.185	12.160	12.135	12.113	12.092	12.072	12.053	12.035
12	12.413	12.388	12.365	12.343	12.323	12.304	12.286	12.269
12.25	12.642	12.618	12.596	12.575	12.555	12.537	12.519	12.503
12.5	12.872	12.849	12.827	12.807	12.788	12.770	12.754	12.738
12.75	13.103	13.081	13.060	13.040	13.022	13.005	12.989	12.974
13	13.335	13.313	13.293	13.274	13.257	13.241	13.225	13.211
13.25	13.567	13.547	13.527	13.509	13.492	13.477	13.462	13.448
13.5	13.801	13.781	13.762	13.745	13.729	13.714	13.700	13.686
13.75	14.035	14.016	13.998	13.981	13.966	13.951	13.938	13.925
14	14.270	14.252	14.234	14.218	14.204	14.190	14.177	14.165
14.25	14.506	14.488	14.472	14.456	14.442	14.429	14.416	14.405
14.5	14.742	14.725	14.709	14.695	14.681	14.668	14.656	14.645
14.75	14.980	14.963	14.948	14.934	14.921	14.908	14.897	14.887
15	15.217	15.202	15.187	15.173	15.161	15.149	15.138	15.128
15.25	15.456	15.441	15.427	15.414	15.401	15.390	15.380	15.370
15.5	15.695	15.680	15.667	15.654	15.643	15.632	15.622	15.613
15.75	15.934	15.920	15.907	15.895	15.884	15.874	15.865	15.856
16	16.174	16.161	16.149	16.137	16.127	16.117	16.108	16.100
16.25	16.415	16.402	16.390	16.379	16.369	16.360	16.351	16.343
16.5	16.656	16.644	16.632	16.622	16.612	16.603	16.595	16.588
16.75	16.898	16.886	16.875	16.865	16.856	16.847	16.839	16.832
17	17.140	17.128	17.118	17.108	17.099	17.091	17.084	17.077
17.25	17.382	17.371	17.361	17.352	17.343	17.336	17.329	17.322
17.5	17.625	17.614	17.605	17.596	17.588	17.581	17.574	17.568
17.75	17.868	17.858	17.849	17.840	17.833	17.826	17.819	17.813
18	18.111	18.102	18.093	18.085	18.078	18.071	18.065	18.059
18.25	18.355	18.346	18.338	18.330	18.323	18.317	18.311	18.306
18.5	18.599	18.591	18.583	18.575	18.569	18.563	18.557	18.552
18.75	18.844	18.835	18.828	18.821	18.815	18.809	18.804	18.799
19	19.089	19.081	19.073	19.067	19.061	19.055	19.050	19.046
19.25	19.334	19.326	19.319	19.313	19.307	19.302	19.297	19.293
19.5	19.579	19.572	19.565	19.559	19.554	19.549	19.544	19.540
19.75	19.825	19.818	19.811	19.806	19.800	19.796	19.791	19.787
20	20.070	20.064	20.058	20.052	20.047	20.043	20.039	20.035
20.25	20.316	20.310	20.304	20.299	20.294	20.290	20.286	20.283

TABLE A (*continued*)

% Interest	Years 28.5	29	29.5	30	30.5	31	31.5	32
20.5	20.563	20.557	20.551	20.546	20.542	20.538	20.534	20.531
20.75	20.809	20.803	20.798	20.793	20.789	20.785	20.782	20.779
21	21.056	21.050	21.045	21.041	21.037	21.033	21.030	21.027
21.25	21.303	21.297	21.293	21.288	21.284	21.281	21.278	21.275
21.5	21.550	21.545	21.540	21.536	21.532	21.529	21.526	21.524
21.75	21.797	21.792	21.788	21.784	21.780	21.777	21.774	21.772
22	22.044	22.040	22.035	22.032	22.029	22.026	22.023	22.021
22.25	22.292	22.287	22.283	22.280	22.277	22.274	22.271	22.269
22.5	22.539	22.535	22.531	22.528	22.525	22.522	22.520	22.518
22.75	22.787	22.783	22.780	22.776	22.774	22.771	22.769	22.767
23	23.035	23.031	23.028	23.025	23.022	23.020	23.018	23.016
23.25	23.283	23.279	23.276	23.273	23.271	23.268	23.266	23.265
23.5	23.531	23.528	23.525	23.522	23.519	23.517	23.515	23.514
23.75	23.779	23.776	23.773	23.770	23.768	23.766	23.764	23.763
24	24.027	24.024	24.022	24.019	24.017	24.015	24.013	24.012
24.25	24.276	24.273	24.270	24.268	24.266	24.264	24.263	24.261
24.5	24.524	24.522	24.519	24.517	24.515	24.513	24.512	24.510
24.75	24.773	24.770	24.768	24.766	24.764	24.762	24.761	24.760
25	25.022	25.019	25.017	25.015	25.013	25.012	25.010	25.009

TABLE A (*continued*)

% Interest	Years 32.5	33	33.5	34	34.5	35	35.5	36
8	8.648	8.621	8.595	8.570	8.546	8.523	8.501	8.481
8.25	8.862	8.836	8.811	8.787	8.764	8.742	8.721	8.701
8.5	9.079	9.053	9.029	9.006	8.983	8.962	8.942	8.923
8.75	9.297	9.272	9.249	9.226	9.205	9.184	9.165	9.146
9	9.516	9.492	9.470	9.448	9.428	9.408	9.389	9.372
9.25	9.737	9.714	9.692	9.672	9.652	9.633	9.615	9.598
9.5	9.960	9.938	9.917	9.896	9.877	9.859	9.842	9.826
9.75	10.184	10.162	10.142	10.123	10.104	10.087	10.071	10.055
10	10.409	10.388	10.369	10.350	10.333	10.316	10.300	10.285
10.25	10.636	10.616	10.597	10.579	10.562	10.546	10.531	10.517
10.5	10.863	10.844	10.826	10.809	10.793	10.778	10.763	10.749
10.75	11.092	11.074	11.057	11.040	11.025	11.010	10.996	10.983
11	11.322	11.305	11.288	11.272	11.258	11.243	11.230	11.218
11.25	11.554	11.537	11.521	11.506	11.491	11.478	11.465	11.453
11.5	11.786	11.769	11.754	11.740	11.726	11.713	11.701	11.690
11.75	12.019	12.003	11.989	11.975	11.962	11.950	11.938	11.927
12	12.253	12.238	12.224	12.211	12.198	12.187	12.176	12.165
12.25	12.488	12.473	12.460	12.447	12.436	12.424	12.414	12.404
12.5	12.724	12.710	12.697	12.685	12.674	12.663	12.653	12.644
12.75	12.960	12.947	12.935	12.923	12.912	12.902	12.893	12.884
13	13.197	13.185	13.173	13.162	13.152	13.142	13.133	13.125
13.25	13.435	13.424	13.412	13.402	13.392	13.383	13.374	13.366
13.5	13.674	13.663	13.652	13.642	13.633	13.624	13.616	13.608
13.75	13.914	13.903	13.892	13.883	13.874	13.866	13.858	13.851
14	14.154	14.143	14.133	14.124	14.116	14.108	14.101	14.094
14.25	14.394	14.384	14.375	14.366	14.358	14.351	14.344	14.337
14.5	14.635	14.626	14.617	14.609	14.601	14.594	14.587	14.581
14.75	14.877	14.868	14.859	14.852	14.844	14.838	14.831	14.826
15	15.119	15.110	15.102	15.095	15.088	15.082	15.076	15.070
15.25	15.362	15.353	15.346	15.339	15.332	15.326	15.321	15.315
15.5	15.605	15.597	15.590	15.583	15.577	15.571	15.566	15.561
15.75	15.848	15.841	15.834	15.827	15.822	15.816	15.811	15.807
16	16.092	16.085	16.078	16.072	16.067	16.062	16.057	16.053
16.25	16.336	16.329	16.323	16.317	16.312	16.307	16.303	16.299
16.5	16.581	16.574	16.568	16.563	16.558	16.553	16.549	16.545
16.75	16.826	16.819	16.814	16.809	16.804	16.800	16.796	16.792
17	17.071	17.065	17.060	17.055	17.050	17.046	17.043	17.039
17.25	17.316	17.311	17.306	17.301	17.297	17.293	17.290	17.286
17.5	17.562	17.557	17.552	17.548	17.544	17.540	17.537	17.534
17.75	17.808	17.803	17.799	17.795	17.791	17.787	17.784	17.781
18	18.054	18.050	18.045	18.042	18.038	18.035	18.032	18.029
18.25	18.301	18.296	18.292	18.289	18.285	18.282	18.279	18.277
18.5	18.548	18.543	18.540	18.536	18.533	18.530	18.527	18.525
18.75	18.794	18.790	18.787	18.784	18.781	18.778	18.775	18.773
19	19.042	19.038	19.034	19.031	19.028	19.026	19.024	19.021
19.25	19.289	19.285	19.282	19.279	19.277	19.274	19.272	19.270
19.5	19.536	19.533	19.530	19.527	19.525	19.522	19.520	19.518
19.75	19.784	19.781	19.778	19.775	19.773	19.771	19.769	19.767
20	20.032	20.029	20.026	20.024	20.021	20.019	20.017	20.016
20.25	20.280	20.277	20.274	20.272	20.270	20.268	20.266	20.265

TABLE A (*continued*)

% Interest	Years 32.5	33	33.5	34	34.5	35	35.5	36
20.5	20.528	20.525	20.523	20.520	20.518	20.517	20.515	20.514
20.75	20.776	20.773	20.771	20.769	20.767	20.765	20.764	20.763
21	21.024	21.022	21.020	21.018	21.016	21.014	21.013	21.012
21.25	21.273	21.270	21.268	21.266	21.265	21.263	21.262	21.261
21.5	21.521	21.519	21.517	21.515	21.514	21.512	21.511	21.510
21.75	21.770	21.768	21.766	21.764	21.763	21.762	21.760	21.759
22	22.018	22.017	22.015	22.013	22.012	22.011	22.010	22.009
22.25	22.267	22.265	22.264	22.262	22.261	22.260	22.259	22.258
22.5	22.516	22.514	22.513	22.511	22.510	22.509	22.508	22.507
22.75	22.765	22.763	22.762	22.761	22.760	22.759	22.758	22.757
23	23.014	23.012	23.011	23.010	23.009	23.008	23.007	23.006
23.25	23.263	23.262	23.260	23.259	23.258	23.257	23.257	23.256
23.5	23.512	23.511	23.510	23.509	23.508	23.507	23.506	23.505
23.75	23.761	23.760	23.759	23.758	23.757	23.756	23.756	23.755
24	24.011	24.009	24.008	24.007	24.007	24.006	24.005	24.005
24.25	24.260	24.259	24.258	24.257	24.256	24.255	24.255	24.254
24.5	24.509	24.508	24.507	24.506	24.506	24.505	24.504	24.504
24.75	24.759	24.758	24.757	24.756	24.755	24.755	24.754	24.754
25	25.008	25.007	25.006	25.006	25.005	25.004	25.004	25.003

TABLE A (*continued*)

% Interest	Years 36.5	37	37.5	38	38.5	39	39.5	40
8	8.461	8.442	8.424	8.406	8.390	8.374	8.358	8.344
8.25	8.682	8.664	8.646	8.629	8.613	8.598	8.584	8.570
8.5	8.905	8.887	8.870	8.854	8.839	8.824	8.810	8.797
8.75	9.129	9.112	9.096	9.081	9.066	9.052	9.039	9.026
9	9.355	9.338	9.323	9.308	9.294	9.281	9.268	9.256
9.25	9.582	9.566	9.552	9.538	9.524	9.512	9.499	9.488
9.5	9.810	9.795	9.781	9.768	9.755	9.743	9.732	9.721
9.75	10.040	10.026	10.012	10.000	9.988	9.976	9.965	9.955
10	10.271	10.258	10.245	10.233	10.221	10.210	10.200	10.190
10.25	10.503	10.490	10.478	10.466	10.455	10.445	10.435	10.426
10.5	10.736	10.724	10.712	10.701	10.691	10.681	10.672	10.663
10.75	10.971	10.959	10.948	10.937	10.927	10.918	10.909	10.901
11	11.206	11.195	11.184	11.174	11.165	11.156	11.147	11.140
11.25	11.442	11.431	11.421	11.412	11.403	11.395	11.387	11.379
11.5	11.679	11.669	11.659	11.651	11.642	11.634	11.627	11.619
11.75	11.917	11.907	11.898	11.890	11.882	11.874	11.867	11.860
12	12.156	12.146	12.138	12.130	12.122	12.115	12.108	12.102
12.25	12.395	12.386	12.378	12.370	12.363	12.357	12.350	12.344
12.5	12.635	12.627	12.619	12.612	12.605	12.599	12.593	12.587
12.75	12.876	12.868	12.861	12.854	12.847	12.841	12.836	12.830
13	13.117	13.110	13.103	13.096	13.090	13.084	13.079	13.074
13.25	13.359	13.352	13.345	13.339	13.333	13.328	13.323	13.318
13.5	13.601	13.595	13.588	13.583	13.577	13.572	13.568	13.563
13.75	13.844	13.838	13.832	13.827	13.822	13.817	13.812	13.808
14	14.088	14.082	14.076	14.071	14.066	14.062	14.058	14.054
14.25	14.331	14.326	14.321	14.316	14.311	14.307	14.303	14.299
14.5	14.576	14.570	14.565	14.561	14.557	14.553	14.549	14.546
14.75	14.820	14.815	14.811	14.806	14.802	14.799	14.795	14.792
15	15.065	15.061	15.056	15.052	15.048	15.045	15.042	15.039
15.25	15.311	15.306	15.302	15.298	15.295	15.291	15.288	15.286
15.5	15.556	15.552	15.548	15.545	15.541	15.538	15.535	15.533
15.75	15.802	15.798	15.795	15.791	15.788	15.785	15.783	15.780
16	16.049	16.045	16.041	16.038	16.035	16.033	16.030	16.028
16.25	16.295	16.292	16.288	16.285	16.283	16.280	16.278	16.276
16.5	16.542	16.538	16.535	16.533	16.530	16.528	16.526	16.524
16.75	16.789	16.786	16.783	16.780	16.778	16.776	16.773	16.772
17	17.036	17.033	17.030	17.028	17.026	17.024	17.022	17.020
17.25	17.283	17.281	17.278	17.276	17.274	17.272	17.270	17.268
17.5	17.531	17.528	17.526	17.524	17.522	17.520	17.518	17.517
17.75	17.779	17.776	17.774	17.772	17.770	17.768	17.767	17.765
18	18.027	18.024	18.022	18.020	18.019	18.017	18.016	18.014
18.25	18.275	18.272	18.270	18.269	18.267	18.266	18.264	18.263
18.5	18.523	18.521	18.519	18.517	18.516	18.514	18.513	18.512
18.75	18.771	18.769	18.768	18.766	18.765	18.763	18.762	18.761
19	19.020	19.018	19.016	19.015	19.013	19.012	19.011	19.010
19.25	19.268	19.266	19.265	19.264	19.262	19.261	19.260	19.259
19.5	19.517	19.515	19.514	19.513	19.511	19.510	19.509	19.508
19.75	19.766	19.764	19.763	19.762	19.760	19.759	19.759	19.758
20	20.014	20.013	20.012	20.011	20.010	20.009	20.008	20.007
20.25	20.263	20.262	20.261	20.260	20.259	20.258	20.257	20.257

TABLE A (*continued*)

% Interest	Years 36.5	37	37.5	38	38.5	39	39.5	40
20.5	20.512	20.511	20.510	20.509	20.508	20.507	20.507	20.506
20.75	20.761	20.760	20.759	20.758	20.758	20.757	20.756	20.756
21	21.011	21.009	21.009	21.008	21.007	21.006	21.006	21.005
21.25	21.260	21.259	21.258	21.257	21.256	21.256	21.255	21.255
21.5	21.509	21.508	21.507	21.507	21.506	21.505	21.505	21.504
21.75	21.758	21.757	21.757	21.756	21.755	21.755	21.754	21.754
22	22.008	22.007	22.006	22.006	22.005	22.004	22.004	22.004
22.25	22.257	22.256	22.256	22.255	22.255	22.254	22.254	22.253
22.5	22.507	22.506	22.505	22.505	22.504	22.504	22.503	22.503
22.75	22.756	22.755	22.755	22.754	22.754	22.753	22.753	22.753
23	23.006	23.005	23.004	23.004	23.004	23.003	23.003	23.003
23.25	23.255	23.255	23.254	23.254	23.253	23.253	23.253	23.252
23.5	23.505	23.504	23.504	23.503	23.503	23.503	23.502	23.502
23.75	23.754	23.754	23.753	23.753	23.753	23.752	23.752	23.752
24	24.004	24.004	24.003	24.003	24.003	24.002	24.002	24.002
24.25	24.254	24.253	24.253	24.253	24.252	24.252	24.252	24.252
24.5	24.503	24.503	24.503	24.502	24.502	24.502	24.502	24.501
24.75	24.753	24.753	24.753	24.752	24.752	24.752	24.752	24.751
25	25.003	25.003	25.002	25.002	25.002	25.002	25.001	25.001

TABLE B.

Constant Annual Percents for Loans with Annual Payments

To be used only in the event of 1 payment made annually or semiannually.

% Interest	Years 1	1.5	2	2.5	3	3.5	4	4.5
6	106.001	71.692	54.544	44.261	37.411	32.522	28.859	26.014
6.25	106.250	71.901	54.735	44.441	37.584	32.691	29.025	26.177
6.5	106.501	72.112	54.926	44.622	37.758	32.860	29.190	26.340
6.75	106.751	72.323	55.118	44.803	37.932	33.029	29.357	26.504
7	107.001	72.533	55.309	44.983	38.105	33.198	29.523	26.669
7.25	107.251	72.744	55.501	45.164	38.280	33.368	29.690	26.834
7.5	107.500	72.954	55.693	45.345	38.454	33.538	29.857	26.999
7.75	107.751	73.166	55.885	45.526	38.629	33.709	30.024	27.164
8	108.000	73.376	56.077	45.708	38.803	33.879	30.192	27.330
8.25	108.251	73.588	56.270	45.890	38.979	34.050	30.360	27.497
8.5	108.501	73.799	56.462	46.072	39.154	34.221	30.529	27.664
8.75	108.750	74.010	56.654	46.254	39.330	34.393	30.698	27.831
9	109.001	74.221	56.847	46.436	39.506	34.565	30.867	27.998
9.25	109.250	74.432	57.040	46.618	39.682	34.737	31.036	28.166
9.5	109.501	74.644	57.233	46.801	39.858	34.909	31.206	28.334
9.75	109.750	74.855	57.426	46.984	40.035	35.082	31.377	28.503
10	110.001	75.067	57.619	47.167	40.212	35.255	31.547	28.672
10.25	110.250	75.278	57.812	47.350	40.389	35.428	31.718	28.841

TABLE B (*continued*)

% Interest	Years 5	5.5	6	6.5	7	7.5	8	8.5
6	23.740	21.882	20.336	19.031	17.914	16.947	16.104	15.361
6.25	23.901	22.043	20.496	19.190	18.073	17.107	16.263	15.521
6.5	24.064	22.204	20.657	19.351	18.233	17.267	16.424	15.682
6.75	24.226	22.366	20.818	19.511	18.394	17.428	16.585	15.843
7	24.389	22.528	20.980	19.673	18.555	17.590	16.747	16.006
7.25	24.553	22.690	21.142	19.835	18.718	17.752	16.910	16.169
7.5	24.717	22.853	21.305	19.997	18.880	17.915	17.073	16.332
7.75	24.881	23.017	21.468	20.161	19.043	18.078	17.237	16.497
8	25.046	23.181	21.632	20.324	19.207	18.243	17.401	16.662
8.25	25.211	23.346	21.796	20.489	19.372	18.408	17.567	16.828
8.5	25.377	23.511	21.961	20.654	19.537	18.573	17.733	16.995
8.75	25.543	23.676	22.126	20.819	19.703	18.739	17.900	17.163
9	25.709	23.843	22.292	20.985	19.869	18.906	18.068	17.331
9.25	25.876	24.009	22.458	21.152	20.036	19.074	18.236	17.500
9.5	26.044	24.176	22.625	21.319	20.204	19.242	18.405	17.670
9.75	26.211	24.343	22.793	21.486	20.372	19.411	18.574	17.840
10	26.380	24.511	22.961	21.655	20.541	19.580	18.744	18.012
10.25	26.548	24.680	23.129	21.823	20.710	19.750	18.915	18.183

TABLE B (*continued*)

% Interest	Years 9	9.5	10	10.5	11	11.5	12	12.5
6	14.702	14.115	13.587	13.111	12.679	12.287	11.928	11.599
6.25	14.863	14.275	13.748	13.273	12.842	12.450	12.092	11.763
6.5	15.024	14.437	13.911	13.436	13.006	12.614	12.257	11.929
6.75	15.186	14.600	14.074	13.600	13.170	12.780	12.423	12.096
7	15.349	14.763	14.238	13.764	13.336	12.946	12.590	12.264
7.25	15.512	14.927	14.403	13.930	13.502	13.113	12.759	12.434
7.5	15.677	15.092	14.569	14.097	13.670	13.282	12.928	12.604
7.75	15.842	15.258	14.735	14.264	13.838	13.451	13.098	12.775
8	16.008	15.425	14.903	14.433	14.008	13.621	13.270	12.948
8.25	16.175	15.593	15.071	14.602	14.178	13.793	13.442	13.121
8.5	16.342	15.761	15.241	14.773	14.349	13.965	13.615	13.296
8.75	16.511	15.930	15.411	14.944	14.522	14.139	13.790	13.471
9	16.680	16.101	15.582	15.116	14.695	14.313	13.965	13.648
9.25	16.850	16.271	15.754	15.285	14.869	14.488	14.141	13.825
9.5	17.021	16.443	15.927	15.463	15.044	14.664	14.319	14.004
9.75	17.192	16.615	16.100	15.637	15.220	14.841	14.497	14.183
10	17.364	16.789	16.275	15.813	15.396	15.019	14.676	14.364
10.25	17.537	16.963	16.450	15.989	15.574	15.198	14.857	14.545

TABLE B (*continued*)

% Interest	Years 13	13.5	14	14.5	15	15.5	16	16.5
6	11.296	11.017	10.759	10.519	10.296	10.089	9.895	9.714
6.25	11.462	11.183	10.926	10.687	10.465	10.259	10.066	9.886
6.5	11.628	11.351	11.094	10.856	10.635	10.430	10.238	10.059
6.75	11.796	11.519	11.264	11.027	10.807	10.602	10.411	10.233
7	11.965	11.689	11.435	11.199	10.979	10.776	10.586	10.408
7.25	12.135	11.860	11.607	11.372	11.154	10.951	10.762	10.586
7.5	12.306	12.033	11.780	11.546	11.329	11.127	10.939	10.764
7.75	12.479	12.206	11.954	11.721	11.505	11.305	11.118	10.944
8	12.652	12.380	12.130	11.898	11.683	11.483	11.298	11.125
8.25	12.827	12.556	12.306	12.076	11.862	11.663	11.479	11.307
8.5	13.002	12.733	12.484	12.255	12.042	11.845	11.661	11.491
8.75	13.179	12.911	12.663	12.435	12.223	12.027	11.845	11.675
9	13.357	13.089	12.843	12.616	12.406	12.211	12.030	11.862
9.25	13.535	13.269	13.025	12.799	12.590	12.396	12.216	12.049
9.5	13.715	13.450	13.207	12.982	12.774	12.582	12.404	12.238
9.75	13.896	13.633	13.390	13.167	12.960	12.769	12.592	12.427
10	14.078	13.816	13.575	13.353	13.147	12.958	12.782	12.618
10.25	14.261	14.000	13.760	13.539	13.336	13.147	12.972	12.810

TABLE B (*continued*)

% Interest	Years 17	17.5	18	18.5	19	19.5	20	20.5
6	9.545	9.385	9.236	9.095	8.962	8.837	8.718	8.607
6.25	9.717	9.559	9.410	9.270	9.138	9.014	8.896	8.785
6.5	9.891	9.733	9.585	9.446	9.316	9.192	9.076	8.966
6.75	10.066	9.910	9.763	9.625	9.495	9.372	9.257	9.148
7	10.243	10.087	9.941	9.804	9.675	9.554	9.439	9.331
7.25	10.421	10.266	10.121	9.985	9.857	9.737	9.624	9.516
7.5	10.600	10.447	10.303	10.168	10.041	9.922	9.809	9.703
7.75	10.781	10.629	10.486	10.352	10.226	10.108	9.997	9.891
8	10.963	10.812	10.670	10.537	10.413	10.296	10.185	10.081
8.25	11.146	10.996	10.856	10.724	10.601	10.485	10.375	10.273
8.5	11.331	11.182	11.043	10.913	10.790	10.675	10.567	10.465
8.75	11.517	11.370	11.231	11.102	10.981	10.867	10.760	10.660
9	11.705	11.558	11.421	11.293	11.173	11.060	10.955	10.855
9.25	11.893	11.748	11.612	11.485	11.367	11.255	11.150	11.052
9.5	12.083	11.939	11.805	11.679	11.561	11.451	11.348	11.251
9.75	12.274	12.131	11.998	11.874	11.757	11.648	11.546	11.450
10	12.466	12.325	12.193	12.070	11.955	11.847	11.746	11.651
10.25	12.660	12.520	12.389	12.267	12.153	12.047	11.947	11.854

TABLE B (*continued*)

% Interest	Years 21	21.5	22	22.5	23	23.5	24	24.5
6	8.500	8.400	8.305	8.214	8.128	8.046	7.968	7.894
6.25	8.680	8.580	8.486	8.396	8.311	8.230	8.153	8.079
6.5	8.861	8.763	8.669	8.580	8.496	8.416	8.340	8.267
6.75	9.044	8.947	8.854	8.766	8.683	8.604	8.528	8.457
7	9.229	9.132	9.041	8.954	8.871	8.793	8.719	8.648
7.25	9.415	9.319	9.229	9.143	9.062	8.984	8.911	8.841
7.5	9.603	9.508	9.419	9.334	9.254	9.177	9.105	9.036
7.75	9.792	9.699	9.610	9.526	9.447	9.372	9.301	9.233
8	9.983	9.891	9.803	9.721	9.642	9.568	9.498	9.431
8.25	10.176	10.084	9.998	9.916	9.839	9.766	9.697	9.631
8.5	10.370	10.279	10.194	10.113	10.037	9.965	9.897	9.832
8.75	10.565	10.476	10.391	10.312	10.237	10.166	10.099	10.035
9	10.762	10.674	10.591	10.512	10.438	10.368	10.302	10.240
9.25	10.960	10.873	10.791	10.714	10.641	10.572	10.507	10.446
9.5	11.159	11.074	10.993	10.917	10.845	10.777	10.713	10.653
9.75	11.360	11.276	11.196	11.121	11.050	10.984	10.921	10.862
10	11.562	11.479	11.401	11.327	11.257	11.192	11.130	11.072
10.25	11.766	11.684	11.606	11.534	11.465	11.401	11.340	11.283

TABLE B (*continued*)

% Interest	Years 25	25.5	26	26.5	27	27.5	28	28.5
6	7.823	7.755	7.690	7.629	7.570	7.513	7.459	7.408
6.25	8.009	7.943	7.879	7.818	7.760	7.704	7.651	7.600
6.5	8.198	8.132	8.069	8.010	7.952	7.898	7.845	7.795
6.75	8.389	8.324	8.262	8.203	8.147	8.093	8.041	7.992
7	8.581	8.517	8.456	8.398	8.343	8.290	8.239	8.191
7.25	8.775	8.712	8.652	8.595	8.541	8.489	8.439	8.392
7.5	8.971	8.909	8.850	8.794	8.740	8.689	8.641	8.594
7.75	9.169	9.108	9.050	8.994	8.942	8.892	8.844	8.798
8	9.368	9.308	9.251	9.196	9.145	9.096	9.049	9.004
8.25	9.569	9.510	9.454	9.400	9.350	9.301	9.256	9.212
8.5	9.771	9.713	9.658	9.606	9.556	9.509	9.464	9.421
8.75	9.975	9.918	9.864	9.813	9.764	9.718	9.674	9.632
9	10.181	10.125	10.072	10.021	9.974	9.928	9.885	9.844
9.25	10.388	10.333	10.281	10.231	10.184	10.140	10.098	10.058
9.5	10.596	10.542	10.491	10.443	10.397	10.354	10.312	10.273
9.75	10.806	10.753	10.703	10.655	10.611	10.568	10.528	10.490
10	11.017	10.965	10.916	10.870	10.826	10.784	10.745	10.708
10.25	11.229	11.178	11.130	11.085	11.042	11.002	10.963	10.927

TABLE B (*continued*)

% Interest	Years 29	29.5	30	35	40
6	7.358	7.310	7.265	6.897	6.646
6.25	7.552	7.505	7.460	7.101	6.857
6.5	7.747	7.702	7.658	7.306	7.069
6.75	7.945	7.900	7.857	7.514	7.284
7	8.145	8.101	8.059	7.723	7.501
7.25	8.346	8.303	8.262	7.935	7.720
7.5	8.550	8.508	8.467	8.148	7.940
7.75	8.755	8.714	8.674	8.363	8.162
8	8.962	8.921	8.883	8.580	8.386
8.25	9.170	9.131	9.093	8.799	8.611
8.5	9.381	9.342	9.305	9.019	8.838
8.75	9.592	9.555	9.519	9.241	9.066
9	9.806	9.769	9.734	9.464	9.296
9.25	10.020	9.984	9.950	9.688	9.527
9.5	10.236	10.201	10.168	9.914	9.759
9.75	10.454	10.420	10.387	10.141	9.992
10	10.673	10.640	10.608	10.369	10.226
10.25	10.893	10.860	10.830	10.598	10.461

TABLE C.

1979 Tax Rate Schedules

If you cannot use one of the Tax Tables, figure your tax on the amount on Schedule TC, Part I, line 3, by using the appropriate Tax Rate Schedule on this page. Enter the tax on Schedule TC, Part I, line 4.

Note: *Your new zero bracket amount has been built into these Tax Rate Schedules.*

SCHEDULE X–Single Taxpayers

Use this schedule if you checked Filing Status Box 1 on Form 1040–

If the amount on Schedule TC, Part I, line 3, is: | Enter on Schedule TC, Part I, line 4:

Not over $2,300........ –0–

Over–	*But not over–*		*of the amount over–*
$ 2,300	$ 3,400	14%	$ 2,300
$ 3,400	$ 4,400	$ 154+16%	$ 3,400
$ 4,400	$ 6,500	$ 314+18%	$ 4,400
$ 6,500	$ 8,500	$ 692+19%	$ 6,500
$ 8,500	$ 10,800	$ 1,072+21%	$ 8,500
$ 10,800	$ 12,900	$ 1,555+24%	$ 10,800
$ 12,900	$ 15,000	$ 2,059+26%	$ 12,900
$ 15,000	$ 18,200	$ 2,605+30%	$ 15,000
$ 18,200	$ 23,500	$ 3,565+34%	$ 18,200
$ 23,500	$ 28,800	$ 5,367+39%	$ 23,500
$ 28,800	$ 34,100	$ 7,434+44%	$ 28,800
$ 34,100	$ 41,500	$ 9,766+49%	$ 34,100
$ 41,500	$ 55,300	$13,392+55%	$ 41,500
$ 55,300	$ 81,800	$20,982+63%	$ 55,300
$ 81,800	$108,300	$37,677+68%	$ 81,800
$108,300	....	$55,697+70%	$108,300

SCHEDULE Y–Married Taxpayers and Qualifying Widows and Widowers

Married Filing Joint Returns and Qualifying Widows and Widowers

Use this schedule if you checked Filing Status Box 2 or 5 on Form 1040–

If the amount on Schedule TC, Part I, line 3, is: | Enter on Schedule TC, Part I, line 4:

Not over $3,400........ –0–

Over–	*But not over–*		*of the amount over–*
$ 3,400	$ 5,500	14%	$ 3,400
$ 5,500	$ 7,600	$ 294+16%	$ 5,500
$ 7,600	$ 11,900	$ 630+18%	$ 7,600
$ 11,900	$ 16,000	$ 1,404+21%	$ 11,900
$ 16,000	$ 20,200	$ 2,265+24%	$ 16,000
$ 20,200	$ 24,600	$ 3,273+28%	$ 20,200
$ 24,600	$ 29,900	$ 4,505+32%	$ 24,600
$ 29,900	$ 35,200	$ 6,201+37%	$ 29,900
$ 35,200	$ 45,800	$ 8,162+43%	$ 35,200
$ 45,800	$ 60,000	$ 12,720+49%	$ 45,800
$ 60,000	$ 85,600	$ 19,678+54%	$ 60,000
$ 85,600	$109,400	$ 33,502+59%	$ 85,600
$109,400	$162,400	$ 47,544+64%	$109,400
$162,400	$215,400	$ 81,464+68%	$162,400
$215,400	....	$117,504+70%	$215,400

TABLE C (*continued*)

SCHEDULE Y—Married Taxpayers and Qualifying Widows and Widowers

Married Filing Separate Returns

Use this schedule if you checked Filing Status Box 3 on Form 1040—

If the amount on Schedule TC, Part I, line 3, is:	Enter on Schedule TC, Part I, line 4:
Not over $1,700........	—0—

Over—	*But not over—*		*of the amount over—*
$ 1,700	$ 2,750	14%	$ 1,700
$ 2,750	$ 3,800	$ 147.00+16%	$ 2,750
$ 3,800	$ 5,950	$ 315.00+18%	$ 3,800
$ 5,950	$ 8,000	$ 702.00+21%	$ 5,950
$ 8,000	$ 10,100	$ 1,132.50+24%	$ 8,000
$ 10,100	$ 12,300	$ 1,636.50+28%	$ 10,100
$ 12,300	$ 14,950	$ 2,252.50+32%	$ 12,300
$ 14,950	$ 17,600	$ 3,100.50+37%	$ 14,950
$ 17,600	$ 22,900	$ 4,081.00+43%	$ 17,600
$ 22,900	$ 30,000	$ 6,360.00+49%	$ 22,900
$ 30,000	$ 42,800	$ 9,839.00+54%	$ 30,000
$ 42,800	$ 54,700	$16,751.00+59%	$ 42,800
$ 54,700	$ 81,200	$23,772.00+64%	$ 54,700
$ 81,200	$107,700	$40,732.00+68%	$ 81,200
$107,700	....	$58,752.00+70%	$107,700

SCHEDULE Z—Heads of Household (including certain married persons who live apart (and abandoned spouses) . . .

Use this schedule if you checked Filing Status Box 4 on Form 1040—

If the amount on Schedule TC, Part I, line 3, is:	Enter on Schedule TC, Part I, line 4:
Not over $2,300........	—0—

Over—	*But not over—*		*of the amount over—*
$ 2,300	$ 4,400	14%	$ 2,300
$ 4,400	$ 6,500	$ 294+16%	$ 4,400
$ 6,500	$ 8,700	$ 630+18%	$ 6,500
$ 8,700	$ 11,800	$ 1,026+22%	$ 8,700
$ 11,800	$ 15,000	$ 1,708+24%	$ 11,800
$ 15,000	$ 18,200	$ 2,476+26%	$ 15,000
$ 18,200	$ 23,500	$ 3,308+31%	$ 18,200
$ 23,500	$ 28,800	$ 4,951+36%	$ 23,500
$ 28,800	$ 34,100	$ 6,859+42%	$ 28,600
$ 34,100	$ 44,700	$ 9,085+46%	$ 34,100
$ 44,700	$ 60,600	$13,961+54%	$ 44,700
$ 60,600	$ 81,800	$22,547+59%	$ 60,600
$ 81,800	$108,300	$35,055+63%	$ 81,800
$108,300	$161,300	$51,750+68%	$108,300
$161,300	....	$87,790+70%	$161,300

SCHEDULE Y–Married Taxpayers and Qualifying Widows and Widowers

Married Filing Separate Returns

Use this schedule if you checked Filing Status Box 3 on Form 1040–

If the amount on Schedule TC, Part I, line 3, is:		Enter on Schedule TC, Part I, line 4:	
Not over $1,700........		–0–	
Over–	*But not over–*		*of the amount over–*
$ 1,700	$ 2,750	14%	$ 1,700
$ 2,750	$ 3,800	$ 147.00+16%	$ 2,750
$ 3,800	$ 5,950	$ 315.00+18%	$ 3,800
$ 5,950	$ 8,000	$ 702.00+21%	$ 5,950
$ 8,000	$ 10,100	$ 1,132.50+24%	$ 8,000
$ 10,100	$ 12,300	$ 1,636.50+28%	$ 10,100
$ 12,300	$ 14,950	$ 2,252.50+32%	$ 12,300
$ 14,950	$ 17,600	$ 3,100.50+37%	$ 14,950
$ 17,600	$ 22,900	$ 4,081.00+43%	$ 17,600
$ 22,900	$ 30,000	$ 6,360.00+49%	$ 22,900
$ 30,000	$ 42,800	$ 9,839.00+54%	$ 30,000
$ 42,800	$ 54,700	$16,751.00+59%	$ 42,800
$ 54,700	$ 81,200	$23,772.00+64%	$ 54,700
$ 81,200	$107,700	$40,732.00+68%	$ 81,200
$107,700	....	$58,752.00+70%	$107,700

SCHEDULE Z–Heads of Household (including certain married persons who live apart (and abandoned spouses) . . .

Use this schedule if you checked Filing Status Box 4 on Form 1040–

If the amount on Schedule TC, Part I, line 3, is:		Enter on Schedule TC, Part I, line 4:	
Not over $2,300........		–0–	
Over–	*But not over–*		*of the amount over–*
$ 2,300	$ 4,400	14%	$ 2,300
$ 4,400	$ 6,500	$ 294+16%	$ 4,400
$ 6,500	$ 8,700	$ 630+18%	$ 6,500
$ 8,700	$ 11,800	$ 1,026+22%	$ 8,700
$ 11,800	$ 15,000	$ 1,708+24%	$ 11,800
$ 15,000	$ 18,200	$ 2,476+26%	$ 15,000
$ 18,200	$ 23,500	$ 3,308+31%	$ 18,200
$ 23,500	$ 28,800	$ 4,951+36%	$ 23,500
$ 28,800	$ 34,100	$ 6,859+42%	$ 28,600
$ 34,100	$ 44,700	$ 9,085+46%	$ 34,100
$ 44,700	$ 60,600	$13,961+54%	$ 44,700
$ 60,600	$ 81,800	$22,547+59%	$ 60,600
$ 81,800	$108,300	$35,055+63%	$ 81,800
$108,300	$161,300	$51,750+68%	$108,300
$161,300	....	$87,790+70%	$161,300